CHRIS MARKER

CHRIS MARKER

EARLY FILM WRITINGS

CHRIS MARKER

EDITED BY STEVEN UNGAR

TRANSLATED BY SALLY SHAFTO

University of Minnesota Press
Minneapolis
London

The University of Minnesota Press and Steven Ungar thank Sally Shafto for her translation and significant editorial assistance on this project.

Published by the University of Minnesota Press
111 Third Avenue South, Suite 290
Minneapolis, MN 55401–2520
http://www.upress.umn.edu

ISBN 978-1-5179-1319-9 (pb)

A Cataloging-in-Publication record for this book is available from the Library of Congress.

Printed in the United States of America on acid-free paper

The University of Minnesota is an equal-opportunity educator and employer.

31 30 29 28 27 26 25 24   10 9 8 7 6 5 4 3 2 1

For my mentors
Helen Richard, Raymond Riva, Germaine Brée, Elaine Marks,
Philip Lewis, David Grossvogel, and Walter Strauss
—S.U.

CONTENTS

ACKNOWLEDGMENTS

A BOOK IS ALWAYS A RECORD OF THE INTERACTIONS THAT mark its inception and making. Some of these interactions are brief. Others extend lifelong dialogues. For their encouragement and assistance this time around, I thank Paula Amad, Clara Bleuzen, Peter Bloom, Hannah Bonner, Colin Burnett, Ivan Cerecina, Corey Creekmur, Pierre Delaunay, Sam Di Iorio, Benn Dunnington, Bernard Eisenschitz, Marie Ferran-Wabbes, Patrick Ferran, Rebecca Fons, Dr. Frederick Frank, Anahita Ghazvinizadeh, Miriam Gilbert, Paul Greenough, Tom Gunning, Christopher Harris, Mike Hendrickson, Matthew Hipps, Alice Kaplan, Dorothy Johnson, Jonathan Lack, Herman Lebovics, Julia Anna Morrison, Kathleen Newman, Marshall Olds, Richard Sjolund, Kyle Westphal, and Chang-Min Yu.

Dudley Andrew and Chris Darke provided astute feedback on early drafts of the manuscript.

Catherine Beaumont welcomed me at the Paris headquarters of Peuple et culture and facilitated access to archival materials. Mme Ghislaine Raynfeld and Mme Mabel Nicolaÿ Duflo guided me on behalf of the Marker estate in obtaining translation and distribution rights. Jean-Michel Frodon provided moral and practical support from start to finish.

At the University of Minnesota Press, Douglas Armato, Zenyse Miller, and Laura Westlund were clearheaded and generous at every phase of the writing and production process.

Sally Shafto drew on her understanding of film, art history, and literature to produce a model translation. Her intellectual energy and editing skills have contributed immeasurably to the tone and substance of this book.

Robin Ungar lived the ups and downs of this project on a daily basis for four years. As she has done so often in the past, she kept everything in a healthy perspective.

—S.U.

EDITOR'S INTRODUCTION
WRITING, FILM, AND THE MARKER MOMENT
STEVEN UNGAR

Chris Marker is of this new generation of writers who believe that the time of the image has come, but who do not find it necessary to sacrifice the powers and virtues of a language that remains the privileged interpreter of intelligence. Which means that for Chris Marker, the commentary is not what is added to images chosen and edited in advance, but almost the primary, fundamental element that nonetheless acquires meaning and usefulness only with reference to the images that accompany it.

—ANDRÉ BAZIN, "Letter from Siberia"

With Marker, words came before images, writing before filmmaking.
—CHRIS DARKE, *La Jetée*

Subject, Period, Corpus

Chris Marker (1921–2012) reputedly described himself as the best-known author of unknown movies. This designation holds true, as his most acclaimed films failed to receive the worldwide acclaim achieved by younger New Wave counterparts François Truffaut and Jean-Luc Godard. Nevertheless, it is hard for me to imagine French cinema without *La Jetée* (1962), Marker's time-travel short feature composed almost entirely of still images. Or *Lettre de Sibérie* (1958, *Letter from Siberia*), whose quirky commentary redirects conventions of the travelogue toward those of the filmed essay. Or the epic account of the global left's failed revolutions in *Le Fond de l'air est rouge* (1977, *A Grin without a Cat*). Or the synth-generated effects in his experimental *Sans Soleil* (1982). Or the nods to Marcel Proust and Alfred Hitchcock in his interactive CD-ROM *Immemory* (1997).

Still, even the most ardent of Marker's fans have yet to contend with the full import of a simple truth: Chris Marker wrote. In fact, he wrote a lot, especially between 1945 and 1955, when his publications included a play, a novel, short stories, a literary monograph, poetry, radio scripts, film commentaries, translations, and roughly one hundred articles, essays, and book entries.

The attention generated by Marker's photographs, films, videos, installations, and digital projects often reduces his writings—and his early writings, in particular—to passing mention or summary. A decade after his death, critics continue to discover—or rediscover—the man whom Jean-Louis Comolli called "the writing Marker" *("Marker l'écrivant")*. François Crémieux argues that Marker's publications in the Parisian monthly *Esprit* starting in 1946 largely form the basis of his subsequent work over the next six decades: "His *Esprit* writings make of him what he will be." Catherine Lupton notes that Marker's early writings are striking in their diversity and their permeability to the influence of other media. She rightly casts him as a multimedia pioneer active across writing, photography, film, video, radio, and digital media. Marker stated as much when he wrote that multimedia "was not just an entirely new language; it's the language I've been waiting for all my life."[1]

The moment when Christian Hippolyte François Georges Bouche-Villeneuve adopts the pen name Chris Marker coincides with his initial postwar publications, a majority of them in *Esprit*. Marker becomes Marker through his *Esprit* writings. Yet as early as 1938, the teenage Bouche-Villeneuve adopts the pen name Marc

Dornier for his contributions to *Le Trait d'union* (The Hyphen), the literary journal he cofounds at the Lycée Pasteur in Neuilly.[2] Jean-Michel Frodon notes that the precocious seventeen-year-old is already citing the painter Giorgio de Chirico, the animator-producer Walt Disney, and the actress Viviane Romance. Equally striking in the same piece is Dornier's assertion that he is writing reflections rather than criticism. For the adolescent Dornier, writing on films was already a means to reflect on the world.[3]

The word "writings" as it appears throughout this book conveys the priority Marker assigns to language and forms of written expression. It is a matter of what Sam Di Iorio and Michael Chaikin call the author behind the *auteur*. Nora Alter agrees when she notes that Marker's auteurism derives more from his literariness and essayistic tendencies than from any cultivation on his part of a director-as-genius myth.[4] It is significant that Marker describes himself as an author of movies, especially when the term *author* reinforces the proposition that Marker's cinematic imaginary—the various ways he thinks and writes about films—is distinctly literary. Michèle Firk catches the essence of this authorship across media when she playfully describes *Letter from Siberia* as an epistolary film in which Marker is "constantly improvising and spontaneously composing his letter—with his pen (sorry, his camera)."[5]

This book began as a study of nine film-based articles Marker wrote for *Esprit* between 1948 and 1955. Its initial form was a paper I presented at a 2015 Yale University conference Dudley Andrew organized on André Bazin, postwar French journals, and the politics of popular culture. The current project developed after I commissioned French film scholar and translator Sally Shafto to translate Marker's film writings in *Esprit,* along with others he contributed during the same period to the newly launched *Cahiers du cinéma* and *Positif* monthlies and two anthologies. These twenty texts track Marker from his midtwenties to midthirties as he thinks about (reflects on) film form, style, and history as well as adaptation, animation, new technologies, national film industries, and pedagogy. They document his contributions to the cinephilia Antoine de Baecque characterizes as the invention of a gaze and the history of a culture from 1944 to 1968. Finally, they sketch a portrait of the writing Marker—more of a self-portrait, really—in the guise of what Jacques Rancière via Roland Barthes might have called a pensive spectator (Rancière) attuned to the emotional charge (Barthes) of still and moving images.[6]

Caveats are in order. First, I make no claim that the texts translated in this book comprise a definitive listing of Marker's film-based writings during the period in question. Research conducted during completion of this project has turned up two additional texts. One, *"Der Trickfilm"* (Animated film), was published in the German-language journal *DOK*. The other, on the filmmaker Wolfgang Staudte, appeared in *Cinéma 55*.[7] Additions to this list are likely. Second, although these twenty texts form a coherent set organized on the basis of chronology and print venue, they were never reprinted together in French. While many of them call to mind specific times, places, and events, it would be inaccurate to refer to them as ephemera.

The translations in this book record Marker's early postwar reflections on films and film culture understood as art, industry, and social practice. But what kind of thinking do they signal? And what might be at stake in assembling them—if only provisionally—as a distinct set? Marker offered a revealing take on these questions when he observed that the playwright, novelist, essayist, and diplomat Jean Giraudoux was the first to approach cinema *as a writer* (*en écrivain,* C.M.'s emphasis).[8] This supports the hypothesis that by 1952 Marker could be described as a writer who also made films. When Florence Delay ranked Marker's multiple professions of photographer, filmmaker, videographer, multimedia tinkerer, publisher, traveler, musician, essayist, critic, and writer, the last topped the list, "because [his] first invention was to be a writer in all the arts and crafts he practiced."[9]

Perhaps nowhere does Marker acknowledge the productive

entanglement of words and moving images more pointedly than in a sequence in *Letter from Siberia* during which he films four street workers in the city of Yakutsk. Marker loops the sequence three times, each time with a different commentary read in voice-over by the actor-director Georges Rouquier:

For example:

Yakutsk, capital of the Soviet Socialist Republic of Yakoutia, is a modern city, where comfortable buses available for use by the local population repeatedly cross paths with powerful Zyms, the triumph of the Soviet car industry. In joyous emulation of Socialist labor, happy Soviet workers, whom we see crossing paths with a striking representative of the northern climes, take pains to make Yakoutia a country where life is good!

Or perhaps:

Yakutsk, with its sinister reputation, is a gloomy city in which local populations crowd uncomfortably onto blood-red buses, while powerful members of the regime insolently show off their costly and uncomfortable Zyms. In the posture of slaves, the unhappy Soviet workers, among whom we see an alarming Asian-type, undertake a symbolic labor: the leveling of a new road surface from below!

Or simply:

Yakutsk, where modern houses are gaining bit by bit on the gloomy older neighborhoods, a bus less crammed with passengers than those during Paris rush hours, crosses paths with a Zym, an excellent car whose rarity restricts it to members of the civil service. With courage, tenacity, and under very demanding conditions, Soviet workers, among whom we see a squinting local afflicted with strabismus, make an effort to improve their city, which needs it.[10]

André Bazin labels the three commentaries communist, reactionary, and impartial. Chris Darke notes that they range from conventional Communist-era propaganda and Voice of America–style misinformation to a bland "neutral" tone.[11] The fact that each commentary emits its own ideological charge implies that the

Urban transit in Sakha (Yakutsk), Soviet Republic in Eastern Siberia, in *Letter from Siberia* (1958), Marker's feature-length documentary.

Street laborers at work modernizing Sakha in *Letter from Siberia*.

Passerby returning the camera's gaze in *Letter from Siberia*.

meaning produced across the looped sequences is cumulative and grounded in difference. Objectivity, Marker continues, lacks the energy and diversity of Siberia's reality that his imaginary newsreel conveys *in phrasings fashioned through images* (my emphasis).[12]

Only days before his death in November 1958, Bazin wrote that Marker had wanted the looped sequences to demonstrate the capacity of words to destabilize the fixed meaning of images through a lateral editing whose back-and-forth movement from eye to ear he considered a distinctive feature of the cinematic image:

> Deprived of its soundtrack, *Letter from Siberia* has no meaning in a narrow sense, with the text alone nothing more than a fireworks of gratuitous ideas. If some spectators find this radically new conception of "the documentary" unsettling, it is because cinema has accustomed us more to the comfort of the eye than to intellectual attention.[13]

A year earlier, Bazin had described Marker's documentary short *Dimanche à Pékin* (1956, *Sunday in Peking*) as neither a poem, nor a reportage, nor a film, but a dazzling synthesis of all three. Darke validates Bazin's assertion when he writes that with Marker, "we move constantly from word to image, page to screen, book to film and back again, sometimes even in the same work. [...] The screen has the attributes of a page, and the page those of a screen."[14]

The goal of this book is to provide anglophone readers access to a formative yet understudied dimension of Chris Marker's postwar activities. Long after the fact, the questions he raises in his early film writings still speak to ongoing reflections on what cinema was, is, and might become. These writings place Marker alongside Bazin, Jean Rouch, Alain Resnais, and Agnès Varda as a tutelary figure for the "Young Turk" film critics and filmmakers at *Cahiers* who would soon launch the French New Wave. Over a longer duration, they inform the movement across medium and format that Marker would explore over the following seven decades.

Who was Chris Marker? Contending with his professional and personal activities remains a work in progress. Marker is often the subject of anecdotal accounts, yet nothing close to a full biography exists. His adopted daughter, Maroussia Vossen, writes that because her father compartmentalized his relationships, those who knew him could speak with authority only of their "Chris."[15] And Marker purposely and perhaps gleefully muddled matters, as when he claimed that he was born in the Mongolian capital of Ulaanbaatar rather than the upscale Paris suburb of Neuilly.[16] Capsule portraits of him vary to the point of contradiction. Film director Costa-Gavras characterizes his longtime friend as an outlier *(un irrégulier)*, simultaneously present while also slightly marginal to his era, as much observer and archivist as participant and memorialist. Ben Lerner describes him as never turning his back on the present. I think of Marker as a polymath as well as a man of twists and turns, which is how Robert Fagles translates Homer's description of Odysseus *polytropos* at the start of *The Odyssey*.[17]

Florence Tissot's chronology in the catalog of the Cinémathèque française's 2018 Marker exhibition complements period-focused articles in the same volume by Jean-Michel Frodon and Thomas Tode.[18] Tissot is especially helpful for the period from Bouche-Villeneuve's 1936 enrollment at the Lycée Pasteur to his initial postwar publications, films, and travels. Equally informative are details concerning the 1940–44 German occupation and its aftermath through May 1945—that is, from Bouche-Villeneuve/Dornier's involvement with the Vichy regime's Jeune France (Young France) movement at Uriage-les-Bains to his stints in resistance groups, the Free French Forces, and the U.S. military.

Of special note is Tissot's reference to a lost 1947 film, *La Fin du monde vue par l'ange Gabriel* (The end of the world seen by the angel Gabriel). Marker described it as his first film, shot in Berlin on an 8mm movie camera purportedly borrowed from Bazin. Elsewhere, Tode imagines Marker during his initial visits to Berlin, photographing bombed-out buildings on the banks of the river Spree. A decade and a half later, Marker would recycle some of these photographs in a montage sequence in *La Jetée* evoking a post–World War III Paris.[19]

La Jetée, World War III ruins. *La Jetée; Sans Soleil,* Criterion Collection, 2014.

When Tissot and Tode reset Maker's initial filmmaking back three to five years, they support the idea that his film-based publications are more than a preliminary phase that ends once he begins to make films.[20] The matter is more complex. As early as 1947, Marker is writing and filming while he adapts the fictions he publishes in *Esprit* to other formats.[21] A half-century later, he would dismiss the films he completed prior to *Le Joli Mai* (1962) and *La Jetée* as rudimentary and no longer worthy of screening in public.[22] (It is unclear whether the dismissal extends to his concurrent film writings.) Darke refers to a "lost period" through the early 2000s when sporadic access to Marker's early films fuels the idea that they are obscure and difficult. He also notes long before Crémieux that the films Marker would later dismiss as "tyro efforts" contain all the tropes, tricks, strategies, and obsessions that recur throughout his subsequent films, videos, and media projects.[23]

Marker's accounts of two childhood experiences qualify as origin stories. The first, in his 1997 CD-ROM *Immemory*, focuses on a sequence in Marco de Gastyne's silent feature *La Merveilleuse Vie de Jeanne d'Arc* (1929, Saint Joan the Maid), in which close-ups of the actress Simone Genevois projected on a large screen triggered a state of exaltation expressed by the seven- or eight-year-old Bouche-Villeneuve in comic-strip onomatopoeias "Wham," "Thud-thud," "Bump-bump," and "Shudder!"[24] Sixty years later, the adult Marker would confess that this primal scene of romance coincided with his discovery of cinema:

> This is the image that taught a child of seven how a face filling the screen was suddenly the most precious thing in the world, something that has haunted you ceaselessly, that slipped into every nook and instant of your life, until pronouncing its name and describing its traits became the most necessary and delicious occupation possible—in a word, that image taught you what love is. The deciphering of these bizarre symptoms came only later, along with the discovery of the cinema, so that for the child who had grown, cinema and woman

became two inseparable notions, and a film without a woman is still as incomprehensible to him as an opera without music. Why this face and this gaze remained unknown for almost sixty years is yet another mystery.[25]

Soon after (*Immemory*, 3:16:01), Marker recalls standing less than ten yards away from Genevois at a 1986 Palais de Chaillot screening of de Gastyne's film.[26] Like his protagonist in *La Jetée*, the adult filmmaker was indelibly marked by a childhood image.

A second formative moment centers on the Pathéorama, a device outfitted with a celluloid strip of hand-painted images that viewers could scroll and watch through a small peephole lens. (The images could also be projected onto a screen or wall by an ancillary apparatus.) The young Bouche-Villeneuve used scissors, tracing paper, and glue to fashion a blank strip of celluloid on which he drew images of his cat Riri ("who else?") that alternated with intertitles: "And all of a sudden, the cat belonged to the same universe

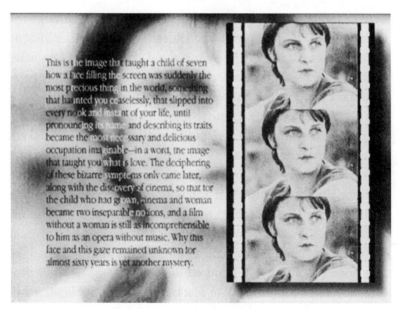

Simone Genevois in Marco de Gastyne's *Saint Joan the Maid* (1929). From *Immemory: a CD-ROM* (Exact Change, 2008).

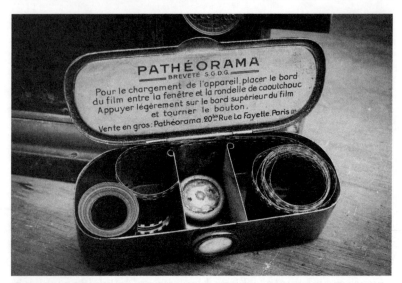

Pathéorama: Marker's childhood filmmaking apparatus. Photograph
courtesy of Pierre Delaunay.

as the characters in *Ben-Hur* or *Napoleon*. I had gone through the
looking glass."[27] These proto-film slideshows launched a lifelong
series of moments in which Marker would adapt new technologies
to creative ends of his own.

Marker was not the only cinephile in early postwar Paris; nor
was he the only one who came to filmmaking via writing. His trajectory recalls those of *Cahiers* film-critics-turned-filmmakers
Jean-Luc Godard and François Truffaut. In fact, it is closer to that
of Éric Rohmer (1920–2010), an older *Cahiers* figure who also came
to filmmaking via journalism and fiction. And much as the man
born Maurice Schérer adopts the pseudonym Éric Rohmer in his
midthirties, Christian-François Bouche-Villeneuve is ever-present
in the Chris Marker persona he assumes in his midtwenties.

A book collecting two hundred film writings by Rohmer provides evidence that much like Marker, Rohmer's publications in
La Revue du cinéma and *Les Temps modernes* did not prevent him
from writing about mainstream releases in other print venues."[28]

Where Marker wrote on Robert Montgomery's *Lady in the Lake*, Robert Cannon's *Gerald McBoing-Boing*, and Irving Lerner's *Man Crazy*, Rohmer reviewed Robert Rossen's *Alexander the Great*, Fred M. Wilcox's *Forbidden Planet*, and Frank Tashlin's *Will Success Spoil Rock Hunter?* Despite their proximity in age and trajectory, Rohmer could muster only a lukewarm review of *Letter from Siberia*, saying that whether one found the film annoying or pleasing, it would leave no spectator indifferent.[29]

Some of the 179 articles Rohmer writes for the cultural weekly *Arts* are short takes on commercial U.S. releases. Others tackle challenging films by S. M. Eisenstein, D. W. Griffith, Carl Theodor Dreyer, Fritz Lang, and Alfred Hitchcock. Yet others advance the young Turks' ongoing polemic against French "cinema of quality" productions.[30] Crossovers between Marker and Rohmer extend to venues and publication dates. The January 1952 issue of *Cahiers* includes Marker's short piece on Jiří Trnka's animated film *Prince Bayaya* and another on Rohmer's "Renoir américain" ("American Renoir"). A year later, the July 1953 *Cahiers* issue containing Marker's "Letter from Hollywood" features a contribution by Rohmer (signing as Schérer) on Roberto Rossellini's *Europa '51.*

A key difference setting Marker apart from Rohmer and the *Cahiers* Young Turks was his affiliation with the activist postwar movements Peuple et Culture (People and Culture, hereafter PEC) and Travail et Culture (Labor and Culture, hereafter TEC). The importance of this affiliation for Marker cannot be overstated. The terms "people," "popular," and "culture" refer here neither to the mass-circulation press, radio, and television nor to the Popular Front–era Maisons de la Culture (Houses of Culture). Instead, educational initiatives undertaken by PEC and the Communist Party–affiliated TEC targeted rural and urban workers living in state-subsidized housing projects.[31] Alain Resnais recalled that TEC-organized meetings, lectures, and screenings were modeled on Vichy-era resistance groups: "There you could pick up reduced-price theater and concert tickets. It was an organization open to everyone. Chris Marker had an office there and that was how I got to know him."[32]

PEC and TEC shared a mission to create a public sufficiently informed to ask more from education than book-based learning. Filmgoers were encouraged to make film culture central to a lifelong education whose scope was political, social, and—on occasion—spiritual. Starting in 1947, Marker (signing as C. B.-Villeneuve) and Joseph Rovan coedited PEC/TEC's joint publication, *DOC*, whose ten issues included contributions by Bazin, Roger Leenhardt, and André Malraux.[33] In 1946 Marker and his fiancée, Yvonne-Yacinthe ("Yéva") Berton, accompanied Rovan to Germany to attend a PEC-sponsored residency *(stage)*, promoting Franco-German cultural relations. Marker's subsequent travels to Mexico and the United States led to letters from Mexico City and Hollywood. Over the next two decades, they generated dispatches and reports—some in print, others on celluloid—from China, Moscow, Siberia, Korea, Israel, Cuba, Japan, Brazil, Chili, Prague,

Cover of the PEC/TEC journal edited by Chris Marker and Joseph Rovan.

and Washington, D.C. Shortly after Marker's death, J. Hoberman described him as a foreign correspondent in the guise of "a romantic leftist in the Malraux mode travelling the world from West Africa to Siberia."[34]

Marker confided to Colin MacCabe that his time at TEC's offices had been one of real joy, "like May '68 every day." So much so that he considered *Esprit* and its offshoots the most interesting intellectual groupings of the early postwar years in Paris.[35] The remark echoes what the historian François Dosse calls the meteoric rise of the prophetic intellectual carried toward action by the breath of history. He names Jean-Paul Sartre as the major embodiment of this figure between 1944 and 1968.[36] Marker's support of educational reform likewise echoes what Sartre prescribes in *Qu'est-ce que la littérature?* (1948, *What Is Literature?*) as the imperative for the committed writer to act in and on the historical moment.

Esprit and the Éditions du Seuil

Emmanuel Mounier, Georges Izard, André Déléage, and Louis-Émile Galey founded *Esprit* in 1932. Its origins were akin to those of groups formed among Catholic intellectuals disaffected after Pope Pius XI condemned the neo-royalist Action française movement and banned its eponymous daily newspaper. The pope's actions precipitated a generational and ideological break with what Mounier called the established disorder of liberal parliamentary democracies. *Esprit* drew on Mounier's philosophy of personalism focused on fostering human development through political change, social communities, and spiritual conviction.[37] Its positions on political, social, economic, and cultural topics during the 1934–38 Popular Front extended to anarchist and communist efforts to rebuild communitarian sensibilities.[38] *Esprit*'s initial run temporarily halted in September 1939. It remained in print under Vichy censorship until August 1941 before reappearing in December 1944.

The *Esprit* of the 1930s featured extensive coverage of the arts, with designated columns for literature, theater, music, and film. Early contributors included Maurice Jaubert and René Leibowitz on music and Roger Leenhardt and Valéry Jahier on film. Bazin assumed duties as film critic shortly after *Esprit* resumed publication in December 1944. After Bazin's death in 1958, Michel Mesnil and Marie-Claire Ropars-Wuilleumier shared the film column over the next decade.[39] The early postwar *Esprit* was united by a dream of liberation prompted by the certainty of living "an objectively revolutionary situation" in symbiosis with the Éditions du Seuil publishing house.[40] Marker's role in this symbiosis extends to his involvement in three of the publishing house's book collections. The first of the three, "Regards neufs sur . . ." ("New perspectives on . . ."), was launched in 1951 in conjunction with PEC. Over the next sixteen years, it grew to twenty-six titles on topics ranging from tourism and reading to sports, dance, cinema, and television. Marker and Benigno Cacérès wrote the volume on the workers' movement.[41]

In 1953, Marker contributed entries on René Clair's *Entr'acte*

Cover of monograph published by Seuil in 1953 as *Regards neufs sur le cinéma* (A new look at the cinema), no. 8, Collection Peuple et Culture, ed. Jacques Chevallier. Copyright 1953 Éditions du Seuil.

(1924), Luis Buñuel's *Un chien andalou* (1929, *An Andalusian Dog*), Cocteau's *Le Sang d'un poète* (1930, *The Blood of a Poet*), Carl Theodor Dreyer's *La Passion de Jeanne d'Arc* (1928, *The Passion of Joan of Arc*), and an afterword to PEC's multi-authored volume on cinema.[42] A year after that, he participated in a companion volume on song. Writing in 1954, Bazin praised PEC's cultural activism, which upheld the moral stance of a shared renewal often rocked by the partisan politics of postwar France. Bazin also referred to Marker's layout, whose ingenious interaction of text and photos he considered the book's most instructive aspect.[43]

In 1951, Seuil assigned Francis Jeanson to direct its new book series, "Écrivains de toujours" (Eternal Writers), on domestic and foreign writers. The following year, Marker's volume on Jean Giraudoux appeared. Titles in the collection featured the name of the writer followed by the phrase *par elle/lui-même* (by herself/himself). Notable for the period was the inclusion of monographs on female writers Madame de Sévigné, Madame de la Fayette, Colette, and Virginia Woolf.[44] Volumes typically included a biographical section, an overview of major themes, selected excerpts, and a bibliography. Innovative layouts gave the books a distinctive look. A looser translation of "X par-elle/lui-même" as "X in Her/His own words" better conveys what amounted to a portrait in words and images. Roland Barthes would take this format to a new level in 1975 in his *Roland Barthes par Roland Barthes*. Pushing reflexivity toward irony, Barthes reviewed his own book in the *Quinzaine littéraire*.[45] Twenty-one years earlier, he had contributed a monograph in the collection on the historian Jules Michelet.

In 1954, Marker initiated a third monograph collection, "Petite Planète" (Small Planet), based on the model of "Écrivains de toujours" and devoted to individual countries. He oversaw the release of eighteen titles over the next four years.[46] Subsequent directors of the series—Juliette Caputo, Jacqueline Trabuc, Mathilde Rieussec, and Simone Lacouture—augmented the collection to sixty-three titles. They also added a subset of eight monographs devoted to major world cities including Amsterdam, Athens, Hong Kong, Naples, New York, Peking, Rome, and Venice. Following up on Bazin's praise of Marker's layouts in the "Regards neufs" collection, Susanna S. Martins praises Petite Planète's striking layouts of drawings, postcards, engravings, and ads: "This interplay of all kinds of images, artistic and popular, in the most various sizes, dates, positions and associations (between each other and between the text) reinforced their impact and unquestionably promoted the emergence of a plurality of meanings."[47]

The small planet motif was more than a marketing ploy. The summer 1954 issue of Seuil's promotional publication, "27, rue Jacob," includes a short text in which Marker identifies the collection with efforts to launch a new kind of tourism as a component of self-knowledge. The statement links the collection to the model of PEC and TEC's educational programs. At the turn of the century, the Michelin tire company published guidebooks to exploit the growing market of motorists, tourists, and travelers. By contrast, Marker considered each volume in the Petite Planète collection "a conversation one might like to have with someone intelligent and well-versed in the country of interest."[48]

Yet another notable example of Marker's prolific editorial work during this period is "Clair de Chine" (China Light), a 1956 photo supplement he created for *Esprit* as a film in the guise of a greeting card. Lupton describes the project as an open-ended relay that presented affinities with *Sunday in Peking*. She adds that the creation of "'China Light' was evidence of Marker's position that a film did not necessarily take the form of a projection on celluloid."[49] The same holds for the 1959 photo book, *Coréennes* (Compositions in the Korean Style), which Marker described as the first in a series of *courts-métrages* (short films).

Marker never fully abandons words for images. After the initial Berlin film, his filmmaking in *Statues* and *Olympia 52* is less a break with writing than a shift from written essays about film toward filmed essays. What Nora Alter calls an essayistic impulse

Cover of *Coréennes* (Compositions in the Korean Style, 1959), a book Marker considered a new kind of short subject film.

remains a constant throughout the interplay of word and image on paper, celluloid, and digital media.[50] The commentaries Marker writes for *Le Mystère Koumiko* (1965, *The Koumiko Mystery*), *Cuba sí!* (1961, *Cuba Yes!*), and *Si j'avais quatre dromadaires* (1966, *If I Had Four Dromedaries*) through the mid-60s are reprinted in the second volume of *Commentaires*. A decade later, the leftist writer, publisher, and bookshop owner François Maspero releases a print book of the commentary Marker had written for *A Grin without a Cat*. Curiously, the book contains no illustrations whatsoever. Seven years earlier, Marker had portrayed Maspero in a twenty-minute documentary, *On vous parle de Paris: Maspero, les mots ont un sens* (1970, Speaking to you from Paris: Maspero, words have a meaning). The trajectory of Marker's film-related writings through the mid-1960s includes his commentaries for films by

Mario Ruspoli, Resnais, Paul Paviot, Joris Ivens, and Haroun Ta-zieff.[51]

The commentaries Marker writes for *Letter from Siberia, La Jetée*, and *Sans Soleil* reaffirm his ongoing attention to written and oral expression, mainly in the form of voice-overs. The critic Roger Tailleur highlights this attention when he urges his readers to peruse

> absolutely any text by Marker: if this passion for words is not evident to you, then you clearly have never been instilled with it. Moreover, if Chris gladly takes up his pen (for Resnais, Mario Ruspoli, Paul Paviot), he never presses others into the task of speaking for him. The long-term balance between words and images may favor the latter, but Marker's commitment to writing persists.[52]

Jean-Luc Godard states in a 1963 *Cahiers* interview that he considers himself someone who produces essays in novel form, "only instead of writing, I film them." Susan Sontag notes that Godard's idea-ridden state of mind—which she describes as literary—treats cinema as an exercise in intelligence.[53]

The editorial roles Marker undertakes with Seuil's book collections tap into a design ethos in which graphic layout on the printed page *(mise-en-page)* is transposed to the arrangement of everything visible *(mise-en-scène)* in the cinematic frame. The transposition recalls modernist experimentation in silent-era films such as Walther Ruttmann's series of *Lichtspiel Opus* (1921, *Lightplay Opus*) and *Berlin: Die Sinfonie der Großstadt* (1927, *Berlin: Symphony of a Metropolis*). Michael Cowan writes:

> Modernism, in both its "high" and "low" forms, was traversed by an ethos of design, where the "surface" (the page, the poster or—we should add in this context—the screen) came to be seen as a space for proposing new life; a space for forging "types" that could help to reorder perception and redistribute the shared space of a world where the traditional forms of religious and courtly ceremony no longer held sway.[54]

Marker never cites this design ethos outright; yet its traces persist throughout his print creations. An early example of this ethos graces the cover of the German-language issue of *DOK 50* in which a medium closeup of a woman is bisected along a vertical axis. The left half of the cover features what appears to be a photonegative of an Archaic Greek or Etruscan sculpture. A photo to its right shows a woman facing the camera. She turns her head to the right while her torso remains in diagonal profile. Here typeface and layout straddle high art and advertising. The effect of this amalgam is one Rancière considers integral to the unified equivalence between forms of art, object, and image.[55] Other examples of this ethos include collages by Cubist, Dada, and Weimar-era figures Pablo Picasso, Georges Braque, Leonor Fini, and Man Ray.

A more direct influence on Marker's practices of collage and graphic design was the writer and film director Nicole Vedrès, of whom he once wrote, "Je lui dois tout" (I owe everything to her).[56]

Collage layout for *DOK 50*. From the Cinémathèque française catalog for the 2018 Chris Marker exhibit (page 42).

Film scholar Bamchade Pourvali notes that even if Marker was referring primarily to the innovative editing in Vedrès's 1947 feature-
length documentary *Paris 1900,* she had done essentially the same
thing two years earlier in a print book, *Images du cinéma français*
(1945, Images of French cinema), which she assembled from photos in the Cinémathèque française archives. The interplay of word
and image over 144 pages and 260 photos creates an album of images that is also an essay on cinematic art. Jérôme Allain notes
that *Images* was the first book on cinema published in France in
which frame grabs and photographs neither embellished nor illustrated the text.[57] The remark recalls Bazin's words cited in the epigraph to this introduction. The film producer Pierre Braunberger
was so taken with the innovative layouts throughout Vedrès's book
that he commissioned her to undertake a film project.[58] The result
was *Paris 1900.*

Where might Marker have seen the films that prompted his
publications in *Esprit* and related print venues? Did he see them
at ciné-clubs, perhaps alongside Bazin and Cocteau? Or at the
Cinémathèque française screenings organized by Henri Langlois? Marker told *Cinéaste* editor Gary Crowdus that after his
Free French unit was placed under temporary U.S. command,
he watched a brand-new copy of Vincente Minnelli's *Meet Me in
St. Louis* (1944) somewhere in the ruins of a German city. (This
was probably between February and July 1945.)[59] Laurent Mannoni sets Marker alongside postwar figures Alexandre Astruc
and Georges Sadoul, whose knowledge of film history acquired at
Cinémathèque and ciné-club screenings prompted a "certain conception of image layout based on aesthetic options, moral choices,
and extreme repulsions.[60] Eric Smoodin writes that in late October
1945 there were around 275 commercial cinemas in Paris, a number he bases on listings in the film weekly *Cinévie.* The twenty-six
films showing that week at thirty-five first-run venues ranged from
U.S. features such as Alfred Hitchcock's *Shadow of a Doubt* (1943)
to French releases such as Léon Mathot's *La Route du bagne* (1945,

The Road to Jail), starring Viviane Romance. Neighborhood venues
often programmed prewar films such as Marcel Carné's *Drôle de
drame* (1937, *Bizarre Bizarre*), with audience favorites Louis Jouvet and Michel Simon.[61]

Nearly half of the 200 or so films Marker mentions in the texts
translated in this volume were U.S.-based productions, including some directed by Orson Welles, John Huston, and Elia Kazan.
Other countries of production listed are Germany, France, Italy,
Denmark, Mexico, the United Kingdom, and Soviet Russia. The
large number of U.S. films results from terms of the May 1946
Blum–Byrnes agreement that erased nearly three billion dollars
of France's wartime debt in exchange for opening the French commercial film market to American releases. The agreement required
French exhibitors to adhere to a programming cycle comprising
four consecutive weeks of domestic films exclusively, followed by
nine weeks of unrestricted programming, which often meant recent and older Hollywood releases.

Marker at *Esprit*

Esprit's website lists ninety-four texts attributed to Chris Marker,
Chris Mayor, or C.M. These include two short fictions, two poems,
and ninety nonfiction prose works.[62] Many appeared in a back-
section digest, "Journal à Plusieurs Voix" (Digest in multiple
voices), whose open-ended format suited Marker's taste for mixing cultural and rhetorical registers. The digest grew out of weekly
meetings at Seuil's offices on the rue Jacob, where participants
brought in materials to generate discussions and develop their
professional skills.

Marker's film writings make up less than 10 percent of his total
contributions to *Esprit*. Approximately 40 percent address literary
topics, with the remaining 50 percent devoted to social and political issues. In sum, his *Esprit* articles chronicle French politics
and culture during the often rocky transition from the liberation to
Cold War politics and state-run modernization. Positions all along

Year	1946	1947	1948	1949	1950	1951	1952	1953	1954	1955
Number of articles	2	37	37 (F2)	7 (F2)	2 (F1)	6 (F2)	2 (F1)	0	0	1 (F1)
Running total	2	39	76	83	85	91	93	93	93	94

A timeline of Chris Marker publications in *Esprit* from 1946 to 1955. The parenthetical numbers indicate the number of film-related publications published each year, while the main number shows the total number of publications.

the partisan spectrum often shifted the stakes of debate from symbolic prestige to policy dominance. This helps to explain *Esprit*'s crucial role during the period as a footbridge between Catholic intellectuals and the French Communist Party.[63]

Postwar pen-and-ink debates coincided with trial-based purges of politicians, writers, actors, artists, musicians, publishers, and film directors suspected of wartime collaboration. Two of Marker's first three publications in *Esprit* during this Janus-like period are short fictions set in wartime and early postwar locales. The first, "Les Vivants et les morts" (The living and the dead) features an angel named Gabriel who finds himself in an unnamed city under military surveillance. Midway through the story, the refrain of the popular World War II song "Lili Marleen" heard in the distance evokes wartime France under German occupation. Several pages later, a woman named Kristel says to Gabriel:

> Until now the nearest beings I have known were at unbelievable distances, and we . . . we suffered a lot to arrive where we are. And it is by the evil that we do unto each other that we have recognized each other.[64]

Marker's decision to cast his initial publication in *Esprit* as a wartime fiction points to the priority he places on contending with France's recent past. It is likely no coincidence that the name Gabriel reappears a year later in the title of Marker's first film. In

Abrahamic religions, Gabriel is an archangel with power to an-
nounce God's will to men. He is mentioned in the Hebrew Bible,
the New Testament, and the Quran. It is Gabriel who announces
to the Virgin Mary that she would have a child.

Marker's third *Esprit* publication, "Till the End of Time," is also
a fiction whose temporal setting on the day after V-J Day may
have drawn on Marker's brief service in the U.S. military. Tissot's
chronology mentions an unpublished 1945 short story whose title,
"Le Jour de la victoire" (Victory Day), suggests possible links to
the subsequent *Esprit* publication. "Till the End of Time" features
American soldiers, Pat and Jerry, whose clipped exchanges recall
contemporary dialogue in pulp and detective fiction by Dashiell
Hammett, Raymond Chandler, and James M. Cain. Marker sprin-
kles the dialogues with cultural details, including racial slurs that
were unacceptable at the time and remain so today. Pat, for example, talks of going to a jazz club to hear a Black trumpet player
"drool into his instrument."[65]

The following description of a young woman could pass for
that of a film noir *femme fatale* such as Barbara Stanwyck's Phyllis Dietrichson in Billy Wilder's *Double Indemnity* (1944) or Jane
Greer's Kathie Moffat in Jacques Tourneur's *Out of the Past* (1947):

> The woman stood near him, her mouth hot and defenseless like a
> dead bird. He realized he hadn't even been able to make out her body
> lost in the shadows and obscured by the muddled lights, yet from it
> rose something that was both a promise and a threat. He dared not
> look her in the eyes, but on the breath approaching closer and closer
> he smelled the scents of a body wet with rain, of bitten fruit, and of
> something like the taste of annihilation.[66]

I have yet to find evidence confirming that Marker had seen
the Wilder and Tourneur films before completing "Till the End
of Time." It is more probable that he knew Sabine Berritz's 1936
French translation of James M. Cain's *The Postman Always Rings
Twice (Le Facteur sonne toujours deux fois),* for which Irène

Barbara Stanwyck as Phyllis Dietrichson and Fred MacMurray as Walter
Neff in Billy Wilder's classic film noir *Double Indemnity* (1944).

Jane Greer as Kathie Moffat and Robert Mitchum as Jeff Bailey on the run
in Jacques Tourneur's *Out of the Past* (1947).

Némirovsky wrote a preface. The same may be the case for the previous cinematic adaptation of *Postman* by Pierre Chenal (1939, *Le Dernier Tournant*). The 1946 U.S. release directed by Tay Garnett stars Lana Turner and John Garfield; the French release date was November 12, 1947.

Marker's Non-Film Related Publications in *Esprit*

The composer Pierre Schaeffer was a major proponent of midcentury *musique concrète*. He was also the author of *Amérique, nous t'ignorons* (1946, America, we misunderstand you), which prompted Marker's earliest nonfiction article in *Esprit*. Schaeffer and Marker met six years earlier at Jeune France (Young France), a cultural movement whose Radio-Jeunesse (Radio-Youth) broadcasts Schaeffer directed. Jeune France was founded in August 1940 in Uriage, a town near Grenoble; it was part of the École nationale des cadres de la jeunesse d'Uriage (The National School for Youth Administrators at Uriage), created to train elite administrators for the Vichy regime. Uriage faculty and students, however, soon deviated from Vichy policies, especially those concerning antisemitism.

Vichy's Prime Minister Pierre Laval retaliated by closing the school in March 1942. Within two years, former Uriage students Hubert Beuve-Méry (the future founder of the postwar daily *Le Monde*) and Jean-Marie Domenach (the future editor-in-chief of *Esprit*) had joined resistance groups. Benigno Cacérès and Joffre Dumazedier cited Uriage as a model for what they hoped to achieve when they launched PEC.[67] Schaeffer's vision of Jeune France as a political and cultural movement may also have been a factor in Marker's later commitment to TEC and PEC's educational programs. Additional members of the Uriage group included pianist Alfred Cortot, actors Pierre Fresnay and Pierre Renoir, and theatrical impresario Jean Vilar.

Marker's affiliation with Uriage sparked debate seventy years after the fact. Despite what sounded loosely like a disclaimer—"This intervention on a former life of Chris Marker is intended neither to denounce nor accuse"—Éric Marty's notice in *Le Monde* less than three weeks after Marker's death was ill-timed, to say the least. Marty did little to support any claims to objectivity when he wrote of Marker: "Loath, as was Maurice Blanchot, to being photographed, he leaves on this period some shadow and many enigmas." In reply to Marty, Jean-Michel Frodon wrote that "only in retrospect and with a romanticism and naïveté that poorly mask a desire to annihilate, could someone be inspired to make the case long after the fact against the man who, under the pseudonym Marc Dornier, cofounds *La Revue française* in 1941."[68]

The seventy-four texts Marker published in *Esprit* in 1947 and 1948 document a period of sustained reflection on the politics and culture of postwar France. Even when film is cited only in passing, it remains a frequent nexus. This is the case in a brief notice on the earthly paradise in which Marker refers to the Hollywood comics Stan Laurel and Oliver Hardy. Lupton considers the reference an example of Marker's ability to compose brief and arresting sketches covering "a breathtaking range of topics: from religious questions to cinema, from song to Cold War ideology, and cat shows to literary scandals."[69] Phillip Lopate discerns a tension in Marker's films between "the politically committed, self-effacing, left-wing documentarist style of the [Joris] Ivens tendency and an irrepressibly Montaignesque personal tone."[70] Lopate is referring specifically to Marker's later documentaries such as *Le Joli Mai, A Grin without a Cat,* and *Sans Soleil.* But that tension is already present in Marker's *Esprit* writings.

A penchant for acerbic reportage appears in Marker's coverage of a Louis Aragon lecture that he describes as a spectacle of provocation between speaker and audience. He writes that the sight of this "well-dressed apologist for the French Communist Party" makes him yearn for the extravagance the same man had displayed twenty years earlier as a Parisian surrealist.[71] Since Aragon's period as an active surrealist coincides with the first decade

of Marker's life, it is unclear whether the remark is straightfor-
ward, ironic, or a bit of both. A similar edge permeates a notice
on the death of Al "Scarface" Capone in which Marker quips that
the notorious Chicago crime boss had received extreme unction
twice, the second time for good measure.[72] The notice's subtitle
"La Mort de Scarface, ou les Infortunes de la vertu" (The death of
Scarface, or the misfortunes of virtue) and its evocation of D. A. F.
Sade's 1791 novel *Justine ou les infortunes de la vertu (Justine, or the
Misfortunes of Virtue)* set the tone for remarks that evoke Howard
Hawks's 1932 talkie *Scarface*. Not properly an example of film writ-
ing, the notice is best read as a tongue-in-cheek obituary. (The real
Al Capone died in 1947.)

A lighter touch dominates "Du Jazz considéré comme une
prophétie" (On jazz considered as prophecy), in which Marker covers a TEC-sponsored talk by the writer and musician Boris Vian:

> The cornet player Boris Christopher Vian has the nonchalant and
> thoughtful demeanor of a Russian wolfhound who might have read
> Kierkegaard, the scornful pout of Louis XIV, and the deep-set eyes
> of Prince Drubetskoy, a vast and radiant forehead around which his
> hair is admirably parted, and—above all—the commendable charm
> and simplicity of a young man already in possession of his personal
> legend.[73]

Ever attentive to wordplay, Marker quips that *Esprit*'s readers
might relish the fact that pronouncing New Orleans's Basin Street
as though it were a French word would transform it into Bazin
Street. In a more expository mode, Marker posits affinities between Duke Ellington's pre-bebop compositions and harmonics
associated with Alban Berg's twelve-tone works. (Vian was a serious jazz fan and an accomplished cornetist. He wrote reviews for
Le Jazz hot and brokered Paris gigs for Hoagy Carmichael, Ellington, and Miles Davis.)

Marker's remarks on the emergence of bebop read as a short
lesson in musicology:

We know how contemporary music has rediscovered Medieval scales and assorted trinkets with unprecedented pleasure. Now it seems bebop has left contemporary music far behind, and that an encounter between [Dizzy] Gillespie and [René] Leibowitz would pulverize the latter. [...] It is certainly not by chance that the most memorable recording of this memorable evening event, a sort of catastrophe for seventeen instruments by Dizzy Gillespie, grandmaster of the bebop order, was entitled "Choses à venir" (Things to come) and the trumpet of the [Last] Judgment would play a bebop phrase, which would not really be all that shocking.[74]

Once again Marker resorts to swipes and slams when he concludes by setting bebop alongside atomic bomb tests, abstract painting, fashion, and Rita Hayworth as an element of postwar life capable of annoying those set in their ways by reminding them of the world's fragility and its potential for self-destruction. Marker's musical knowledge makes him Vian's equal.

Marker's reportage articles in *Esprit* evoke a cross between cultural critic Siegfried Kracauer's Weimar-era journalism in the *Frankfurter Zeitung* and items in the *New Yorker*'s "Talk of the Town" column. They also anticipate Roland Barthes's "Petite Mythologie du mois" (Little mythology of the month) column whose first installment, "Le Monde où l'on catche" ("In the Ring") appears in *Esprit*'s October 1952 issue. For *Esprit*'s 13,000 readers, the urbane and often mordant tone of Marker's reportages expresses his perspective on France's postwar politics and culture.

Marker's Imaginary Film Archive

Marker's film-based articles in *Esprit* typically start as reportages prompted by screenings, retrospectives, and—in one instance—a dissertation defense. They often broaden toward essay-like reflections on medium specificity, film history, film style, animation, and pedagogy. A shift occurs from 1951 to 1953 when Marker supplements his film-based publications in *Esprit* with others in *Cahiers du cinéma* and *Positif* monthlies and two multiauthored books. The shift coincides with the increased emphasis he assigns to filmmaking and film culture as social activities linked to national practices in Germany, France, Mexico, and Hollywood. For Germany, Marker addresses the obstacles associated with filmmaking in the aftermath of World War II. For Mexico, he identifies the negative role of monopolies complicit with films that promote a so-called way of life built on sexuality and violence. Articles on Hollywood and the United States focus on censorship and an industry-wide crisis for which 3-D and wide-screen technologies are seen as remedies to declining box-office figures linked to the rise of home television.

The shift to multiple print venues also coincides with Marker's collaboration on *Statues* with Resnais as well as a 1952 trip to Finland where he films the Helsinki Olympic Games on assignment for PEC. The material product of this trip is *Olympia 52,* Marker's first feature-length documentary, whose commentary and shot/ countershot sequences of athletes and spectators add human elements to an otherwise straight reportage.[75] Subsequent visits to North America provide on-location settings for Marker's articles "Letter from Mexico City," "Letter from Hollywood," "Cinerama," and "Hollywood on Location." Visits to Germany dating back to 1946 likewise inform reportages such as "Siegfried and the Gaolers" and "Farewell to German Cinema?" Marker often reconfigures ongoing concerns and topics. He first addresses animation in conjunction with pedagogy in a 1951 *Esprit* reportage of a dissertation defense at the Sorbonne's Institut de Filmologie. He returns to animation in texts devoted to Robert Cannon's *Gerald McBoing-Boing,* Jiří Trnka's puppet animation feature *Prince Bayaya,* and the United Productions of America (UPA) studio. Similar clusters appear in Marker's reflections on postwar Hollywood, from his early piece on Robert Montgomery's *Lady in the Lake* to his 1955 article on Elia Kazan's *On the Waterfront.* The four single-film pieces he writes for *Esprit* are offset by the two essay-type "letters" in *Cahiers* and a third on Cinerama reprinted more or less word-for-word in *Cinéma 53*.

Marker's earliest film-based article in *Esprit* links Laurence Olivier's 1944 adaptation of Shakespeare's *Henry V* to issues of medium specificity by characterizing painting and theater as two roads leading to the *cinématographe*. Where the former derives from cave paintings, the Bayeux Tapestry, and Baroque-era painting, the latter draws on theatrical performance. Marker clarifies his use of the term *cinématographe* in place of the more conventional *cinéma* when he writes that movement in theatrical performance awaited cinema's invention of the close-up to convey the inner—emotional—movement of subjects. References to Orson Welles and Sergei Eisenstein as well as Fred Niblo's *Ben-Hur* (1925) and Roberto Rossellini's *Paisà* (1946) align Marker's remarks on adaptation and directorial style. Marker's quips and barbs provoke minor jolts, as when he describes a four-minute tracking shot at the end of act 4 as an abrupt shift from the late medieval painter Jean Fouquet to Buffalo Bill.

Later the same year, Marker discredits Robert Montgomery's adaptation of Raymond Chandler's detective novel, *Lady in the Lake*, in which camera placement purportedly matches the point-of-view of Chandler's protagonist Philip Marlowe. Marker challenges this claim when he cites a sequence in which Marlowe improbably sees his reflection in a mirror . . . with his eyes closed! How much more subjective, Marker counters, is the scene in Edward Dmytryk's *Murder, My Sweet* (1944) in which a drugged Marlowe (Dick Powell) is enveloped in a web of smoke. Or the final tracking shot in Welles's *The Lady from Shanghai* (1947) that achieves more visually in a few seconds than all of Montgomery's clumsy efforts. The antecedents of a truly subjective film, which Marker considers yet to be made, are the literary efforts of Marcel Proust, Raymond Radiguet, André Malraux, and Guillaume Apollinaire. The statement reconfirms the extent to which Marker's early film-based writings draw on literary sources.

Robert Montgomery as Philip Marlowe pretends to see his reflection with his eyes closed in his dubious efforts at subjective cinema in Montgomery's *Lady in the Lake* (1947).

Audrey Totter as Adrienne Fromsett mugs for the camera in *Lady in the Lake.*

Instead of relishing Audrey Totter's facial contortions, Marker suggests that spectators would do well to ponder why Montgomery's experiment had failed. The title of the piece, *"L'imparfait du subjectif,"* announces Marker's reservations, since the French word *imparfait* is both an adjective ("imperfect") and a noun referring to the past indicative tense. Marker plays on these two meanings by echoing the more familiar *imparfait du subjonctif* (imperfect subjunctive), an outdated verb form whose usage is increasingly rare. A decade later, Raymond Borde and Étienne Chaumont would note that although *Lady in the Lake* was disappointing, Montgomery's notion of a subjective camera, "when judiciously used" in films such as *Murder, My Sweet* and Delmer Daves's *Dark Passage,* had yielded excellent moments.[76]

Marker inflects medium specificity via pedagogy and adaptation in a reportage on female high school students *(lycéennes)* assigned to offer advice for a proposed film based on Pierre Corneille's 1640 tragedy *Horace.* He starts by praising the instructor for finding inventive ways to motivate his students by asking them whom they might cast in various roles. The names they suggest—Pierre Blanchar, Michèle Morgan, and Jean Marais— display a precocious sophistication. Another reportage later the same year shifts the site of pedagogy to a Cinémathèque française retrospective Marker describes as an immersive initiation capable of turning adolescents into cinephiles.

A third take on pedagogy is prompted by a screening of Cocteau's 1950 *Orpheus* for young filmmakers moved to silence, as though they suddenly found themselves in a radioactive zone. Film audiences watch *Orpheus,* Marker declares, much as one reads Kafka; that is, for the prefiguration of grace revealed through Cocteau's ability to project his personal obsessions onto his protagonist. By the time *Orpheus* was released, Cocteau had cofounded the Objectif 49 ciné-club and headed the jury at the 1949 Festival du film maudit (Festival of Damned Films) in Biarritz. Frédéric Gimello-Mesplomb places Marker alongside Alexandre Astruc,

Éric Rohmer, Jean Douchet, Jean-Luc Godard, François Truffaut, and a cohort of adolescent cinephiles on a train from Paris to Biarritz.[77] Three years later, Marker returns to Cocteau in PEC's *Regards neufs sur le cinéma* when he sets *The Blood of a Poet* within a silent-era avant-garde.

Animated films are the starting point of four texts Marker published between 1951 and 1954. Two appear in *Esprit*, the third in *Cahiers*, and the last in *Cinéma 53*. The first of the four, inflected again by pedagogy, is prompted by a dissertation defense directed by the aesthetician Étienne Souriau at the Sorbonne's Institute of Filmology.[78] Marker first describes the dissertation as a welcome change from stodgy literary types for whom cinema is an unsettling return to barbarity. Yet he soon contests the viability of a quantitative approach to account for the emotions these films generate. Marker adopts strident words to chide the dissertator, Marie-Thérèse Poncet, for relying on Disney studio productions to support her comparison of medieval illustrations and animated films. He continues by asking disingenuously whether what the Bayeux Tapestry prefigures is closer to Disney's *The Three Little Pigs* or to Eisenstein's *Alexander Nevsky*.

Marker pushes irony toward ridicule when he questions to what degree Poncet's argument might extend to the Fleischer Studios' Betty Boop or to Popeye, Woody Woodpecker, Tom and Jerry, or to works by the animators Paul Grimault, Walter Lantz, Tex Avery, Saul Steinberg, and Émile Cohl, all of whom Poncet overlooks.[79] Three months later he responds to a gentle admonition from Alain Resnais for having failed to mention Robert Cannon's animated short *Gerald McBoing-Boing*. Is the reprimand sincere? Or a shared joke among friends? Either way, Marker sides with Cannon's Oscar-winning cartoon by citing it as a counterexample to Disney's cheap rubbish. A 1952 *Cahiers* piece on Jiří Trnka's *Prince Bayaya* allows Marker to develop his views on animation in conjunction with cinema's capacity to mobilize duration in ways that transcend distinctions among visual and performing arts: "No more false distinctions between theatre and cinema, painting, and cinema."[80] Marker prefers the simplicity of Trnka's *Prince Bayaya* to the lyrical bruises that keep the universe Walt Disney strives to create in *Fantasia* (1940) closed in on itself. When Marker refers to Trnka's animated films as a form of ornament, he ascribes to it a value of civilization and a constant homage to the act of creation.

A third motif in Marker's writings explores avant-garde practices dating back to the silent era. Carl Theodor Dreyer's *La Passion de Jeanne d'Arc* (1928, *The Passion of Joan of Arc*) merits this designation through its pairing of cinematic style and cast performances, especially that of the female lead Renée Falconetti. Marker writes twice about the film, first in *Esprit* and again in PEC's *Regards neufs sur le cinéma*. The *Esprit* piece is prompted by a newly discovered negative whose pristine prints heighten spectator emotion. Image clarity also results from the attention Dreyer and cinematographer Rudolph Maté pay to the close-up achieved through framing.[81] For Marker, the new prints mark a technical and artistic achievement in which:

> Skin texture, tears, drool, whites of the eyes *perform,* and where the human figure is no longer rendered a black and white ideogram by orthochromatic film, which brilliantly showed off Chaplin, but the equivalent, in relation to the screen, of a crowd or of a landscape—this possibility is much more than just a film historian's satisfaction. It's a gift to the spectator. And spectators make no mistake, since this silent film from 1928 has been showing continuously for several weeks in a cinema usually reserved for short runs (true, it does have a soundtrack, but it's just discreet enough so that in 1952, the audience, accustomed to muttering in their seats, stays quiet and doesn't hear the silence). Moral of the story: adding a soundtrack is the only way to make a truly silent film.[82]

Shots of Jeanne framed by halo effects contrast with unframed extreme close-ups of Bishop Pierre Cauchon. Two medium close-ups shot from below monumentalize three of Joan's judges. A year

Extreme close-up of a tearful Joan (Renée Falconetti) on trial in Carl Theodor Dreyer's *The Passion of Joan of Arc* (1928).

Close-up of the cruel Bishop Cauchon (Eugène Silvain) in *The Passion of Joan of Arc*.

later, Marker compares Dreyer's image compositions and editing
favorably to the childish stylizations in Fritz Lang's *Metropolis*.
Also of note are references to facial close-ups in Robert Bresson's
Journal d'un curé de campagne (1951, *Diary of a Country Priest*)
and a remark that Maté's framed shots in Charles Vidor's 1946 film
noir *Gilda* draw on his collaboration with Dreyer two decades earlier.

Marker devotes his final film-based text in *Esprit* to Elia Kazan's 1954 feature *On the Waterfront*, whose cinematography and
editing he praises as conveying psychological complexities previously found only in the novel. As in his piece on the Sorbonne
dissertation, Marker's initial praise for *On the Waterfront*'s photographic style does not stop him from criticizing the use of a hand-
held camera to dramatize Brando's unsteady gait in the film's
climactic sequence. Repeated references to the actor Brando suggest that Marker's reservations concerning Terry Malloy's crisis of
conscience might derive from Kazan's efforts to justify his naming
of names before the House Un-American Activities Committee's

Terry Malloy (Marlon Brando) dons Edie Doyle's (Eva Marie Saint) glove so
that he can keep talking to her in Elia Kazan's *On the Waterfront* (1954).

Kazan uses the theatrical convention of a dropping stage curtain to convey a sense of closure in the final shot of *On the Waterfront.*

hearings on communists in Hollywood. Marker also speculates on a subplot in which Brando's Malloy is a converted homosexual burdened with the heavy conscience of a repentant informer. Three decades later, James Naremore would write that Terry's slipping on Edie's mitten during the urban park sequence supports what Kazan once described as a "bisexual" element of Brando's on-screen image.[83] The closure implied by the film's final shot of a warehouse door dropping like a stage curtain turns out to be nothing more than a change from one boss to another.

New Venues: *Cahiers, Positif,* and Beyond

The five articles Marker contributes to *Cahiers du cinéma* between July 1951 and October 1953 address conditions affecting film and filmmaking as social and political phenomena. Three provide overviews of postwar practices in Germany, Mexico, and Hollywood. A fourth article, on Cinerama, boosts wide-screen technologies among Hollywood's efforts to regain market share among filmgoers drawn to home television.

The title of the first *Cahiers* essay, "Siegfried and the Gaolers, or German Cinema in Chains," places a figure of German mythology alongside an outdated French term for a prison guard or policeman. It also resonates with *Siegfried et le Limousin* (1922, *My Friend from Limousin*), the title of a novel by Jean Giraudoux who is the subject of Marker's 1952 monograph in Seuil's "par lui-même" collection. Six years after the end of World War II, Marker argues, Italian releases are receiving the wide distribution and critical attention systematically denied to films by German directors Wolfgang Staudte and Helmut Käutner.

Staudte's *Die Mörder sind unter uns* (1946, *The Murderers Are among Us*) was released by the Deutsche Film-Aktiengesellschaft (DEFA), the postwar production company established in Berlin's Soviet-occupied zone of what was soon to become the German Democratic Republic (GDR). *Murderers* is also an early example of the rubble film (*Trümmerfilm*), which Eric Rentschler describes as a cycle of some sixty feature films that share a historical situation, a production context, and a political mission.[84] Rubble in the film is both literal and figurative. Staudte conveys its cinematic expression in long shots of towerlike ruins. In line with the subsequent division of Third Reich Germany into two republics, Staudte conceived of *Murderers* in the West but shot it in the East. Five years later, Marker writes, East German cinema is coming to terms with a reality that West Germany continues to skirt: "On the one hand, life with all its compromises and imperfections, and on the other, a flower-covered void."[85]

Two articles cast as letters from Mexico City and Hollywood focus on federal and industry-wide policies affecting film production, distribution, and exhibition. Marker was in Mexico at a UNESCO-funded training program to eradicate global illiteracy. A 1952 report on a UNESCO seminar held in Paris refers to Mr. Christian Bouche-Villeneuve as an author, translator, instructor, and director of a short subject whose application for support includes a two-month stay in Ottawa and a three-month residency at the Pátzcuaro Center in Mexico.[86] In "Letter from Mexico City,"

Marker notes that the priority assigned to the commercial content most likely to maximize box-office numbers led one newspaper to assert that there was no such thing as Mexican cinema, only cinema made in Mexico. Marker likewise questions a predilection for melodrama whose plots sketch a so-called Mexican way of life based on machismo, submissive women, and tequila-fueled excess. He concludes that only infrequent productions by non-Mexicans such as John Huston, John Ford, Paul Strand, and Sergei Eisenstein hold promise of making a memorable film.

"Letter from Hollywood: On Three Dimensions and a Fourth" and "Hollywood on Location" continue Marker's critique of Hollywood studio efforts to promote 3-D and wide-screen technologies. He begins by challenging film industry claims equating the impact of 3-D with those of sound and color. The new technology, he asserts, is nothing in itself and would begin to exist only through the use to which it is put. Marker emphasizes the point when he concludes that 3-D would be aesthetic or not be at all. The sentence plays on André Breton's call for convulsive beauty in the last lines of *Nadja* (1928): "Beauty will be CONVULSIVE or will not be at all."[87]

Marker's counterexample to Hollywood's infatuation with new technologies is Irving Lerner's *Man Crazy*. The film in two rather than three dimensions features what Marker calls a fourth dimension in the form of a story. His plot recap of *Man Crazy* centers on three teenage women in a small American city who discover a box containing $17,000 while babysitting at the home of a local doctor. The teenagers steal the money to finance a shopping spree in New York City. (Plot details vary among sources. The American Film Institute's entry on the film replaces the doctor with a pharmacist and has the babysitters heading out to Hollywood.) The police arrest the women and an investigation reveals that the money they stole came from illegal abortions the doctor had performed. The doctor kills himself, while the young women, Marker opines, are jailed for believing that money held the key to everything.

Suggestive lobby poster—"Bold! Blunt! Brutal!"—for Irving Lerner's exploitation feature *Man Crazy* (1953), which exposes the hypersexualized treatment of young women. Courtesy of Wisconsin Center for Film and Theater Research.

Man Crazy was a low-budget ("B-film") release whose depictions of sexuality and lessons in morality located it alongside youth exploitation films of the period. A poster promoting the film as "Bold! Blunt! Brutal!" reduces the babysitters to sex objects. I have yet to see anything more than the film's trailer. But the Irving Lerner who directs *Man Crazy* has a backstory of his own in conjunction with radical U.S. filmmakers' groups of the 1930s such as the Workers' Film and Photo League. The same is true for *Man Crazy*'s screenwriters Philip Yordan and Sidney Harmon and for the filmmaker Willard Van Dyke, all three of whom Marker cites in the article.[88] Marker lists Lerner's professional credits, including Van Dyke's 1940 *Valley Town* and Robert Flaherty's 1942 *The Land*. The UCLA arts library holdings include a file containing

Lerner's 1954–55 correspondence with Marker and his wife concerning future collaborations. The correspondence likely drew on Marker's interactions with Lerner during his spring 1953 stay in Los Angeles.[89]

What might have prompted Marker to compare Lerner's *Man Crazy* to a 3-D release such as *Bwana Devil*? Kyle Westphal notes that Lerner's social sphere during the 1930s and 1940s existed on the radical Communist–Popular Front axis.[90] Marker's reflections on Lerner resonate with the militant stances he adopts not only in his own filmmaking, from *Statues* to *A Grin without a Cat*, but also in conjunction with the SLON and ISKRA filmmaking collectives in which he is active from the mid-1960s to mid-1970s. An early instance of this resonance appears toward the end of *Statues* in two newsreel clips. One shows U.S. Marshals shooting at labor union organizers. The other is of Communist Party members Eugene Dennis, Henry Winston, and others entering a police van. For Sam Di Iorio, the critique of cultural appropriation in *Statues* "[has] become a sign of transnational resistance to the domination of a broadly framed possessor class."[91] Another explanation for what Marker sees in *Man Crazy* points to what he considers its realist depiction of social and economic class. Antecedents here might be the films of Italian Neorealist directors Roberto Rossellini and Vittorio De Sica as well as depictions of economic and educational tensions in Jean Vigo's *À propos de Nice* (1930, *Concerning Nice*), *Zéro de conduite* (1933, *Zero for Conduct*), and *L'Atalante* (1934, a.k.a. *Le Chaland qui passe*, *The Passing Barge*).

Marker describes Lerner as a man of the documentary whose work for the Motion Picture Division of the U.S. Office of Wartime Intelligence included credits for the shorts *A Place to Live* (1941) and *Hymn of the Nations* (1944).[92] Yet Marker makes no mention of allegations that Lerner had been a mole for Soviet military intelligence. The allegations stemmed from an incident in which a counterintelligence agent purportedly observed Lerner photographing the University of California at Berkeley's cyclotron without the proper security clearance. Lerner never faced formal charges, and his name never appeared alongside those of Hollywood Ten figures such as Edward Dmytryk, Albert Maltz, and Dalton Trumbo. Even so, his postwar career was uneven. He died in 1976 while working as an uncredited advisor on *New York, New York,* which the film's director Martin Scorsese dedicated to him.

For Marker, "Hollywood on Location" provides the political backstory to Hollywood's postwar crisis by tracking federal investigations of the Screenwriters' Guild between 1934 and 1947. Yet not even this serious-minded account of film industry politics prevents Marker from the occasional quip or barb, as when he dismisses Gene Kelly and Stanley Donen's screenplay for *Singin' in the Rain* as trite. Or, when he notes that Louis Calhern's performance as Caesar in Joseph Mankiewicz's *Julius Caesar* is heightened by his physical resemblance to General Charles de Gaulle.

"Cinerama" in *Cahiers'* October 1953 issue reviews a feature-length advertisement for the new wide-screen process made possible by the coordination of three projectors. Its inclusion in *Cinéma 53* makes it the only text in our corpus to be reprinted virtually verbatim. Minor differences between the two versions include a change in title from "Cinerama" in the *Cahiers* version to "And Now This Is Cinerama" in *Cinéma 53.* The latter invokes words spoken by on-screen narrator Lowell Thomas just as the film switches from black-and-white to color and from the standard 1.37:1 aspect ratio to wide-screen 2.65:1. A second difference adds a parenthetical phrase asserting that "investigations" is a dangerous word to use at the time, an overt reference to HUAC's activities. It appears in the *Cahiers* version but not in the *Cinéma 53* reprint. A final difference takes the form of a four-page addition in the latter by the screenwriter and film critic Gavin Lambert, for whom Cinerama and Cinemascope extend a cinema of attractions initiated during the silent-film era by the Lumière brothers and by Abel Gance.

A climactic sequence in *This Is Cinerama* tracks an airplane flying west toward the Pacific coast over scenic territory. Saccharine arrangements of "America the Beautiful" on the soundtrack tone down traces of midcentury jingoism in Thomas's commentary. Marker is no dupe: "In short, not a single cliché is spared: the presentation is nonchalant and the effect crude. The imagery stops at postcards, art with opera, and the universe with America."[93] The piece asserts Marker's preference for the potential merits of wide-screen technologies over 3-D's promise of increased depth. It is fair to ask what Marker might have thought about 21st-century 3-D releases such as Werner Herzog's *Cave of Forgotten Dreams* (2010), Wim Wenders's *Pina* (2011), and Jean-Luc Godard's *Adieu au langage* (2014, *Goodbye to Language*).

This book documents a formative phase of what Catherine Lupton calls Marker's involvement with activities undertaken with a view toward cultural renewal and political revolution.[94] "Cinema, Art of the Twenty-first Century?" is the afterword Marker writes for PEC's *Regards neufs sur le cinéma*. Its title recasts the assertion set forth in the book's subtitle ("Cinema, Art of the Twentieth Century") into a question. The result redirects the temporal scope of Marker's reflections from the current crisis related to home television toward the long-term effects of new technologies on the future of what he calls the cinematic spectacle. The afterword does not detract from Marker's critique of Hollywood's capitalism. More to the point, it announces Marker's recognition that Hollywood's incessant commercial reflex might eventually produce aesthetic techniques such as those associated with wide-screen explorations undertaken by Abel Gance and Raymond Spottiswoode.

Marker hints at the nature of this renewal when he writes that major Hollywood producers have begun to look for novelty *(se sont mis à chercher du nouveau)*. The italicized phrase recalls the final verse of Charles Baudelaire's 1859 poem *Le Voyage* ("The Voyage"): *"Au fond de l'Inconnu pour trouver du nouveau!"* ("To the depths of the unknown to find the new!").[95] The antecedent he provides for this aesthetic-based change is the deep focus in Welles's

Citizen Kane: deep focus I. Director Orson Welles and cinematographer Gregg Toland use deep focus in the classic *Citizen Kane* (1941) to stage two pivotal sequences in three planes of action.

Citizen Kane: deep focus II. Shot of Kane at typewriter in foreground and Jedediah Leland in middleground.

Citizen Kane (1941). He might also have cited Jean Renoir's use of the same technique in *La Règle du jeu* (1939, *Rules of the Game*). Marker's critique of Hollywood's infatuation with 3-D and widescreen technologies is inseparable from the long-term impact on cinematic representation searching for its true aesthetic forms: "The spectacle taking shape amidst so many upheavals might be an instrument of the twenty-first century's great collective celebration: the culmination of film, theatre, and mural painting, the veritable new vision of an entire people."[96]

As I complete this introduction, only a fraction of the materials donated to the Cinémathèque française by Marker's literary heirs has been processed for consultation. Additional insights will surely follow as more materials become available. It is my hope that the translations at the core of this book will generate new projects. These might include translating the full run of Marker's *Esprit* publications through 1955. Or taking a closer look at Marker's film-based publications alongside those in *André Bazin's New Media*.[97] Or even comparing Marker's film writings of the period to those of Georges Sadoul, Jean-Luc Godard, and François Truffaut. I close my remarks with a popular slogan from May '68: This is only the start: let's continue. *Ce n'est qu'un début. Continuons . . .*

Notes

1. Jean-Louis Comolli, "Les *Coréennes* de Chris Marker," *Trafic*, no. 109 (Spring 2019): 95; François Crémieux, "Chris Marker, nouvelle plume de la revue *Esprit*," in *Chris Marker, l'homme monde*, ed. Raymond Bellour, Jean-Michel Frodon, and Christine Van Assche (Paris: Cinémathèque française, 2018), 46; Catherine Lupton, *Chris Marker: Memories of the Future* (London: Reaktion, 2005), 14; and Chris Marker, *Libération* (January 8, 1999), n.p. Translations of Marker's articles are by Sally Shafto. All other translations are mine, unless otherwise noted.

2. Additional pen names attributed to Marker include Palotin Giron, Chris Mayor, Joéle Lelanceur, Jacopo Berenizi, Christian Berger, Fritz Markassin, Christof Marker, Toulanov, Dolorès Walfisch, Knick Garter, Chris Krazyka-tovich, Nicholas Carter, Sandor Krasna, Hayao Yamaneko, Boris Villeneuve, Sergei Murasaki, and C.-B. Villeneuve (Florence Tissot, "Chronologie," in *Chris*

Marker, l'homme monde, 2–3. Credits for Alain Resnais's *Toute la mémoire du monde* (1956, *All the World's Memory*) list "Chris and Magic Marker." A 2008 Second Life posting attributed to Murasaki states that he chose the pen name Chris Marker because it was easy to pronounce in most languages and because he intended to travel: "Marker, then, like Kodak—chosen with movement, many languages, and the world in mind," cited in Florence Delay, "L'invention de Marker," in *Chris Marker, l'homme monde,* 25. Marker uses the initials C.M. for all but one of his *Esprit* film publications. Nine others in various venues are signed Chris Marker, with his *Cahiers du cinéma* piece on Jiří Trnka's *Prince Bayaya* attributed to Christian Marker. The C.M. signatures in *Esprit* confirm Marker's status as an in-house contributor. Those signed Chris Marker and Christian Marker attest to his heightened visibility beyond *Esprit*.

3. Frodon, "1939–1946, Fragments biographiques et littéraires," in *Chris Marker, l'homme monde,* 31. First in *Le Trait d'union* (June 1939): 14. A facsimile appears in *Chris Marker, l'homme monde,* 56–57.

4. Michael Chaiken and Sam Di Iorio, "Printed Matter: The Author behind the Auteur: Pre-Marker Marker," *Film Comment* 39, no. 4 (July–August 2003): 42–43; and Nora M. Alter, *Chris Marker* (Urbana: University of Illinois Press, 2006), 4.

5. Michèle Firk, "*Letter from Siberia (Lettre de Sibérie, 1958),*" trans. Jennifer Wallace, in *The French New Wave: Critical Landmarks,* ed. Peter Graham and Ginette Vincendeau (London: BFI, 2022), 237. First in *Cinéma 58,* no. 32 (December 1958): 111.

6. Antoine de Baecque, *La Cinéphilie* (Paris: Fayard, 2003), 9–11; and *André Bazin's New Media,* ed. and trans. Dudley Andrew (Berkeley: University of California Press, 2014), 1. See Jacques Rancière, "The Pensive Image," in *The Emancipated Spectator,* trans. Gregory Elliott (London: Verso, 2009), 110; and Roland Barthes, *Camera Lucida,* trans. Richard Howard (New York: Hill and Wang, 1981), 51–57.

7. The texts are Marker, "Der Trickfilm," DOK 50 *Sondernummer Film und Kultur* (1950) [DOK 50, special issue Film and Culture] (1950): 75–76, and Marker, "Wolfgang Staudte, un cinéaste de l'Allemagne d'aujourd'hui," *Cinéma 55* (November 1954): 33–36.

8. Marker, *Jean Giraudoux par lui-même* (Paris: Seuil, 1952), 5.

9. Delay, "L'Invention de Marker," in *Chris Marker, l'homme monde,* 25.

10. Marker, "*Lettre de Sibérie,*" in *Commentaires* (Paris: Seuil, 1961), 63. The sequence runs from about 26:00 to 27:39. Rouquier's feature-length documentaries *Farrebique* (1946) and *Biquefarre* (1983) portray the lives of a farming family over nearly four decades.

11. André Bazin, "*Lettre de Sibérie,*" in *Écrits complets II,* ed. Hervé

Joubert-Laurencin (Paris: Macula, 2018), 2501; and Chris Darke, "Eyesight," *Film Comment* 39, no. 3 (May–June 2003): 48–49.

12. Marker, "*Lettre de Sibérie,*" in *Commentaires,* 64.

13. Bazin, "*Lettre de Sibérie,*" in *Écrits complets II,* 2507.

14. Bazin, "*Dimanche à Pékin,* un film modèle," in *Écrits complets, II,* 2218, and Darke, *La Jetée* (London: BFI/Palgrave, 2016), 17.

15. Maroussia Vossen, *Chris Marker (le livre impossible)* (Paris: Le Tripode, 2016), 9. See also Adrian Martin, "Chris Marker, Posthumously All Bets Are Off," *Cinéaste* 43, no. 3 (2018), 7.

16. For additional information, see chrismarker.ch.

17. Costa-Gavras, Frédéric Bonnaud, and Joël Daire, "Exposer Chris Marker," in *Chris Marker, l'homme monde,* 13; Ben Lerner, "Introduction," in Adam Bartos and Colin MacCabe, *Studio: Remembering Chris Marker* (New York: Or Books, 2017), 3; and Homer, *The Odyssey,* trans. Robert Fagles (New York: Penguin, 1997), 77.

18. Tissot, "Chronologie," in *Chris Marker, l'homme monde,* 1–9. See also Jean-Michel Frodon, "1939–1946, fragments biographiques et littéraires," 30–37; and Thomas Tode, "Un Après-guerre promis à l'apocalypse et à l'utopie," 38–43, both in *Chris Marker, l'homme monde.*

19. Bernard Eisenschitz, "Quelquefois les images," *Trafic,* no. 19 (Summer 1996), 47; Darke, *La Jetée,* 31; Frodon, "1939–1946"; and Tode, "Un Après-guerre," 39. Tode notes that the montage of rubble shots in *La Jetée* includes images not only of the bombed Notre Dame cathedral in Le Havre and the Arc de Triomphe in Paris, but also of Hiroshima following the August 1945 atomic bombing. Some of the photographs are included in Raymond Bellour, "*Le Coeur net,*" in *Chris Marker, l'homme monde,* 72–77. Thirty years later, Marker's subtitle for *A Grin without a Cat* is *Scenes from World War III, 1967–1977.*

20. Tissot, "Chronologie," in *Chris Marker, l'homme monde,* 2. The figure of the angel Gabriel appears in Marker's first publication in *Esprit,* a short story "Les Vivants et les morts" (The living and the dead), signed Chris Mayor, *Esprit,* no. 122 (May 1946): 768–85. See also Nora M. Alter, *Chris Marker,* and Sarah Cooper, *Chris Marker* (Manchester: Manchester University Press, 2008). Alain Resnais told Birgit Kämper and Thomas Tode in 1995 that he remembered seeing *La Fin du monde vue par l'ange Gabriel* at Marker's house in Ville d'Avray: "It was a sequence of images that weren't always identifiable, he used a lot of out of focus shots and techniques like that, but the commentary was fabulous and I was completely swept away by this film"; cited in Lynn A. Higgins, ed., *Alain Resnais Interviews,* trans. T. Jefferson Kline (Oxford: University Press of Mississippi, 2021), 141. Based on Tissot's timeline, this screening likely

occurred between 1948 and the early 1950s. Tissot lists the film as lost. But the fact that the catalog for the Centre Georges Pompidou's 2013 "Planète Marker" exhibition refers to it as unfindable *(introuvable)* does not exclude the possibility that one or more copies of the film may have circulated among Marker's friends (cited in Darke, *La Jetée,* 31).

21. For Darke, the proximity of "Les Vivants et les morts" to *La Fin du monde vue par l'ange Gabriel,* shot in Berlin a year later, indicates that Marker was already working in multiple formats. See Darke, *La Jetée,* 32. The same is true for another of Marker's short fictions, "Till the End of Time" (dated October 1945 and published in *Esprit*'s January 1947 issue) that he adapts for radio broadcast in 1950. An English translation of "Till the End of Time" appears in Darke and Habda Rashid, eds., *Chris Marker: A Grin without a Cat* (London: Whitechapel Gallery, 2014), 117–23.

22. "Marker mémoire" (Cinémathèque française, 7 janvier–1 février 1998), in *Images documentaires,* no. 31 (1998): 75–85 (cited in Cooper, 38). Adrian Martin observes that Marker regarded these early films as trial efforts, "Chris Marker, Posthumously All Bets are Off," *Cinéaste* 43, no. 3 (Summer 2018): 5.

23. Darke, "Chris Marker: Eyesight," 48.

24. Marker, "The Rest Is Silent," in *Silent Movie* (Columbus: Wexner Center for the Arts, 1995), 16.

25. *Immemory,* 3:14:19. I have slightly altered the wording midway through the passage.

26. A pamphlet for Marker's 1995 "Silent Movie" video installation at the Wexner Center for the Arts includes an addendum stating that the charming old lady (Simone Genevois) whom he saw at the Cinémathèque screening "didn't suspect for one minute she had been, literally, my first love." See Marker, "The Rest Is Silent," 16.

27. See the Criterion Collection, no. 387 (2007): 17–18. The same account appears in French and English in the 2003 Arte DVD of *La Jetée* and *Sans Soleil.* The Arte version contains prose left untranslated in the notes for the Criterion release. First in *Film Quarterly* 52, no. 1 (Fall 1998): 66.

28. Éric Rohmer, *Le Sel du présent: Chroniques du cinéma,* ed. Noël Herpe (Bordeaux: Capricci, 2020).

29. Rohmer, *Le Sel du présent,* 499. First in *Arts,* no. 695 (November 8, 1958).

30. De Baecque, "Eric Rohmer at *Arts:* A Cinema Writer," *Film Criticism* 39, no. 1 (Fall 2014): 67–68.

31. Brian Rigby, "The *Vivre son temps* Collection: Intellectuals, Modernity, and Mass Media," in Brian Rigby and Nicholas Hewitt, eds., *France and the Mass Media* (London: Macmillan, 1991), 143.

32. Cited in Tode, "Le Détonateur de la culture cinématographique

allemande d'après-guerre: les rencontres cinématographiques franco-allemandes (1946–1953)," *1895,* no. 60 (2010): 107.

33. Rovan (born Joseph Adolph Rosenthal, 1918–2004) served on *Esprit*'s editorial board and promoted postwar cultural relations between France and Germany. See his *Mémoires d'un Français qui se souvient d'avoir été Allemand* (Paris: Seuil, 1999) and *Peuple et culture: 50 ans d'innovations au service de l'éducation populaire* (http://www.peuple-et-culture.org/IMG/pdf/pec_50_ans .pdf; accessed July 20, 2019).

34. J. Hoberman, "The Lost Futures of Chris Marker," *New York Review of Books,* August 23, 2012. https://www.nybooks.com/online/2012/08/23/lost-futures-chris-marker/.

35. MacCabe, 12–13. Tissot's timeline for 1952 lists Marker's May 15–22 stay in Germany, a two-month visit to Ottawa, Canada, and a July visit to Helsinki where he films *Olympia 52.* For 1953, she includes a two-month trip to the United States (notably New York and Los Angeles) as well as a three-month residency at the Pátzcuaro Center in Mexico. The trips to Canada, the United States, and Mexico were funded by UNESCO.

36. François Dosse, *La Saga des intellectuels français, 1944–1989,* volume I, *À l'Épreuve de l'histoire (1944–1968)* (Paris: Gallimard, 2018), 11–13. Dosse's equivalent figure for 1968–89 is Michel Foucault.

37. Lupton, 16.

38. B. Jaye Miller, "Anarchism and French Catholicism in *Esprit,*" *Journal of the History of Ideas* 37, no. 1 (January–March 1976): 163. See also David L. Schalk, *The Spectrum of Political Engagement: Mounier, Benda, Nizan, Brasillach, Sartre* (Princeton: Princeton University Press, 1979).

39. Jaubert (1900–1940) wrote film scores for Jean Vigo (*L'Atalante* [1934]) and Marcel Carné (1938, *Hôtel du Nord*), *Le Quai des brumes* (1938, *Port of Shadows*), and *Le Jour se lève* (1939, *Daybreak*). Leibowitz (1913–1972) was a composer, theorist, and teacher whose composition students included future composer, theorist, and conductor Pierre Boulez (1925–2016). Roger Leenhardt (1903–1985) was a film critic whose credits as a director included *Les Dernières Vacances* (1948, *The Last Vacation*). Jahier (1899–1939), Mesnil (n.d.), and Ropars (1936–2007) were respected film scholars.

40. Dosse, 58 and 57. Dosse cites "the objectively revolutionary situation" in Goulven Boudic's *Esprit 1944–1982: Les Métamorphoses d'une revue* (Paris: Éditions de l'Imec, 2005), 52.

41. Pourvali, "Chris Marker, éditeur-monteur," in *Chris Marker, l'homme monde,* 155.

42. The 1963 re-edition of *Regards neufs sur le cinéma* combines Marker's 1953 entries on the French avant-garde into a single unsigned section titled

"Repères" (benchmarks). It also switches the order of entries, with an entry on Dreyer's film following those on Clair, Buñuel, and Cocteau. Marker's afterword to the 1953 edition does not appear in the re-edition, which also replaces his signed entries on the Clair, Buñuel, Cocteau, and Dreyer films with shorter pieces by Jean Sémolué, Georges Sadoul, Robert Bresson, Francis Picabia, and Ado Kyrou. The section (on pages 123–31 of the revised edition) begins with the following unsigned statement:

"Each film requires a specific mode of approach. The originality and richness of the following works prohibit all systematic access. As a result, we have preferred to grant full freedom to the filmmaker by replacing an index card *(fiche)* of facts and information with selected opinions and judgments on *La Passion de Jeanne d'Arc, Entr'acte, Un chien andalou,* [and] *Le Sang d'un poète.*"

The reprint miscites the title of Cocteau's film on pages 130, 349, and 351 as *Le Sang du poète* (Blood of the Poet). The absence of documentation concerning changes in the reprint leads me to attribute them at least for now to the reprint's editor Jacques Chevallier.

43. Bazin, "Deux Livres utiles," in *Écrits complets,* II, 1314.

44. Bernard Pingaud, author of *Madame de la Fayette par elle-même,* was Marker's classmate at the Lycée Pasteur and a contributor to *Le Trait d'union.*

45. See Roland Barthes, "Barthes puissance trois," *Quinzaine littéraire,* no. 205 (1–15 March 1975): 1–5. Barthes may have taken a cue from Jean-Luc Godard's 1968 *Godard par Godard (Godard on Godard).*

46. Arnaud Lambert writes that Marker's name is replaced by that of Juliette Caputo between the 1958 monograph no. 18 devoted to Belgium and no. 19 devoted to India. See Lambert, *Also Known as Chris Marker* (Paris: Le Point du Jour, 2008), 279.

47. Susana S. Martins, "Petit Cinéma of the World or the Mysteries of Chris Marker," *Image (&) Narrative* 11, no. 1 (2010): 92–110. I thank Sally Shafto for alerting me to *A Zoo for Chris Marker,* a book by Richard Bevan and Tamsin Clark collecting images of animals from each of the thirty-one Petite Planète books whose production Marker oversaw. The book's cover and layout evoke those of volumes in the original collection, and the volume's absence of ISBN number and publication information exude the kind of ludic intelligence evident in Marker's graphic designs and layouts.

48. Marker, "Petite Planète," "27, rue Jacob," 10 (Summer 1954): n.p. See also "Isabel Stevens on Chris Marker's 'Petite Planète,'" *Aperture* (December 24, 2014), accessed January 6, 2020. https://aperture.org/blog/isabel -stevens-chris-markers-petite-planete/.

49. Lupton, 62.

50. Alter, *Chris Marker,* 4.

51. See Mario Ruspoli, *Les Hommes de la baleine* (1956, *The Whalers*), *Le*

Mystère de l'atelier quinze (1957, *The Mystery of Workshop Fifteen*); Paul Paviot, *Django Reinhardt* (1959); Joris Ivens, *À Valparaíso* (1963); and Haroun Tazieff, *Le Volcan interdit* (1966, *The Violent Earth*). Paviot's film is available online at https://www.youtube.com/watch?v=dT3_o8jvLn4 (accessed April 8, 2020).

52. Roger Tailleur, "Markeriana," https://chrismarker.org/chris-marker-2/markeriana-by-roger-tailleur/ (accessed January 24, 2022). First in *Artsept* (January–March 1963).

53. Jean-Luc Godard, *Godard on Godard*, trans. and ed. Tom Milne (New York: Da Capo, 1986), 171. First in *Cahiers du cinéma* (December 1962) and reprinted in *Jean-Luc Godard par Jean-Luc Godard, vol. 1 (1950–1984)* (Paris: Cahiers du cinéma, 1998), 215; and Susan Sontag, "Godard," *Styles of Radical Will* (New York: Farrar, Straus and Giroux, 1969), 153.

54. Michael Cowan, *Walter Ruttmann and the Cinema of Multiplicity: Avant-Garde—Advertising—Modernity* (Amsterdam: Amsterdam University Press, 2014), 28.

55. Rancière, "The Surface of Design," in *The Future of the Image*, trans. Gregory Elliott (London: Verso, 2007), 99.

56. Cited in Pourvali, "Philosophie de la photographie et mise en page chez Chris Marker," in Vincent Jacques, ed., 15. Marker's statement appears in the program for the Centre Pompidou's 1998 retrospective of his films. Pourvali and Marc Cerisuelo organized a June 2022 conference, "Chris Marker, écrivain en premier" (Chris Marker, First of All a Writer).

57. Jérôme Allain, "*Images du cinéma français* (1945) de Nicole Vedrès: Un discours par l'image," n.p. Accessed September 8, 2022. https://hal.archives-ouvertes.fr/hal-01326678v1. See also Bernard Eisenschitz, "Le Film de papier," *Trafic*, no. 100 (December 2016): 35–39.

58. Braunberger (1905–1990) produced films on both sides of the Atlantic. His filmography includes Robert Fleury's *La Route est belle* (1930, *The Road Is Beautiful*), Alain Resnais's *Toute la Mémoire du monde* (1956, *All the World's Memory*), and Jean Rouch's *Moi un Noir* (1958, *I, a Black Person*).

59. Gary Crowdus, "Emails from Chris Marker," *Cinéaste* 43, no. 3 (Summer 2018): 9.

60. Laurent Mannoni, *Histoire de la cinémathèque française* (Paris: Gallimard, 2006), 224.

61. Eric Smoodin, *Paris in the Dark: Going to the Movies in the City of Light, 1930–1950* (Durham: Duke University Press, 2020), 131.

62. See Chris Marker, "Till the End of Time," *Esprit*, no. 129 (January 1947): 141–51; "Romancero de la montagne," *Esprit*, no. 135 (July 1947): 90–98; and "Les Séparés," *Esprit*, no. 162 (December 1949): 921–22. I base these numbers on documentation in *Chris Marker, l'homme monde* and in Clara Bleuzen, "Chris Marker à *Esprit* (1946–1952), mémoire d'étude 1er année de 2e cycle,

École du Louvre (May 2017)." Bleuzen attributes two additional unsigned texts to Marker: "La Vie quotidienne accablée" (Daily life overwhelmed) in *Esprit*, no. 136 (August 1947) and "Lumière pour tous" (Light for everyone) in *Esprit*, no. 147 (August 1948). These figures are likely to change as research continues.

63. Bleuzen, 8.

64. Marker (under the pseudonym Chris Mayor), "Les Vivants et les morts," *Esprit*, no. 122 (May 1946): 784–85.

65. "Till the End of Time," in Darke and Rashid, eds., *Chris Marker: A Grin without a Cat* (London: Whitechapel Gallery, 2014), 118 and 120. Tissot incorrectly lists "Till the End of Time" as Marker's first *Esprit* publication, appearing in the monthly's January 1945 issue. The *Esprit* website confirms the article's publication date in issue no. 129 (January 1947).

66. Marker, "Till the End of Time," 122.

67. Lupton, 16.

68. Éric Marty, "Un Moment pétainiste dans la vie de Chris Marker," *Le Monde*, August 15, 2012. https://www.lemonde.fr/idees/article/2012/08/15/un-moment-petainiste-dans-la-vie-de-chris-marker_1746314_3232.html. Frodon's reply appears in *Chris Marker, l'homme monde*, 32.

69. Lupton, 18. The text by Marker is "À propos du paradis terrestre," *Esprit*, no. 129 (January 1947): 158. Two texts—"Newsreel," *Esprit*, no. 133 (May 1947) and "Newsreel," *Esprit*, no. 145 (July 1948)—imply film topics but focus instead on current events.

70. Phillip Lopate, "In Search of the Centaur: The Essay-Film," in *Totally, Tenderly, Tragically* (New York: Anchor, 1998), 287.

71. Marker, "Une Conférence de Louis Aragon," *Esprit*, no. 129 (January 1947): 172.

72. Marker, "Deux précautions valent mieux qu'une: La Mort de Scarface ou les infortunes de la vertu," *Esprit*, no. 131 (March 1947): 488.

73. Marker, "Du Jazz considéré comme une prophétie" (On jazz as prophecy), *Esprit*, no. 146 (July 1948): 134. The reference is to Prince Boris Drubetskoy, a character in Leo Tolstoy's 1867 novel *War and Peace*.

74. Marker, "On Jazz," 138.

75. In 1952, Seuil published *Regards neufs sur Les Jeux olympiques* under PEC's imprint. The authors listed are Joffre Dumazedier, Maurice Bacquet, and Janine Dumazedier. Fifty years later, Julian Faraut's documentary *Regard neuf sur Olympia 52* recounts his efforts to obtain a copy of Marker's film.

76. Raymond Borde and Étienne Chaumeton, *A Panorama of American Film Noir*, trans. Paul Hammond (San Francisco: City Lights, 2002), 58. First in 1954.

77. Frédéric Gimello-Mesplomb, *Objectif 49: Cocteau et la nouvelle avant-garde* (Paris: Séguier, 2013), 107.

78. Filmology was a cultural movement whose study of filmic facts as a positive science drew on methods of inquiry associated with sociology and philosophy. Gilbert Cohen-Séat directed the *Revue internationale de filmologie* from 1947 to 1961.

79. In 1953, The Parisian publishing house A. G. Nizet released Poncet's dissertation in two volumes: *Étude comparative des illustrations du Moyen-Age et du dessein animé* (Comparative Study of Medieval Illustrations and the Cartoon) and *L'Esthétique du dessein animé* (Aesthetics of the Cartoon). A third title, *Le Génie de Walt Disney* (The Genius of Walt Disney), appeared in 1971, drawing on Poncet's 1960s meeting with Disney in Hollywood.

80. Marker, "An Ornamental Form," *Cahiers du cinéma*, no. 8 (January 1952): 66.

81. Maté (1898–1964), born Rudolph Mayer, worked as a director and cinematographer. In Europe, he was cinematographer on Dreyer's *Vampyr*. His work in Hollywood included *Stella Dallas, To Be or Not to Be*, and *The Lady from Shanghai*.

82. Marker, *The Passion of Joan of Arc*, 59 .

83. James Naremore, "Marlon Brando in *On the Waterfront* (1954)," in *Acting in the Cinema* (Berkeley: University of California Press, 1988), 194. Marker's description of Brando's Malloy as a converted homosexual was intolerable in 1955. It remains so today.

84. Eric Rentschler, *The Use and Abuse of Cinema: German Legacies from the Weimar Era to the Present* (New York: Columbia University Press, 2015), 137 and 134.

85. Marker, "Siegfried and the Gaolers, or German Cinema Enchained," 46.

86. I thank Sam Di Iorio for pointing me to the UNESCO seminar report and two companion documents. The first is an unsigned "Pátzcuaro: Première Ecole Régionale pour les Spécialistes de l'Éducation de Base" (Pátzcuaro: First regional school for fundamental education specialists) (February 1951), 8–9. The second, "Premier Q.G. de la lutte contre l'ignorance" (First headquarters for the struggle against ignorance), in *Le Courrier de l'UNESCO* (June 1951) is attributed to Daniel Behrman.

87. André Breton, *Nadja*, trans. Richard Howard (New York: Grove, 1960), 160. The French original reads, "La beauté sera CONVULSIVE ou ne sera pas."

88. On Lerner's activities in conjunction with the Film and Photo League, see Russell Campbell, *Cinema Strikes Back: Radical Filmmaking in the United States, 1930–1942* (Ann Arbor: UMI Research Press, 1982); Jan-Christopher Horak, ed., *Lovers of Cinema: The First American Film Avant-Garde, 1919–1945* (Madison: University of Wisconsin Press, 1995); and Patrick McGilligan and Paul Buhle, *Tender Comrades: A Backstory of the Hollywood Blacklist* (Minneapolis: University of Minnesota Press, 2012). In *The American Cinema* (1968),

Andrew Sarris identifies Lerner among directors deemed "Oddities, One-Shots, and Newcomers."

89. See UCLA Arts Library Special Collections, Irving Lerner papers, 1935–1978, collection number 112, Box 2, Folder 25.

90. Kyle Westphal, "Irving Lerner: A Career in Context," https://www.chica gofilmsociety.org/2013/03/25/irving-lerner-a-career-in-context/.

91. Sam Di Iorio, "The Fragile Present: 'Statues Also Die' with 'Night and Fog,'" *South Central Review* 33, no. 2 (Summer 2016): 19–20.

92. The latter was directed by Alexander Hammid, with appearances by the orchestra conductor Arturo Toscanini and the operatic tenor Jan Peerce. Others credited for the film were May Sarton (screenplay), Burgess Meredith (narration), and Boris Kaufman (editing). Hammid (1907–2004) was a Czech-born photographer who immigrated to the United States in 1938. He is best known for collaborating with his then-wife Maya Deren on the 1943 avant-garde short *Meshes of the Afternoon*.

93. Marker, "Cinerama," 83.

94. Lupton, 13.

95. "Le Voyage," in Charles Baudelaire, *Œuvres complètes completes*, Y. G. Le Dantec, ed. (Paris: Gallimard Bibliothèque de la Pléiade, 1968), 127.

96. Marker, "Cinéma, Art of the Twenty-first Century?" 107.

97. See Dudley Andrew, ed. and trans., *André Bazin's New Media* (Berkeley: University of California Press, 2014).

NOTE FROM THE TRANSLATOR

AFTER HIS DEMOBILIZATION IN OCTOBER 1945, CHRIS MARKER laid down his military weapons to adopt a different arm, that of the pen. Entering into a fruitful collaboration with the journal *Esprit* in May 1946, he began writing extensively on a wide range of topics. This volume is a compilation of his twenty postwar essays on film in French that begin and end with his articles for *Esprit*. In January 1948, he published his first film essay there, a review of Laurence Olivier's *Henry V*. Seven years later, in March 1955, his last film essay was published, a review of Elia Kazan's *On the Waterfront*, marking the end of his work for that review. In between, Marker contributed to the recently founded film magazines *Cahiers du cinéma* and *Positif* and to two anthologies.

Chris Marker's prose is scintillating: every article, even the shorter ones, is filled with his keen insights on cinema and the world. He frequently ends an essay with a sharp, invigorating turn of phrase. Occasionally, he peppers his criticism with English words, a reminder that he was not only fluent in English and had worked as a translator–interpreter for the U.S. Army at the end of World War II but also subsequently translated or cotranslated in the 1950s several books from English to French for Seuil, which also published *Esprit*. Stylistically, his writing is characterized by a penchant for long paragraphs and occasionally sentences of

Proustian proportions, which Marker extends with colons, semi-colons, dashes, and parenthetical asides. Two of the longest ones both clock in at 186 words! This translation occasionally truncates such sentences and long paragraphs to render his writing more dynamic, entirely in keeping with his Man of Action persona à la Malraux. Some of Marker's parentheses have been removed to give these supplemental thoughts their due weight. Marker's numerous ellipses have been greatly reduced in number. Minor errors of dates and spelling have generally been silently emended. Marker frequently italicizes for emphasis or when he employs foreign words, and his usage is usually maintained. His use of the word *auteur* to refer to filmmakers, which predates its appearance in François Truffaut's influential January 1954 *Cahiers du cinéma* essay "A Certain Tendency in French Cinema," is also observed.

Marker cites nearly two hundred films in his writings on film. His film writings are anchored in the time in which they were written with references to other films, to persons, etc. The translator's nonexhaustive endnotes are meant to clarify these references. Very occasionally Marker included a footnote in his writings. These are indicated by asterisks and are treated as footnotes within the text.

It was helpful to consult Marker's two articles that previously appeared in translation. Sophie Lewis's translation of Marker's *Orpheus* review was published in the Whitechapel Gallery exhibition catalog (*Chris Marker: A Grin without a Cat,* edited by Chris Darke and Habda Rashid, London, 2014). For Jean-Michel Frodon's dossier "Chris Marker's Film Criticism" in *Cinéaste* (Summer 2018), Jennifer Cazenave translated Marker's reviews of both Cocteau's *Orpheus* and Elia Kazan's *On the Waterfront.*

The translator would like to thank the following individuals for their support and encouragement: Jean-Michel Frodon, co-curator of the 2018 Cinémathèque française exhibition *Chris Marker, les sept vies d'un cineaste* and coeditor of the accompanying catalog, *Chris Marker, l'homme monde* (Actes Sud; Cinémathèque française); Dr. Lisa Eck of Framingham State

University; Dr. Michael Cramer of Sarah Lawrence College; Dr. Katarzyna Pieprzak of Williams College; and librarians Laurence Moreau and Hervé Grosdoit-Artur of the Bibliothèque nationale de la France. Also special thanks to Dylan Skolnick of the Cinema Arts Center, Kristen Merola of the Film Foundation, and Amanda Smith and Mary K. Huelsbeck of the Wisconsin Center for Film and Theater Research. Film archivist Jeff Joseph who oversaw the film and trailer archive SabuCat productions generously shared the trailer for Irving Lerner's *Man Crazy*. That 1953 film may perhaps be lost, but it lives on in Marker's fine appraisal. Special warm thanks to Jean-Claude Gaubert for being an invaluable sounding board as I worked out this translation. Finally, special warm thanks as well to Steve Ungar for asking me to translate Marker's early film writings.

HENRY V'S WHITE HORSE

ONE PATH TOWARD THE CINEMATOGRAPH STARTS WITH cave paintings, passes through the Bayeux Tapestry, and, *dixit* Malraux, *gets bogged down in the Baroque period.*[1] What's at stake is an attempt to capture movement that painting clearly addresses. But there's another, more haphazard route that runs through the theatre. To the object's movement that it more or less controls, the theatre dreams of adding the subject's movement and its dual conditions of space and freedom.

If it's important that the centurion draws his sword and Jocasta wrings her hands *for everyone,* it is also important that sometimes both remain immobile, while spectators get up from their seats to look into an actress' face or quickly mount a tower to enjoy the sight of an army on the move. Pending the invention of the close-up and the long shot, all of the theatre's dispersed

---

Review of Laurence Olivier's *Henry V* (1944), released in France on September 17, 1947. Signed: C.M.

Source: *Esprit,* n.s., no. 141 (January 1948): 120–27. On the *Esprit* website, this article is mistakenly attributed to another author, Dheur Gabriel, a pseudonym for Henri Fayol (1906–1965), a close friend of Emmanuel Mounier. Instead of the last page of the article, where we would expect Marker's byline "C.M.," there is a scan of page 117, instead of 127.

Marker's title puns on a proverb about King Henry IV (1553–1610), well known to French children: What is the color of Henry IV's horse?

cinematographic effort—once it reaches its limits—will resolve itself in trickery, magic, or surrender. The trickery is quickly exhausted by recourse to machinery; magic by suggestion and illusion (pantomime, expressionism, or Père Ubu's placards); surrender by this same conversion to the inner world (classical tragedy and romantic drama) that painting will also know when, in its turn, it will have triumphed over its problems. Following painting and theatre's mastery over movement and space, the cinema will be recognized as their legitimate heir. While the older arts are left to their own domains, cinema will assume the task of completing their conquests and accomplishing their prophecies.

"The Scriptures must be fulfilled."[2] Laurence Olivier's attempt to adapt Shakespeare for the screen thus brings to mind this prideful humility. Of all *Henry V*'s qualities, the most striking is undoubtedly its fidelity and piety that make the film predictably accessible. And this easy and obvious access, this impression that everything in the film is as it should be and in complete accord with Shakespeare's wishes, this apparent erasure of the director, are ultimately a thousand times more impressive than the addition of any gratuitous ingenuity and numerous effects not found in the original play. While in Orson Welles's *Macbeth* we can expect, for example, to be dazzled by the mise-en-scène's inspiration, even if it means rereading *Macbeth* with a defensive reflex, everything here seems to derive from the play itself. Only after the fact can we admire the ground covered to get there.

Several reasons undoubtedly led Sir Laurence Olivier to begin his Shakespearian cycle (recently continued with his *Hamlet*) with one of the least "universally" famous plays: *Henry V.* First of all, obviously, was the aim to present a singularly suitable work to match England's wartime hopes (the film was shot during the war and is dedicated to the British troops). This parallel with *Ivan the Terrible* is meaningful on more than one count, and this alchemy by which people make their former rulers into democratic heroes can be interpreted quite optimistically.[3] There is also the intention

of freeing *Henry V* and the other historical dramas from an infe-
riority complex vis à vis the Bard's greatest tragedies. But above
all, and here we encounter the prophetic fulfillment mentioned
at the outset, this drive toward the cinema that animates Shakespeare's work beyond theatrical limits is most clearly and explicitly expressed in *Henry V.*

One character, in particular, embodies this effort, which no
other Shakespeare play—apart from the brief introduction in
Romeo and Juliet—possesses: the Chorus. The Chorus who is also
the narrator, this invisible and omniscient voice that openly ac-
knowledges, beseeches, and entrusts the Cinema God to reveal
itself. Just listen to the drama's opening lines:

> Can this cock-pit hold
> The vastly fields of France? Or may we cram
> Within this wooden O the very casques
> that would affright the air at Agincourt?
> [. . .] Piece out our imperfections with your thoughts
> Into a thousand parts divide one man.
> And make imaginary puissance.
> Think, when we talk of horses, that you see them,
> Printing their proud hoofs i' the' receiving earth.[4]

And from one act to the next we will find the same warnings and
invocations. If the Cinema God had a heart, it would have de-
scended to Earth in the seventeenth century.

> Be patient and we will hold in the play this space that stops us. . . . So
> with an imaginary wing, steal our theatre, in a vivid movement like
> that of thought. . . . Come on, put your imagination to work, so that
> it shows you a seat.

When the Chorus becomes transparent, then invisible in the film,
and the scenes that it invokes arise from a dissolve, the sequence
appears natural and deliberate. Better still, when the marvelous
guard of Agincourt finishes by saying "Behold . . . a little touch of

Henry in the night," we can imagine him only in this small patch of light that accompanies the king, becoming larger as the camera draws near, and surrounded with inflated tents like veils, whose glow creates a fleet half-engulfed by the night. It's no longer a question here of suggestion, but of a precise intention contained in the "little touch," and about which generations of Shakespearian directors likely fretted, until the advent of cinema.

So it was entirely logical and even praiseworthy to adopt *Henry V.* Even if it still had to be adapted. The play's length, unusual tone (cinematographically speaking) of its dialogue, and its distant temporal setting, all this Laurence Olivier manages with an intelligence beyond all praise. First of all, the overly long text had to be trimmed, and it certainly is on screen. Then once certain digressions were eliminated, there had to be a ruthless pruning in the subplots. Thus, the entirety of the Lord Scroop conspiracy has disappeared, except for one reply. And if it's to be expected that several episodes developed at length by Shakespeare have been deleted, all that remains is a fragment or a vague allusion, which is completely incomprehensible if the audience that doesn't know the play, as if it were a witty wink exchanged between Laurence Olivier and Shakespeare. On the other hand, the added scene of Falstaff's death, in which we hear the last interview between the dying man and prince Hal, crowned Henry V that very morning, is borrowed from *Henry IV* to shed light on Falstaff's character for those unfamiliar with the story. But because of the abridgment, we fail to learn that his companion Bardolph was hanged for having stolen a chalice. Nor do we learn that the soldier with whom Henry quarrels on the eve of the Battle of Agincourt will be found by him and rewarded for his valor and candor. It's unfortunate, but at least the essential is kept. And if the character of Fluellen, the raging and loyal Welshman, is less important in the film than in the play, his two best scenes survive intact (although the first—a confrontation of accents and tics of a Welshman, Scotsman, and Irishman—apparently confounded the subtitlers). Less regrettable is the elimination of the jokes exchanged between Henry and the Duke of Burgundy at the time of the engagement, and whose "frank gaiety," as the Duke says, could revive, in our chaste century, lovely Renée Asherson's *maiden blushes*.[5]

With the narrative line thus streamlined and abridged, Olivier's aim was to reconstitute a "15th century" mood. Naturally referring to the convention of period documents, he had the idea to remain faithful to this convention, as wonderfully archaic as the text of the play itself. In addition, the film's entire middle section takes place in striking exteriors, half real and half sets, where as they progressively move away, the views finish in a flat background that perfectly reproduces contemporary miniatures.[6] The morning of the Battle of Agincourt is particularly striking: in the dawn light, an image of an illuminated book of hours slowly comes to life. In the landscape a thousand little points, still black and stiff like lead soldiers, become distinguishable. Then the machine switches on, the shots get closer, the soldiers are covered with metal and flesh, and suddenly we jump from Fouquet to Buffalo Bill, with a charge of the French cavalry (to the tune "Awaken Picards"), in what is perhaps the most beautiful tracking shot of a cavalry ride ever filmed.[7]

But it's on the third count, on the difficulty of getting the public—used to colloquial language and Hollywood sets—to accept the style and imagery of the play that Laurence Olivier proves his brilliance. He starts by proposing to reconstitute a performance of *Henry V* at the Globe Theatre, thus creating a spectacle within the spectacle that makes it possible for the spectator to accept, via a discreet parody, what would initially have shocked it. Even better, as the prologue includes a long historical exposé, essential for the plot, but that quickly could have become tedious, he invents simple gags for the public's enjoyment. All without straying from the plot. With the narrator's words, the stage widens, ships appear, then the sea, and we are led, as Shakespeare wished, to France, "after having enthralled the straits of seas" as far as Agincourt (handled, as already noted, as pure cinema). By then the audience is sufficiently "in the mood" to easily follow what might otherwise be some rather baffling scenes: Pistol and his leek, Henry's declaration to the French princess and his charming dialogue. Another long monologue, by the Duke of Burgundy, occurs, thanks to a long panning shot that illustrates his wording. And once again the image and music go so well with the text that one is persuaded to have clearly read this intention in Shakespeare, and that in all his dramatic and human inventions, old Will has added the speaker's more discreet intention. At which point Henry and the princess ascend to the throne, where they are welcomed by the applause... of the *Globe* spectators, because in the meantime, we've returned there by a simple artifice I won't reveal so as not to spoil the surprise for the unsuspecting spectator.

The audience follows, a little astonished, laughing along the way because the princess speaks French with an English accent (which proves, after all, that the transition was sufficiently convincing to make the audience forget it was a play). The public reacts only at the moment of the Battle of Agincourt, because, as Jeanson has said so well, the French of 1947 accept everything—the recently ended war, the one on the horizon, the scandals, hardships, and the exceptional and regular taxes—literally everything, except having been beaten at Agincourt in 1415![8] Despite all precautions! An introductory text informs us that we're about to watch not a historical reconstitution, but a dramatic fiction. (All that's missing is the usual disclaimer in American films: "Any resemblance with real events, persons alive or dead, is purely coincidental.") The copy being screened in France includes an important cut, but the scene is nonetheless described by Shakespeare. The French constable, enraged by the defeat, raids the English camps, slaughters the pages, and loots the treasure. Following this wrongdoing, in the play, the king instructs each soldier to kill his prisoners. But Laurence Olivier has elided and replaced this grim episode by a remarkable battle at the end of which Henry lays out the dead constable with a mere stroke of his gauntlet. He also eliminates the slapstick scene of the French soldier begging Pistol for grace, whom he takes for a "fine captain." Finally, when the king asks for the number of Englishmen killed, the herald answers: "Five and twenty," but the subtitler, solicitous before the ten thousand French massacred, to counter the disaster's epic proportion, writes: "500." Every effort has thus been made so that the valiant French public doesn't feel the brunt of this five-hundred-year-old disgrace, ill-accustomed as this public is since then of all defeat, military or other. . . . Well, no, the audience protests and calms down only at the end, when the king marries the lovely princess, signaling in filmic terms that henceforth all's well.[9]

But, and here's the irony, if Agincourt was unquestionably a massive defeat, it was also an enormous and courageous undertaking. The nobility massacred there, despite its recklessness, demonstrated both valor and a highly respectable patriotism. Whereas this happy marriage that heartens our people in a prelude to the Treaty of Troyes nevertheless earmarks one of our greatest national catastrophes: the establishment of the English royalty in France, which will end only with Joan of Arc.[10] Ultimately the patriotic French public is offended at the moment of courage, smiles at the shameful moment, and surrenders *in honor and dignity,* which is as it should be.

That said, let's not be too demanding with regard to the characters' historical accuracy. Sometimes they have the naïvety of images and always their luster. Admittedly, it will be difficult for a French audience to recognize the Duke of Orléans, this moon-faced aficionado of bilboquet . . . Charles d'Orléans himself. Even more difficult to imagine—under the beautiful velvet robe and the gently melancholic air of the Duke of Burgundy—the abominable scoundrel who delivered France to the English and then, ten years later, delivered Joan of Arc to them. The characterization of the French King is, on the other hand, more complex. We know that he's Charles VI, the mad king (you know, the one who awakened by the sound of a spear on a breastplate, pricked by two in shouting:

"To me, the Auvergnats are enemies. . . ."). Shakespeare, whose play closely follows Holinshed's *Chronicle,* was surely familiar with this matter.[11] Yet in the text nothing indicates the king's character with certainty, and we would even be tempted to attribute to him a "royal" bearing. But Laurence Olivier has chosen to make him ludicrous, which gives to certain replies an ironic edge that they didn't perhaps originally have (for example, the Dauphin's speech beginning with "My most redoubted father " prompts a smile). This is the only real malice for which we can reproach the film. Nevertheless, besides its indisputable theatrical merit, we say that it is a pale reflection of history. The spectacle of this court surrendered to the vassals of a mentally ill monarch, who refuse to testify out of some vague sacrilegious fear, would have been infinitely more trying for our chauvinism. As for the depiction of the French lords as frivolous and unthinking blowhards, we know very well since Kipling's Bandar-Logs what the English think of us.[12] At best we can laugh a little to find on the shoulders of this antipathetic French Dauphin the finest mouth of an Englishman-redhead-burner-of-saints that Monsieur Boutet de Monvel ever dreamed of.[13] More significant are two other aspects that the English display at our expense: piety (none of the French fret over God's existence, while the English king and his army invoke God in their actions) and democracy (the French lords have no contact with their troops and boast of their splendor on the eve of the Battle of Agincourt. In contrast, Henry nurtures informality with his soldiers "and calls them brothers, friends, and countrymen"). And the crosscutting's shocking parallel between the French knights drinking a last cup with an English peasant dripping with sweat as he hammers the stakes on which the first named are impaled neatly sums it up.

To speak of Laurence Olivier the actor, as of Laurence Olivier the filmmaker, discourages praise. Let's just say that he is handsome, with a hard, untarnished beauty all alone in the frame. He adapts to an implausible bowl cut and a crown posed like a wreath of flowers. Let's also say that for the first time we have the feeling of having literally seen *an actor*. Whatever our love of Jouvet, Dullin, and Barrault, there always remains a shadow zone between them and the image we have of a Talma, a Rachel. We end up attributing this shadow zone to the past prestige and legend. And it is perhaps so for some of them. But the others, now that we have seen Laurence Olivier, we know to what race they belong, to what and to whom they might resemble. He possesses the dual function of a great thespian and an "animal of cinema." Around him, this human and divine ambivalence, gravitate irreproachable, seasoned actors of Shakespeare in England, but who are unknown to us, except Leslie Banks (the Chorus) in whom we recognize the dark hero of *The Most Dangerous Game,* and Robert Helpmann (the Bishop of Ely) whose reputation as a dancer has already crossed the Channel.[14]

There's a lot more to say. We can extol the Technicolor (whose quality, so say the naysayers, is inversely proportional to the proximity on set of patent holder Madame Natalie Kalmus). We can say all kinds of good things about William Walton's score, in which we recognize numerous themes familiar to us. And idem, which is rare, of the literary quality of the subtitles—admire the construction of the work, whose apparent disorder of the chronicle, in the style of "Goetz of Berlichingen" or "La Jacquerie," hides a strong shot, causing the prolonged *fortissimo* of the Agincourt Battle (which, for those curious about such things, is situated in the play and in the film at a point corresponding to the golden ratio). The spectator will compensate for it. It is nonetheless important to emphasize that this epic film, which rivals the great mega-productions of American cinema, was made under technical and financial constraints much closer to those of *Paisà* than those of *Ben-Hur.*[15]

If the personality of its director proves—following Malraux, Cocteau, and Orson Welles—the fragility of the concept of a film *auteur,* the film nonetheless confirms our hopes for reinstating the myth of a "rich cinema," a myth that currently paralyzes French production more than the Blum–Byrnes Agreements. The popular quality, adorning the film as much in its origins as in its thesis, naturally marks its making. In an area of Ireland, Laurence Olivier had a camp set up, and the labor board delegated a hundred real Irish soldiers to reinforce his army. Thanks to a local veterinarian, he obtained riders and horses from the neighboring farmers for the French cavalry. Students from the Dublin art schools participated in the production by making costumes, blind students knitted the *faux* mail coats. In short, as Laurence Olivier himself says with a charming naïveté in an article in *Everybody's Weekly,* "the groundbreaking work we undertook required different methods than those generally used in film production."

Another reason too, perhaps, for the film's *difference.*

THE IMPERFECT OF THE SUBJECTIVE

JUST RELEASED IN PARIS IS THE "SUBJECTIVE FILM" *Lady in the Lake*. If the advertising is to be believed, the goal of this endeavor was to achieve the spectator's identification with the adventure's hero. "You will discover the guilty party," declares a newspaper plastered on the wall of the theatre lobby. In order to create this illusion, the protagonist disappears shortly after he first appears by merging with the movie camera itself, which sees with his eyes, hears with his ears, and beholds his face in a mirror. The other actors address it, stare at it, bump up against it, and embrace it. And occasionally the film tries to do one better, as when an arm appears in a corner of the screen, which fills with cigarette smoke, or a cavernous voice echoes out of the blue. "Here at last, we are told, is a film in the first person."

That film critics felt the need to feign astonishment at this spectacle is sufficient proof of the industry's high culture. Because if ever there was an idea in the air, it's definitely this one. So it's not surprising it finally came to fruition. Orson Welles (of

---

Review of Robert Montgomery's *Lady in the Lake*. U.S. release: January 23, 1947. French release: April 14, 1948.

Signed: C.M.

Source: *Esprit*, n.s., no. 148 (September 1948): 387–91.

Marker's title puns on the subjunctive imperfect in French, a literary tense.

course) arrived in Hollywood with a plan to shoot Conrad's *Heart of Darkness* following this method. But Hollywood was intimidated and the project was abandoned. First-person sequences used to appear in many films, more or less successful, and more or less motivated. Experimental cinema tackled it. (It seems that Mr. Cohen-Séat, director of the Filmology Center, filmed subjective shots of a child. And Alain Rodriguez de Berton, a talented young Bolivian filmmaker, showed up in the streets of Paris on all fours wearing a helmet equipped with a camera, while preparing a dog's subjective film.) Amateur cinema has also experimented with it. It seems, however, that Robert Montgomery was the first to think of the idea in 1938, thus two years before Welles. Montgomery has the honor of having made the first "commercial" film, entirely in the first person.

Let's leave him that honor. It's just as well because it's the only good thing to be said about this undertaking. For the rest, it's bewildering—given Hollywood's means, Montgomery's free hand with such an experiment, and all the work invested—that the final film is so bad, heavy-handed, and awkward. I won't dwell on lengthy criticisms, a few examples will suffice: the hero's hand sometimes emerges from the screen's bottom corner, sometimes from the upper corner, as if he were opening a door while holding an inordinately long arm above his head—the slowness and stiffness of his field of vision, which moves around like a good movie camera careful to avoid spinning and thereby fails to approximate human vision—the implausible mirror scene where, after Miss Totter performs an odd detour to the aforementioned mirror in order to avoid the camera's reflection, Montgomery looks at himself, winces, and *closes his eyes*—and is seen closing his eyes. This is no longer subjectivity, but fakirism.

I've concentrated on the technical aspect of the matter, because obviously it alone interested Montgomery and his crew. And this is why I specified that this identification of the hero-spectator with the camera was proposed by the film's advertising and its *auteur.*

The goal of the ideal subjective film, which we shouldn't despair of seeing made one day, is altogether different. I would even say that it's the exact opposite.

First of all, let's note (I'm embarrassed to write it, but since we seem to be engaged in a serious discussion) the impossible challenge of a truly subjective representation: the visual range of the human eye doesn't correspond to a rectangle. It includes, beyond a zone of rather limited focus, a faded halo where objects, although blurry, are perceived with an infinitely greater clarity than in the artifice of the cinematic blur. Furthermore, this field is arranged according to an opening that no lens can approximate. (In writing this, I'm looking at my typewriter roller, and at the same time I sense the existence of objects located within my field of vision, to the right and to the left.) Independently of the head movements that the movie camera can imitate (but not without spinning), the eye continuously performs sudden jumps, goes from the floor to the ceiling (the hero in *Lady in the Lake* never *once* sees his feet). This is simply because of the optical equipment. There is moreover a feeling of presence, the movement of thought, and the emotion that gives to each representation its own quality, and for which seeing the actor's face is the sole means of communicating with the spectator. Here we are at an advanced stage of being "in the position of" a character whose perspective we know only imperfectly and whose reaction we are forced to surmise on others' faces. Instead of identifying ourselves with him, the process depletes and isolates us.

In contrast, how much more "subjective" is a good close-up. When in *Murder, My Sweet* a drugged Dick Powell suddenly appears enveloped in a kind of spider's web or frozen smoke through which he tries to pass, the classic convention of the observer-camera—oriented in this precise moment in observing the representation of a given character—allows for complete identification without any need to conflate object and subject. When in *The Testament of Dr. Mabuse*, a universe of spun glass has been built around the madman, we fail to see him, but we penetrate his madness far better than we would have with his own eyes. In the narrow sense of character identification, true subjectivity consists of using standard cinematic means *in accordance with* the character. And the final tracking shot of Orson Welles's *The Lady from Shanghai* says infinitely more than all of Mr. Montgomery's clumsy virtuosity.

But the true meaning of the subjective procedure lies not in its technical artifice, but rather in its dramatic and psychological utility. *Lady in the Lake*'s every imperfection arises from the fact that the subject hardly justifies the use of the first person. The novel says "I," but beside the fact that Raymond Chandler's choice of it is slightly more arbitrary than, for example, in Proust or Radiguet, a novel's characters can always describe their thoughts and feelings. In contrast, saying "I" in the cinema with the immediate reduction in expressive possibilities that this signifies (we should also think about the impossibility of a logical shot breakdown) would amount instead to the hero's depersonalization. Deprived of a face, a physical presence, and prohibited by their invisibility of all trivial curiosity, their body must coincide with their vision. In it should flow all power of existence and action. A search and persistent attention ought to destroy the attention we pay it, so that no one any longer dreams of demanding their presence. In the midst of this observation, the camera positions itself with its own movements and methods without trying to imitate human beings, but is so well focused on the story that it ends up standing in for it much more convincingly. Instead of being mistaken for a pair of human eyes, it would be regarded as a kind of very sophisticated X-ray machine. In that respect Perken in *The Royal Way,* an "objectively" described character driven by his quest, would be a far better hero for a subjective film than Raymond Chandler's "I."[1] Perhaps Welles intuited the same thing in choosing to adapt *Heart of Darkness,* the story of a mysterious character in the jungle, which is at times reminiscent of Malraux's saga.[2]

Some filmmakers initially thought that they had been "left in the dust" when Montgomery's film was released. They are probably reassured. . . . With the characteristic subtlety for which he is well known since his anticommunist performance before the Rankin committee, the likable former leading man charged right into the most obvious trap set by his technique.[3] A true subjective film is yet to be made, either as a cold and abstract technical performance or as a drama of depersonalization. A lieutenant commander in the U.S. Navy, Montgomery missed his mark (if I dare say so), failing even to provide a faithful illustration of Raymond Chandler's captivating world, as shown, for example, in *The Big Sleep*.[4] So it's in our interest to consult the original novel, which was just published by Gallimard, translated by Boris Vian and his wife (but I assure you Chandler comes through).[5] In Montgomery's *Lady in the Lake*, only the young woman whose bust cleverly evokes this line from a war poem by Apollinaire, "your breasts are the only shells I care about," remains faithful to the work's mythology. She has only to cross the room and for once the camera's movement that follows her to the door seems justified. We even feel the hero hesitate. We think that he's going to follow her. . . . But instead, he turns around to face Audrey Totter's grimaces. We retain of this moment the most subjective of regrets, while telling ourselves that in surrendering to this movement, the film might have been something else, and maybe even good.

CORNEILLE AT THE MOVIES

THIS GENERATION IS LUCKY. I'M TALKING ABOUT THOSE under twenty, those who in America are called *teenagers*.[1] Their teachers sometimes recognize that the most important part of their education isn't in textbooks, and that the use of free time— whether devoted to outdoor sports, romance, or film—is sometimes worthy of consideration. Whence a sharp breath of fresh air and a sudden surge of new blood in an exercise mummified by the French academic tradition, which results, for example, in the following topic recently proposed to students of the Sèvres High School[2]: "With your advice, you're helping a filmmaker adapt [Corneille's] *Horace* for the screen. Together you will choose the sets and costumes, and determine the essential elements to use, or those that are better left out."[3]

Let's wholeheartedly congratulate the pedagogue who dares to conceive such an exercise. It compels sympathy. But its results are worth more than just sympathy, and it's with a certain admiration that I discover in these thirteen-year-old demoiselles the makings of an excellent film-club public. All ten papers I received are interesting. In one, a touch of humor, in another a discovery, and

Signed: C.M.

Source: *Esprit*, n.s., no. 153 (February 1949): 282–85.

elsewhere a commonsensical reflection. While the *bobby-soxers* across the Atlantic faint in step to Frank Sinatra's murmurings, let's listen to Michèle C.: "Our goal is to attract filmgoers with intelligent films that could develop their minds while also entertaining them."[4] And here's Monique: "We parted company, hoping to meet up again in a cinema theatre, watching the film *Horace* as well as seeing the delirious crowd and saying: I have to read this play. Thus, Corneille will be paid his due." And Jacqueline: "The whole film should bask in a vigorous and majestic atmosphere so that our attention never flags. I'm working for the public-at-large to make the Cornelian drama accessible to all."

Some have a film culture that exceeds the cult of actors. For example, here's how Claire, the most gifted of the bunch, begins: "Like Jean Cocteau who, with Jean Marais, adapted *Ruy Blas* for the screen, the director C. plans to adapt Horace—."[5] "Why this initial C.?," I ask. "Well, it can be Clair, Carné, Clouzot, Clément, or Christian-Jacque." She continues: "We could do the film in British colors as in *Henry V.*" "What do you mean by British colors?" asks the teacher. Claire's response: "British Technicolor is far better than American Technicolor." And with a poise no doubt nurtured by her reading of *Écran,* she adds, undoubtedly "because Natalie Kalmus isn't there."[6]

Where culture is lacking, imagination steps in. Do you want a mise-en-scène in depth? Here's Claire, who proposes that when in the first shot old Horatius laments his son's flight, "through the open door, we see Horatius in perspective carried triumphantly." "Are you thinking of *Battleship Potemkin*?" Jacqueline's response: "A woman faints before the bloody battle. Her appalling face seen in close-up, with her upturned eyes, registers her horrified disgust. . . ." Or maybe of *Children of Paradise*? "They can both speak while walking in a noisy and hectic street to emphasize the intensity of the drama occurring within them and the agitated frenzy around them" (Claire). Maryvonne establishes an odd, chromatic symbolism: "Camilla might wear a red tunic trimmed in pink. For the young woman, love is the only thing that matters. Old Horatius would wear a blue tunic, assertive like his character." Finally, Claire again, proposes an ending that evokes both *The Eternal Return* and the vigil in *Henry V:* "We could show the fulfillment of the oracle's prophecy (whereby Curiatius would unite with Camilla): the tomb of Curiatius and Camilla" while we hear the oracle's lines:[7]

> 'Your prayers are answered. The gods have ordained
> Peace for Rome and Alba with tomorrow's sun.
> You and Curiatius shall from all unkind
> Fortune be freed, and eternally made one.'[8]

Jacqueline reinvents the adaptive principle Cocteau chose for *Ruy Blas:* "We will transpose in prose, besides certain famous tirades, such as Camilla's imprecations, and some maxims that from time to time will remind the spectator that Corneille isn't completely forgotten." Maryvonne focuses on the film's rhythm: "We must respect this tragedy's numerous implications of despair and hope." Jacqueline also has a taste for camera movement à la de Santis[9]:

> The battle will be the highlight. . . . There will be a multitude of panting warriors, with people hanging from the walls and towers. The day will be stormy and the sky covered in clouds. Everything will be bathed in tension until the moment when proud and radiant, the combatants will appear. Then the battle will begin. We'll see it from a distance, because the camera will soar and hover above the countryside, the city, the field, and in the middle of an open space where six men are fiercely fighting.

And Marie-Claude updates the story's very imagery, by replacing the "open space" "of Horatius's escape, with a thick forest where nature presents a thousand dangers and a thousand accidents." The combatants' somewhat ridiculous and Olympian confrontation then becomes an obstacle course—and thus much more cinematographic—through the forest. From *Ben-Hur,* we jump to *The Most Dangerous Game.*

Then there's the casting. There was a total consensus concerning Jean Marais in the role of Horatius *fils*. "All are fierce-looking," says Jacqueline. "Personally, I would very much like Jean Marais. . . ." Starting with Curiatius, opinions diverge. The majority choose Georges Marchal (baptized Marshall by Michèle C. who reads too many newspapers) "whose face expresses more gentleness."[10] Several votes go to Jean Desailly. For old Horatius, Pierre Blanchar and Louis Salou are proposed. For the role of Camilla, the following are suggested: Dominique Blanchar, Michèle Morgan, and especially Andrée Clément, "this tempestuous and passionate young woman who has such beautiful braids."[11] For the role of Sabina, Annie Ducaux and Edwige Feuillère.[12] But this last role will be shortened, if Michèle G. is to be believed, who suggests "ending the act with line 1,372. That will avoid one of the many calls for Sabina's death of which there are enough already. . . ." Claire adds the following advice for the actors: "Above all, no emphasis or misplaced theatrical gestures, which would be ridiculous and laughable in the cinema."

For inspired ideas, there are some real pearls, mainly due to the marvelous ease with which these youngsters waltz around the machines and crowd extras. "I think," says Michèle C. with candor, "that we could openly express the public's pleasure in depicting the frenzied Roman crowd on set." The sudden appearance of this frenzied crowd delights me. Michèle G. wants to adjust the lighting: "The openings must be plentiful and I think that with a bright light everything will work." The first Michèle takes us for a stroll across the studio: "We step over electric wires, planks, cables, pianos" (this must be the set of *Hellzapoppin'*).[13] As Flavian leaves, he hangs his military coat on a set panel. Little by little, the panel parts fall to the ground. "Too bad," cries the production coordinator. "Let the Roman decor be set up!" "Horatius suddenly appears carrying three dead bodies." (This line is in Livy, but transposed here, it assumes a comic force.) "Camilla wrings her hands and calls for her dead fiancé. But Curiatius doesn't answer. He's busy

removing his makeup and drinking a well-deserved lemonade."
Finally, here Claire once again takes the cake in her description
of Camilla's murder: "There's an outburst from Horatius, a raging
madman, who attacks and kills her.... A long silence and a release
of tension." Well, it's the least one can say.

Perhaps I am more lenient with female high school students
with admirable legs and comely appearance than with the ma-
ture guild of male critics. But we find here and there among these
girls' essays greater cinematographic instinct than in an article
by.... Let's just say some authors whom I don't have the pleasure
of knowing personally. Compare that with the daily observations
of young girls shimmying to the sound of be-bop and young boys
browsing illustrated books of Matisse and Picasso with delight.
And let's admire this generation that catches up with the advance
that art suddenly took on humanity and finds itself at last on equal
footing with its technique. Let's wait for the films that tomorrow—
when democratic progress will make possessing a camera as natural as that of a pen—Claire, Micheline, Francine, or Elisabeth will
give us, what they are aiming for, like Monique, to make the crowd
go wild, or that, like Jacqueline, they are wise enough to desire
"that the audience might leave the cinema feeling healed after the
tragedy saying simply: 'I won't forget this film.'"

ONE HUNDRED MASTERPIECES OF FILM

IMAGINE AN AUTODIDACT WHOSE ONLY CULTURAL RE-
source is a circulating library, and whose shelves are haphazardly
stocked by publishers, and who consequently reads Gide without
having heard of Montaigne or Valéry or knowing a single line of
Racine—indeed, who judges the novel as defined by Sartre, criticism by Kanapa, and American literature by Vernon Sullivan,[1]
but for whom Stendhal, Sainte-Beuve, and Edgar Allan Poe are
just names, remembered at best thanks to a newspaper article–
–worse still, having casually come across *Dangerous Liaisons* or
Andromache, has no way to reread them or to make any compar-
isons.[2] This unimaginable person exists and can be found in the
film spectator, an autodidact by necessity (since IDHEC's teaching
notes aren't widely distributed). They are poorly informed by virtue of the ill will of those who possess rare film copies and whose
only opportunity to complete their studies is currently screening
at the Cinémathèque française at 7, avenue de Messine, a three-
pronged program of notable works of film history from 1895 to
1934. There they will discover—following initiatory rites next to

---

Signed: C.M.
  Source: *Esprit*, n.s., no. 156 (June 1949): 878–80.

which Eleusis and Freemasonry are as inoffensive as François
Mauriac's wrath—material for rethinking their opinions. Because
despite the modest ticket price of 101 FF, they are unable to access this dark chamber, which recalls the Great Pyramid's mortu-
ary chamber, where the precious mummies of Douglas Fairbanks
and Lillian Gish await us clasped tightly in their celluloid strips.[3]
Irregular screening schedules, forgetful ticket-takers, overcrowd-
ing in gas-chamber-like corridors, and under- and over-sold seats.
All this is orchestrated with panache by the Cinémathèque's invaluable director, Henri Langlois, and puts spectators in an utterly
religious state, torn between a sense of their unworthiness and a
mad hope of finally . . . seeing the film. Spectators are crushed,
churned, laminated, and purified in such a way that binds them to
the screen as if it's their only lifeline. In memory of what they have
just endured, cinema appears as a true Paradise. I rest my case.

At the Cinémathèque, spectators can thus see how film language has developed. With every screening they will realize the
amount of chance, labor, and genius that has gone into its evolution. They will discover Griffith at the origin of everything. They
will learn that Stroheim is not just this actor with Stroheim's face,
but the most prodigious cinematic brain before Welles; that Fairbanks is not just Zorro and d'Artagnan, but that in 1920 he created a prototype for American comedy in *When the Clouds Roll
By;* that Pearl White is altogether different from Betty Hutton; and
that Abel Gance has done better than *Blind Venus.*[4] They will be
astonished to discover genuine masterpieces signed by unknown
names: Murnau, Lupu Pick, Piscator. Even aside from special oc-
casions (like Griffith's *Intolerance* that was shown again, one last
time, on May 3rd), some films better known to a ciné-club public acquire greater meaning by being reinserted in their historical context. Borrowings are acknowledged, influences become
clear, and discoveries gain a foothold. What we praise in the one,
belongs in fact to another, while originality often jumps out and
destroys a legend. (As in *The Assassination of the Duke of Guise,*

whose slick characters continue to laugh in the film's clever presentation of cinema's first example of dramatic editing.)[5] We realize that good feelings make bad cinema. Every time Griffith surrenders to his noble sentiments, inspiration falls flat, while Stroheim's inappropriate feelings "come across" marvelously. We also realize that the best kind of fantasy appears in *Nosferatu*'s real sets and not in *Caligari*'s topsy-turvy decor; that Murnau's armchairs and Eisenstein's staircases are more surprising and unexpected than Fritz Lang's cities, landscapes, and castles. In short, cinema's destiny is not as an escape, but as an analysis of reality. By noticing all this, we might yield to "fancy words" (although it should be possible among honest people to use words like "subjective" and "technical shot breakdown" without offending anything other than a certain snobbery for simplicity). But at least it prevents us from mistaking Piraeus for a man, Figueroa for Goya, *Brute Force* for a realistic film, and the Orson Welles of *Citizen Kane* for the director of *The Stranger*.[6]

ORPHEUS

TOWARD THE END OF THE SUMMER HOLIDAYS I HAD THE opportunity to introduce *Orpheus* to a group of young French and foreign filmmakers. The ensuing silence was on the order of that following a performance of *Parsifal* at the Bayreuth Festival: in such a case, resorting to applause just to be released from the emotions that overcome one would be inappropriate. At best, one is forced to carry these feelings home with oneself. But the producer's spokesperson was present and might have misunderstood our silence. So we clapped. Our applause was genuine. The audience was generally entranced by the film with two exceptions: an Englishman congenitally impervious to all poetry and a progressive Swiss, a post-revolution nouveau riche who desperately critiqued the protagonists' fancy attire and Death's Rolls-Royce to denounce the mythology of a rotting society in decomposition.* Admiration came only later. *Orpheus'* incredible formal beauty was apparent only upon reflection. What mattered was that the film was beginning to cast its spell: we had entered into the radioactive zone

---

Review of Jean Cocteau's *Orpheus,* released in France on September 29, 1950. Signed: Chris Marker. Source: *Esprit,* n.s., no. 173 (November 1950): 694–701.
* Franz Thomassin told him once and for all "death was the poor man's only luxury."

and were affected; we could neither give in nor resist. And some of us *were afraid.*

Orpheus' apparently cool reception during its world premiere is doubtless due to other reasons. Admittedly, the Republican guardsmen, the 15-foot-wide rugs, and the candy favor boxes wrapped in Cocteau's drawings were perhaps not the ideal introduction to a "meditation on death."* But above all how could the film not put a chill on this seasoned audience, the Paris *beau monde* who can't be duped and that freezes in terror at the idea that it might be possible to be hoodwinked when introduced to a work that eludes them. Because *Orpheus* can be unlocked with several keys and on several levels. *Orpheus'* real public, a sensitive one, enters into the film simply by the power of identification, which is cinema's specialty, and may fear for themselves, much like my young foreigners. An initiated public, which holds the first key, and reads in this Cocteau-*Orpheus,* as previously in *The Blood of a Poet,* its most explicit condemnation, can no longer identify with what they see. All projections and harmonics are denied them. Credulity, the first condition of a good spectator, is forbidden to them. They see in this spectacle only what concerns them, namely: their responsibility. If there exists a Cocteau legend, a Cocteau caricature, that turns this worker into a socialite, this monk into an acrobat, and his radiance into something "showy," it's the effect of the audiences that attend these openings. In 1923 Cocteau wrote: "The gestures of a man who walks in death's footpath must appear comical."[1] Since then, if this reverse illusionist shows his hand, reveals his tricks, opens his closets, reveals that his white magic is black magic, his pigeons are alive, his women really are chopped into pieces, and he actually walks in death's footpath, then his public will abandon him. Haughtily excluded from the discussion between Orpheus and his Death, incapable

---

* See, for example, the review in *Le Film français* on October 6, 1950, that takes the cake.

of the humility and detachment through which simple spectators can nonetheless participate in the sacrifice, they "lose interest in a dream that ceases to be theirs."*

TO DOUBT CINEMA'S ABILITY to "formulate problems," as we say, is to doubt its capacity for revelation, as old as spirit, and to forget the very role of myth, which is to refract on and transmit: on a made-to-order template, the patient assesses the mystery. This is the function of fables, apparitions, and miracles. From Mount Sinai to Paramount, the only difference lies in the audience. When it came time for him to make us measure death, during the first *Orpheus,* a stage play, Cocteau went straight for the most *serious* technique, that of the music hall. The sets had the toughness and fragility of fairground stalls; the objects functioned like the props of a tightrope walker, of an Icarian; the characters themselves resorted to metaphors of the tightrope and the safety net. For this undertaking, the relaxed "theatre," made comfortable by luxury and idleness, was unsuitable. Something else was needed besides an actor, who is a man of embonpoint changing costumes in a cozy dressing room. What Cocteau needed were acrobats, thin men who do their makeup in the hallways and risk their lives every evening in a single exercise, constantly perfected. But it meant confusing both the theatregoing audience, who understood not a thing, and the circus audience, who didn't set foot in Cocteau's theatre. Cinema alone facilitates miracles, with its boundless public, its actors, trained creatures who are simultaneously gods, Indians, and undeniable corpses. In his 1926 dedication, Cocteau said that admiration left him cold and that the only thing that mattered was being believed. It seems that cinema alone today affords the artist credibility, and Saint Thomas would have needed only a screening in technicolor to be convinced.

---

* I don't think it necessary to point out the numerous quotes by Cocteau in this article. Inquisitive readers will benefit more by looking for them themselves and to find others.

I don't have at hand the beautiful passage from *The Difficulty of Being* where Cocteau speaks of those who have a hard time believing in the reality of inner adventures.[2] Combat, risk, and a manhunt aren't the sole domain of physical bodies, is what he more or less says. Some are the domain of the soul and are no less real or dangerous. I think that this quotation might illuminate *Orpheus'* strategy for creating myths. A strategy that doesn't operate through "symbols," that is, by substitution, but by development. We watch *Orpheus* the way we read Kafka, without worrying about what the characters "represent," while closely following the story. But in this story, each word resonates from the other side of the wall. And without losing anything of its own architecture, it simultaneously builds an invisible path where the soul's adventures properly come together. So well that the fable is no longer a game of portraits in a morality tale, where each image peels off to deliver its meaning printed underneath—but instead the imitation and the prefiguration of a truth that allows us simply to sense the depth and to measure the distance.

But it is understandable that there more than ever the poet is held to a strict law, to an intensified realism. His microcosm must have detail, the precision of a crystal ball. And Cocteau has often insisted on the fact that the marvelous, too, has its laws. Hence the excess of verisimilitude and attention that we find in *Orpheus*. The horse in the original play and its messages are here replaced by a car equipped with a wireless radio. A real car and a real radio.[3] *The Blood of a Poet*'s magic incantations that the author uttered from behind the image now arrive in the form of personal messages to which the radio has accustomed us. Everywhere this search for the concrete, for the fact, for this poor reality that is not substantially different from the reality of souls, of death, which is as close and foreign to it as the front and back of a cloth. Indeed, it is a reality so very close to us, that of war, radio messages, ruins, and purge trials. Which is not to say that Cocteau "exploits" elements of contemporary life to make us receptive to the myth (and only a lightweight new-style critic from *Combat* could make this mis-take).[4] For if he does employ these things, the era did so first. The notorious messages, so similar in form to those transmitted by the BBC's Radio London, already appeared in Cocteau's *Orpheus* play of 1926. The existence of the radar-like instrument used by François Périer seems completely normal in this time of cyber-netics. But it was already used by the angels Raphael and Azrael in the play, and undoubtedly seemed extravagant at the time. It is widely acknowledged today that one of the characteristics of dreams is their strange freedom with respect to time. It's hardly surprising that a poet wrests forms from the future still impossible to identify, which will remain an object of mystery or of mockery until their formal advent delivers them. By transmitting his mes-sages in short-wave signals, by situating the inside of the mirror in a bombed out Saint-Cyr, by making SS motorcyclists be his angels of death, Cocteau was only taking his cues from the era. Nature doesn't imitate art, but fulfills its prophecies.

It's undoubtedly for the sake of a greater rigor that a decisive role is given to the objects in *Orpheus*. A lot can be done with characters and feelings without, however, convincing anyone. An object, with its weight, its materiality, and its ambiguity as servant-enemy, imposes its presence. The most stunning exam-ple of an object *performing* in cinema seemed to me until now to be the turnstile in Orson Welles's *The Lady from Shanghai:* one of those revolving doors similar to a vertical turnstile, like the one at the Concorde subway station, that allows for passage *in only one direction.* When the sailor Welles goes through this door, leaving Rita to die, it's the turnstile and not him that guarantees he won't turn back, he can't come back, the story's over, and what he leaves behind—woman and chintzy delights—he is leaving for good.

But in *Orpheus* there is the rearview mirror. Whereas in the play, Orpheus was led to look at Eurydice, and thus to lose her again, by an artifice of acting (Orpheus has slipped and turns around only to steady himself), here he sees her in the rearview mirror.

No more accidents or escape are possible. This rearview mirror is a Death trap. We were told that mirrors are his doors and what is a rearview mirror if not another mirror? But above all the mirror possesses this power that objects have over us, preventing us from turning back and forcing us to see what is behind us. Only a moment earlier Orpheus managed to turn away from a photo of Eurydice, caught in this alternative confusing trap of likeness. Finally, how can we forget this height of realism and disorientation: Heurtebise (a real chauffeur) enters the home of Eurydice (a real young woman in a real house) to the tune of Gluck's *Orpheus and Eurydice* (real music played on a real radio). In this picture everything is normal, tangible, reasonable, where the secret architecture of the adventure is nevertheless revealed, where a flesh and blood Heurtebise enters basking in the aura of his true mission, where everything is bathed in a different light, that we can have fun calling supernatural without resorting to another form of the marvelous, which is born from the most natural associations of beings and objects. This is both one of the most moving moments of the film and one where the intention is the clearest, which serves to illustrate the treatment's excellence. I'm reminded of the minor heartaches in a T. S. Eliot poem provoked by a line from Dante incorporated into the banal story. We are at the crossroads of time and eternity, in a present of great significance. A never distant eternity becomes momentarily discernible. What's funny is that those most impervious to this realistic alchemy are ready to accept, without discussion, the crude miracle of invisible violins that flourish all of a sudden, like little chicks, beneath the pillows in a love scene in any old Hollywood film.

I CAN THINK OF ONLY ONE FILM in the history of cinema that can compare to *Orpheus:* Dreyer's *Vampyr* with its embodied metaphysics. But where Dreyer ambitiously tackles the general problem of death, Cocteau tells his own story.

Orpheus's Death is very clear on this point: she is *his* death and

not death *in general*. We all carry death inside of us. Our Guardian
Death, like our Guardian Angel. We recognize a leitmotif in Jean
Cocteau. If, as Welles (it's surely a factor in their friendship) is incapable of a work that doesn't disclose in one way or another his
deepest obsession, or that doesn't relate to his life—there where
Welles—through his incarnations as Kane, Macbeth, and even *The
Lady from Shanghai*'s dialogue—raises for us and for himself the
problem of Evil (up until what point can we live with Evil?), Cocteau reveals his longstanding familiarity with death and unmasks
himself from the start. In the game's fifth minute (as is said in
sports' reporting) Diaghilev's "astonish me" betrays him.[5] We find
then, magnified and in the flesh, many known things. Death's assistants are foreshadowed in *Plain Song*:

> Because it isn't Death herself that kills.
> She has her assassins.[6]

And from one image to the next and one episode to next, echoes
of all his earlier work are juxtaposed within the film and merged
with it like an object placed on a mirror catching its reflection and
becoming one with it. All that's needed is a little memory to clearly
read this delicate mechanism of the poet's relation to his work and
his Death as a question of Death's triumph over love. ("Better than
Venus, O Death, you inhabit our beds") or the poet's power over
his Death and the paradox of immortality ("Death shall not have
me alive. To write is to vanquish death," etc.) And as always this
precautionary exegesis exceeds the work to expand on its context.
Just as the spectators who laugh at *The Blood of a Poet* are forced
to see themselves within the film applauding the torture—and as
a result are judged, here every criticism is already disarmed in advance: When R.S. in the *Observateur* writes: "In no other film ... do
we pass through mirrors so often. But this time no one is fooled,"
he is merely repeating the statue's very words in *The Blood*: "I congratulate you. You wrote that we would be walking through mirrors and you didn't believe it." Therein lies the crux of the drama

and Cocteau is fully aware of the tension. But this is also the poet's function, a constant, exhausting effort to reduce the distance between reality's two opposing sides. Poetry builds its perspective in this gap between the two worlds, like a stereoscope. And it is in this way, too, that the cinematograph becomes our best vehicle for poetic exploration. We don't pass through the mirror. We don't pass through the screen. And yet we do travel via the screen. We live the lives of the characters and inhabit life on the screen. The film becomes the endpoint and the most advanced realm of the demiurge. Of course it may appear crude and even ludicrous from a certain nostalgia for a poetic action in the "real" world. But we might as well reproach humans for not being God. An entirely triumphant poetry would be silence. And it is in its failure, in its imperfect effort toward an impossible reconciliation, that it fills the space to be bridged between these two beautiful corpses where we recognize ourselves.

This is perhaps why the cinema assumes a unique role in Jean Cocteau's work, why it's never thanks to the prestige of a technical novelty or plaything (like Welles's "electric train set") that he enters into his art, but through the ambiguous character of the world closest to ours, the final lie before the truth. In his poetic experiments in all the arts, Cocteau followed the inverse order of Hegel's spectre, that ran from architecture to poetry, presented an itinerary of disembodiment. By contrast, all of Jean Cocteau's work is a struggle toward *gravitas* and the most precise understanding of the world. Amenable at first to the instructions and messages of the invisible, connected to his receiver like a radio operator, revealing in his poems the transcript of his interviews like Orpheus in his car, he keeps on searching in the novel, in the theatre, in drawing, in travel, via language, color, the "snowy brass of a wire sculpture" or the "light's India ink," the means to weigh down the invisible, to trap Death, an ink that reveals the presence of angels and shows us "phantoms suddenly transformed into blue trees." The cinematograph is the last and the richest of these modes of investigation. We know the importance Cocteau ascribes to waves and signals, and all means of mechanical revelation. In Cocteau the poet often appears as a kind of a recording device. And certainly he thinks of the movie camera as a machine for multiplying and sharpening the senses, an X-ray lamp, a tool for catching secrets that reveals more than what we give it. "Photography's surprises" was a subtitle for *The Blood of a Poet,* in which Cocteau "caught in the trap of *his own film,*" attributed to the camera's discernment the revelation of his own face instead of that of his hero. And we remember the photograph of the *Newlyweds on the Eiffel Tower.*[7] A miracle, the reverse of a climbing fakir seen by all but never recorded on film, Cocteau dreams of a film that will be sensitive enough to preserve the figures precisely where the human eye sees only confusion. Meanwhile, he collaborates with the mysterious; it's true he feeds the camera-beast pre-prepared dishes, but whose prodigious metamorphosis he ultimately expects. Then he can say as he did of *The Blood of a Poet:* "How can I reproach anyone for misunderstanding a film I understand so little myself," and distance himself from his film, as far away as sleep, as impossible to recount as a dream, transmissible only by this other miracle of which the cinematograph alone is capable—making others dream it, too.

ALL OF THIS, OF COURSE, does not prove that *Orpheus* is a good or bad film. Here again Cocteau settled the question long ago. "It is neither beautiful nor ugly, it has other merits," is how he concluded one of his poems. It is these other merits that should be, it seems to me, the focus of the discussion and which we might ask the critics to consider, instead of expressing their dismay.* Not because it is necessary to refer to Cocteau's work to pass judgment, nor because it is a film for acolytes. I saw a young German, completely ignorant of Cocteau's oeuvre, discuss *The Blood of a Poet*

---

* See, for example, the film's appalling synopsis in *Aurore.*

by substituting the snowball fight with his own experience as a prisoner in Russia, where the blood of some and the applause of others made him feel a similar "shock." He understood that this was the crux of the film, and starting from this substitution, he reconstructed the whole, clearly misconstruing the meaning of certain details (sometimes rather childishly: he saw in the famous five-pointed star the Soviet star). But no matter: he was no longer telling us about Cocteau's film, but about his own, for which Cocteau had provided the raw material. And ultimately he was perhaps closer, with all his mistakes, to the poem's real purpose, which is not to be read, but to be rewritten silently by readers in their own name.

Such is the state of grace that I wish for *Orpheus*' audience. But if the film's chief virtue is to push to the background a formal beauty that is usually the sole criterion for judging a film, it would be unfair to say nothing about it. Particularly since this beauty is not gratuitous. It coincides thoroughly with Jean Cocteau's method and intentions. The camera's independence and insight, which I spoke of earlier, assert themselves, for example, in Nicolas Hayer's extraordinary compositions, where every image is framed like a picture that never impedes the characters' freedom. It's as if the movie camera allows the actors to move instinctively and assumes the position yielding the most meaning. (Of course it's not just the definition of a good composition that I am giving here. But rather . . .) And what text could be a more appropriate caption for the famous photo of Maria Casarès by the car door than this passage from a story told by Jean Cocteau on the first Christmas eve of the war: "She was frighteningly beautiful, so beautiful that our eyes couldn't bear it and would have found her ugly if it had been possible to envision that."[8] And Jean Marais has never been more handsome nor a better actor, and François Périer, the friendly devil, has been turned inside out like a rabbit offering us an unforgettable angel-face, and Juliette Gréco, with her lioness' marble face, snatched from her dives and taboos is a revelation, as is Édouard Dermit, for once well directed—all this is not nothing.[9] I admire people sufficiently blasé to be unmoved by the incessant spectacle of Cocteau's soul, uncomfortable in its only body, that spreads its genius on everything that nears it and transports and objects to their highest realization—and what's more, with the supreme courtesy of thanking them for it.

SIEGFRIED AND THE GAOLERS, OR GERMAN CINEMA ENCHAINED

IN FILM COMPETITION GENERALLY, FILM CRITICISM HARDLY ever comes into play except in the preliminary round. It doesn't figure in the playoffs. It would be hard to define this first vetting where the mysteries of distribution, curiosity, empathy, fame, and anecdote are decisive for launching a film, an *auteur,* or a school. But it's certain that when a critic brags about their choice, they are dealing with a matter that is already the result of a selection. The critic discovers what they are supposed to discover, arbitrarily following releases and the festival circuit. The critic thus practices their art in a mold already half-hardened, whose contours can only be modified. Their personal tastes can at best lend only a helping hand.

Thanks to a tremendous kick off, due in large part to ignorance concerning its real history, Italian cinema successfully passed

Signed: Chris Marker.

Source: *Cahiers du cinéma: Revue du cinéma et du télécinéma,* no. 4 (July–August 1951): 4–11.

The first half of Marker's title ("Siegfried et les Argousins") riffs on Jean Giraudoux's novel *Siegfried et le Limousin* (1922) and later stage play. A year after this review, Marker published his study *Giraudoux par lui-même* (Giraudoux in his own words).

Early appearance of the swordsman prince Siegfried (Paul Richter) in *Die Nibelungen* (1924, *The Ring Cycle*), the first of director Fritz Lang's two fantasy-adventure films based on the medieval figure of German and Norse mythology.

the written exam. Positive reviews are a foregone conclusion. In contrast, because of its poor start, due almost entirely to circumstances, German cinema continues to go unnoticed. In 1951 Italian cinema, even when it appears in a minor example like Zampa, is guaranteed distribution, reviews, as well as a certain quality of reception and attention, while the work of leading filmmakers like Wolfgang Staudte and Helmut Käutner is systematically neglected. This indifference may result in part from the dissatisfaction in which many German films leave us, but it can also be the cause. After all, the success of Italian Neorealism owes something to the fanfare that greeted it. To some extent, opinion from abroad allowed Rossellini and De Sica to be imposed on a country, which tended in the immediate postwar period to reconnect only with *Cabiria* and *Scipio Africanus*.[1] But even if, after having offered

Germany its own *Paisà* in 1947, with *In Those Days,* Helmut Käutner had devoted himself only to frivolities, we should still hold to
account those who in Germany and elsewhere have failed to appreciate his work.

German cinema is in chains. But this conspiracy of silence isn't
the only ailment afflicting it. It shares the woes of world cinema:
censorship, crisis of subject matter (the latter largely the result
of the former), and is joined to others of a more personal nature:
a confusion of values, an expressionist heritage, the public's general lack of culture, the almost total absence of a knowledgeable
and independent film criticism, a guilt complex, a miscalculation
of competence (an entire article would be needed to condemn
the dominance of university professors over the German documentary). Among the gaolers who keep it shackled, the occupying
forces play their role, less through direct intervention than by the
repercussions of the situation that they have created.

Today, however, truth has quickly caught up with the lie. Germany's partition in two, what in 1945 was only an imaginary behe-
moth, has become a reality. Cinema bears witness to the drawing
and quartering of the country and caricatures it to the extent
that it anticipates, on both sides, a popular, slightly vague conscience, yet marks its undeniable milestones. With specific exceptions (a good craftsman *sans* ideological preoccupations—like
Arthur Maria Rabenalt, the *auteur* of *The Three Codonas*—can the
same year produce a cloak and dagger film in the East and a realist melodrama in the West), there now exists a typical Eastern
production and a typical Western production. From a common
background and an initial problematic identity, two opposing
manifestations have emerged. The line that originates in 1946
with *The Murderers Are among Us*—conceived in the West, but
shot in the East—comes to fruition in the East in 1951, with Staudte's ferocious satire of the German middle class in his *The Kaiser's
Lackey*—and in the West, with Günter Neumann's self-justification
in *Wonderful Times.* Equally scarred by the war, defeat, and anxiety

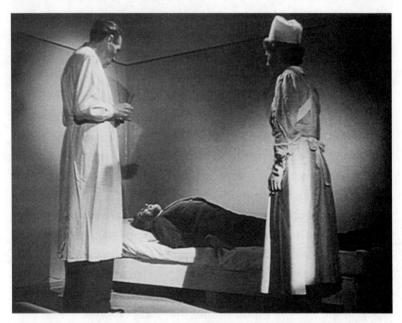

Former German army officer Dr. Hans Mertens (Wilhelm Borchert) under treatment for a painful return to civilian status after a traumatic wartime incident in Wolfgang Staudte's *Die Mörder sind unter uns* (*The Murderers Are among Us*, 1946).

concerning the future, Eastern productions seek to condemn—sometimes summarily—political causes and precise responsibilities, while Western productions blame fate, the Kaiser, Wotan, Mephisto, Adam, and the Good Lord.

In 1946–47, German cinema was dominated spiritually by the presence of the disaster, the need to face and emerge from it, and aesthetically, by a fifteen-year period of stagnation that reconnected it with expressionism. These two dominant strains went hand in hand. Everything that seemed prophetic in the aftermath of the First World War suddenly seemed clear. I remember my emotion in seeing *The Murderers Are among Us:* faced with the protagonist's compelling physical resemblance to the character of Death in Fritz Lang's *Destiny*—who said the exact same things: "I can do nothing. . . . I'm only obeying orders from higher up. . . .

My actions horrify me, but I must obey. . . ." For five years, obeying orders from higher up, the German people were Death's servant. And the character of Mertens, a German military doctor witnessing a massacre ordered by his captain, obsessed by this memory and trying to free himself from it by killing the officer whom he has tracked down after the war, is the image that the German people presents of itself. Yet the real conflict isn't between Mertens and Captain Brückner. Mertens didn't tangle with Brückner in an attempt to prevent him from ordering the massacre. He followed the captain's curt advice "to go outside to get some fresh air." Mertens, who had turned on his heel before his superior, is now portrayed as an avenging angel waiting with gun in hand for an unarmed Brückner. . . . In reality, it wasn't so much Brückner he wanted to kill as himself, the Mertens whose courage had failed him at the right moment. This is the moment he wanted to kill, whose stain he wanted to erase: The moment when *he knew and had done nothing*—the very tragedy of the German people.

The Murderers Are among Us was inconclusive. It certainly raised the question of salvation (Mertens as the German people freed from the sin to which it had been lured by Brückner— Nazism—through Hildegard Knef, or anti-Nazism's intervention), but resulted in the uncertainty affecting all Germany in 1946. At least that's how it was seen in France, where this uncertainty was taken all too easily for a lack of awareness. Next, the vagaries of Parisian film distribution offered us two moving but second-rate films: *The Blum Affair* and *Marriage in the Shadows*, and an anthology film, *The Berliner*—while Germany itself sent great mystagogic machines like *Love '47* or evangelical films like *Keepers of the Night* to international festivals. As if on purpose, the really important films went unnoticed. There was *Wozzeck* (1947), in which the phenomenon of aesthetic stagnation took on a value of laboratory reconstitution and allowed for the experiment of an expressionist sound film, as interesting in its field as that of the Russians dubbing *Potemkin*. There was the already mentioned *In*

Those Days, where via a series of two- or three-person sketches, Käutner delivered a small-scale chronicle of Nazism by lending his voice to a car, ever since the day in 1933, when it leads the female friend of a Jewish artist who must leave the country to a final meeting, until the automobile makes it way in the Berlin ruins. *Paisà* comes to mind, and not only because of its episodic organization and its refraction of historical events in the lives of everyday people. *Paisà* also comes to mind because of its haphazard sets, the rejuvenation of its film technique (everything was shot on location; studios no longer existed; no projectors; no reflectors, and a constant need to improvise) and also for the way it has upset audiences. I don't know a single French person who has seen *In Those Days* and hasn't made the connection.

For this last film Käutner had a young assistant, Rudolf Jugert, who made his directorial debut the following year with another film written by Käutner, *Film without a Title.*[2] Relatively disordered but also relatively distinguished, this *Film without a Title* was a film without a film, or more precisely a film of a film—what the Americans had timidly attempted in *Hellzapoppin'.*[3] Three screenwriters in a trailer try to conceive of a film: an idea for a story emerges, takes shape, and evolves. It finishes brilliantly with three films "to satisfy all tastes," spoofing in turn expressionism, operetta, and themselves (the screenwriters appear in the story, interviewing the characters, etc.). Beyond its success and its exemplary levity, this film is timely: it finishes off German film's two dominant trends. Its humor destroys the mania for and aesthetics of catastrophe, proving that German cinema is making up for lost time. And by a paradoxical progress, rejoined Western cinema in this state of crisis where art becomes its own subject.

It's perhaps no accident that this aesthetic watershed, this liquidation of legacies and influences, coincides with the political change of direction in 1948 and the hardening of positions on both sides of the demarcation line. Until then, Berlin was still a single city. *The Murderers Are among Us,* shot in the Russian zone that

Title figure in feature *Wozzeck* (1947), whose flashback depiction of a deceased soldier's humiliation and betrayal transforms director Georg C. Klaren's adaptation of Georg Büchner's 1837 stage play into a condemnation of postwar Germany society.

offered more facilities, could have been shown interchangeably in the West or in the East. (The Americans even lamented, after the fact, that they hadn't financed it.) *Film without a Title* was still a Berlin film with its idiosyncratic humor fairly unique in the rest of Germany, but at the same time it served as a balance sheet. A fresh start was necessary. The blockade has helped; the separation between East and West was inevitable, and destinies were going to diverge.

The cheery slogan *"Neither right, nor left, but forward!"* is well known, while another slogan, *"In the air!,"* seems specifically to designate West German cinema, where there is an incredible use of angels, ghosts, visions, devils, and good gods. When a film's characters aren't in the clouds, it's clearly the director who is. Since it becomes increasingly difficult to criticize a war that you are asked to renew against the same enemy and for the same propagandistic reasons and since all future paths are closed, one takes to the skies. Plus, Germans are prone to walking on the ceiling, and artistic Wagnerism responds perfectly to its pathos of the eternal adolescent. The Germans were ashamed of the starkness of *In Those Days* and the nonchalance of *Film without a Title*. But from a sober and tense play like Borchert's *The Man Outside,* the director Liebeneiner makes an incredible mishmash of heaven and hell, with a prologue where God wearing a bowler and the Devil in top hat converse among the ruins, with a ten-meter-tall cripple chasing the hero on deserted town squares, with a dream in negative exposure, superimposition every ten meters, and a swirling sound that gives you mussels inside the ear—that's called *Love '47* and it represents Germany in festivals.[4] It comforts Germans who at last detect in it the signs of *Art.*

It's worth repeating that this expressionist slosh, normal in 1945, is no longer innocuous in 1949. It's no longer gratuitous. It doesn't express a conflict between a backward form and a topical background. On the contrary, it is precisely what suits the dissolution of responsibilities and the vague prophecy by which West Germany attempts to express its distress. It is by the same token of mental superimpositions that Germans ascend the ladder of guilt, which they finally discharge . . . on God.

Much could be said about a certain *Christianity of the Defeat.* There are people who discover cathedrals when they can profit from the right to asylum. Their names are Abellio and Malaparte. West German cinema, under the direct impetus of the Church, didn't overlook this admirable emergency exit. That earned us *Keepers of the Night* and *The Falling Star,* where Germany absolves itself with a great deal of wishful thinking and puerility, with angels who fly on the end of thick strings and children whose death on film approximates a human sacrifice. A secular version of forgiveness for offenses led to the theme of the Franco-German reconciliation in *A Day Will Come,* the story of the unfortunate corporal Mombour, a descendant of Protestant immigrants who, during the 1870–71 Franco-Prussian War, after having killed his French cousin and billeted to said family, conquers the heart of his female cousin. Now everything is revealed, but hold on, the mother is on her deathbed. She calls her son. Let's forget the past. The German cousin dons the uniform of his French cousin; the mother thinks she's seeing her own son and dies at peace. But horrors! The French attack, and the Uhlans who don't recognize their disguised corporal kill him. His female cousin collapses weeping on the body of her dead cousin. Female France and Male Germany collaborate in the void. The End. More serious is the fact that *A Day Will Come* was signed by Jugert. For his sake we doubt that the *auteur* of *Film without a Title* could have believed for a minute in such a screenplay. What has happened now to Jugert's acuity, keen understanding, lightness, and agile camerawork? (His incredibly mobile camerawork in *Film without a Title*, where the camera wanders, takes a close look at people, studies characters, sniffs the furniture. . . . After the camera-I and the camera-pen, it's now time for the camera-dog.) Nothing is more futile than the technique of their last works. Next to them, we should be more sensitive to the great narrative qualities of a film like Willi Forst's *The Sinner*. But as we see there a woman of ill repute in a relatively favorable light, the Church went on a rampage; self-censorship was let loose, and the bishops launched commandos of young devotees to attack the theatres. By its prohibitions as by its impulses, Europe's most backward Church wields over the cinema the same disastrous influence as on other activities.

If we look closely at West German film production, starting with its myths, its window dressing, its hallucinated residues, we might be tempted to think of German cinema around 1925 and to draw a conclusion on some kind of German fatality, forever doomed to nighttime and lies. From there to extending this fatality to the German people itself is no stretch, as foreign critics have often pointed out. Fortunately, Eastern film production exists to

Ehe im Schatten (1947, *Marriage in the Shadows*), director Kurt Maetzig's melodrama that chronicles the story of the stage actor Hans Wieland, whose marriage to the Jewish actress Elisabeth Maurer exposed the couple to persecution after Hitler's rise to power.

prove, independently of its specific qualities, that this inevitability doesn't exist, and that German cinema can address additional themes by other means. But two coincidences don't make an inevitability. If twice in a row, after the first technical stammerings, after the Nazi freeze, German cinema attained its maturity in the aftermath of a military defeat, a foreign occupation, a domestic crisis, an explosion of misery and doubt, it would be hard to not ask it to express something and impossible for it to express a gentleness of life that it hardly ever knew. There as elsewhere, "fate" exists only in domestic complicity, and if West German films surrender to it, the East German DEFA films aspire to overcome it. Once again, cinema reveals itself as society's microcosm.

Wolfgang Staudte's films serve here as prime examples. I'm inclined to think of Staudte as Germany's leading filmmaker. First because he's tall, breaks windows when he laughs, and because he and his wife are the most independent and finest people I've ever met. And because his qualities—first and foremost his great honesty—are found in his films. Guided by a not fully formed conscience and disgruntled by his guilt, the image of the German sketched in *The Murderers* takes on fuller form in *Rotation*. If *In Those Days* was his version of *Paisà, Rotation* would be his *Difficult Years*. But we find there neither the transference of guilt in *The Murderers* nor the irresponsible bitterness in *Difficult Years*. This last note occurs rather in the previously mentioned West German film by Günter Neumann, *Wonderful Times,* in which the German petty bourgeois appears overwhelmed, drowned in a hostile universe. In *Rotation,* the problem of personal responsibility is raised with a humanity and a humility full of grandeur. The relationship between the father, a German worker essentially hostile to Nazism, and his son, a Hitler youth, resolves itself neither in a hopeless generational conflict nor in a vague forgiveness, but in a shared desire to construct the future. It brings a new and particularly noble tone to these inextricable postwar settling of scores. We are told that *Rotation* has been banned in France. I would like to know if this is true, and if so, under what pretext. In any event, let's wait for the welcome that our censors will give to *The Kaiser's Lackey,* the film that Staudte is currently completing, based on the Heinrich Mann novel. This return to literary sources is in no way a step backward: the life of a German burgher, his pseudofeudal values, the way in which he conducts his career might situate him during the Empire. Yet the film is timely. Its release coincides in West Germany with a rise of student groups, a renewal of military veterans' traditions, and a resumption of control by the industrial and financial bourgeoisie. A country's film production should be judged on films of this caliber. It matters less that the cinema of a young and unstable republic—compelled to pursue simultaneously a hundred activities of equal importance, slightly mesmerized by the rise of the Russian neighbor—commits errors of taste and sins of oversimplification. If the form of *The Council of the Gods,* which retraces the history of the IG Farben company, borders on caricature, the substance is not far from the historical truth. In contrast, success is nearly total in the wonderful *Heart of Stone* and in the realism of *The Last Year.* East German cinema adheres to current reality, with all its dross that West German cinema skirts or dissolves. On the one hand, life with all its compromises and imperfections, and on the other, a flower-covered void. West and East German cinemas are two brothers sharing a heavy heredity. But if the one copes by writing poems (and by engaging in military preparation), the other is busy learning its craft. It's not difficult to see where the promise of freedom lies.

A ritual toast in *Der Untertan* (1951, *The Kaiser's Lackey*), Wolfgang Staudte's adaptation of Heinrich Mann's 1918 satirical novel about a Prussian subject in pre–World War I Germany, whose rise and fall the film transforms into an object lesson exposing German militarism long before the Third Reich.

THE AESTHETICS OF ANIMATED FILM

AN IMPORTANT EVENT IN THE HISTORY OF FILMOLOGY
took place last April: the Arts Faculty of the Sorbonne accepted
and praised a dissertation defense on "The Aesthetics of Animated
Film."[1] Its author was Mademoiselle Poncet, a collaborator of Mr.
Souriau at the Institute of Art and Archaeology. She has a lively
personality, enormous curiosity, a solid cultural background, and a
passion for animated film. Her thesis is the fruit of both her culture
and her passion. Its very existence is praiseworthy, apart from any
other merit. Her work would console filmmakers from the not-so-
distant past when the literary world, in the words of the Académie
française's Permanent Secretary, used to describe cinema as an
"alarming return to barbarity."

But the value of this dissertation lies not only in its exemplary
and satisfactory nature. It is extraordinarily rewarding and introduces some ideas that deserve greater consideration, if only for
the sake of discussion. The brevity of the excerpts distributed in

Signed: C.M.

Source: *Esprit*, n.s., no. 182 (September 1951): 368–69.

Marker published a related but different article in German: "Der Trickfilm,"
DOK 50, special issue "Film und Kultur," ed. Joseph Rovan (Stuttgart, 1950):
75–76.

mimeographed form during the defense prevents me from elaborating here without distorting the work. Ideally, we would evaluate the thesis *in toto*. Perhaps this discussion will continue once it is published in book form.[2] For now, it's important to emphasize the dual movement by which Mlle Poncet includes animated film within the field of aesthetics. First, she identifies the aesthetic categories she sees at work in animated film. Next, she applies these categories critically and elucidates animated film's internal economy of operations by introducing an order in her empirical study. This is how she creates a table of values: the poetic, the picturesque, the graceful, the pretty. Measured in film footage, these values, in descending order, will offer the *range* of a given animation and its formula. This merits discussion: is footage the only relevant dimension to be considered? Can't intensity compensate for any variation in length? The method is nonetheless significant and absolutely justified in a technique as collaborative as animated film, where after all the musician's work plan appears in a form not far from its diagrams: 100 feet of elegance, 50 feet of comedy, etc. We even sense the application in a less pure perspective than the aesthetics to which Mlle Poncet deliberately confines herself regarding a veritable spectroscope of themes, which calculates and translates into statistics the "values" used in the animated film industry. This would allow technicians to see how and perhaps sociologists to say why.

As for the first criterion, animated film's inclusion within the domain of aesthetics naturally leads Mlle Poncet not only to assign an actual place to it and to offer this kind of consecration, but also to locate it within history and to look for relevant connections. Whence her supplementary point indicated in the subtitle: "A Comparative Study of Pictures from the Middle Ages and Animated Films." Without trying to identify the two phenomena as we might be tempted to do (the conjunction *and* in the subtitle says it all), the author convincingly demonstrates the striving of imagery toward movement that makes the Bayeux Tapestry, for example, an intimate drawing that lacks—as we say of a pooch lacking the ability to speak—only time.

Here too the absence of footnotes in the text raises questions. Otherwise, it might be possible to quarrel with Mlle Poncet regarding the way in which animated film responds to this expectation. After all, a drawing's meaning in the Middle Ages differs from that of a drawing for a twentieth-century artist. On its own, this meaning summarizes all efforts of representation. In addition, photography and cinema per se have come to liberate the draftsman's stroke from its representational obsession. It's perhaps in these practices that we must look for its real legacy. It's difficult to decide: is the Bayeux Tapestry meant to be understood as an ideogram or a chronicle? What does it foreshadow more, animated film or newsreels? *Alexander Nevsky* or *The Three Little Pigs*?[3] Émile Cohl made a real animated film out of it, it's true, and it seems that this is being done again, even if it proves nothing.[4] Isn't film the true culmination of the longing for movement and narrative in our imagery? Isn't animated film just a technical flirtation?, a desired anachronism, in sum a marginal art? Other examples exist of a major technique that makes a game out of adopting the appearance of a minor technique: thus the Acropolis imitates in stone the technique of wood carving, amulet boxes from the Belgian Congo imitate in wood the technique of basket weaving, etc. But cinema's fidelity is perhaps best found not in the imitation of imagery. A horse's posterity is the automobile—not the carousel horse.

These examples help us to see that even those objections, which may disappear after reading the dissertation, support Mlle Poncet's work. Such criticisms prompt questions and promote an understanding of problems as they affect our contemporary mythology. Finally, the sole criticism that can be made doesn't address her directly, but instead the collusion of film distributors and the public for whom the very notion of animated film is equated only with the productions of that color-blind grocer Walt Disney.

He is indeed her main—and unique—reference. Which risks restricting the scope of her argument far below the promise of her more encompassing title. Maybe she should have called her dissertation "The Aesthetics of Walt Disney"? Or are we to believe that Mlle Poncet's apt conclusions apply equally to the psychoanalytic pantomime of the Fleischer brothers, Betty Boop, and Popeye? To the existential ferocity of Woody Woodpecker? Tom and Jerry? Andy Pandy? The savages: Gertie the Dinosaur, Koko the Clown, Crazy-Cat, Oswald the Rabbit? To the abstractions of Fischinger, Len Lye, Norman McLaren? And to the animated engraving of Alexeieff? Or to the political freedom of Anthony Gross? Paul Grimault? And Soviet animated film? Walter Lantz, Tex Avery, Philip Stapp, Saul Steinberg? Without mentioning Émile Cohl, who discovered everything fifty years ago. And what about that great unknown figure, Pat Sullivan, whose Felix the Cat had all the qualities of a character by Disney, plus a *freedom* that this prig removed from them once and for all! The field of animated film is truly vast. We should thank Mlle Poncet for having taken the topic seriously, for having begun to clear and order the field. Let's hope that she will consider her work and extend it to others beyond Mickey, whose existence is insufficient to pardon Mr. Disney's creative impotence, with all his factories, machines, and strikebreakers, this mountain that perpetually gives birth to a mouse.[5]

GERALD MCBOING-BOING

MY RECENT COLUMN ON ANIMATED FILM EARNED ME A reprimand from Alain Resnais, the *auteur* of some of the most appreciated art films currently being made, *Van Gogh* and *Malfray*.[1] He whom Claude Mauriac has called a future master inquired: "How can you cite so many titles in opposition to Disney without ever mentioning the very best of all, *Gerald McBoing-Boing*?" Not knowing *Gerald McBoing-Boing*, I was going to turn into a Buddhist monk, when a chance trip to London revealed it to me.[2] The film was prominently showing in seven or eight cinemas simultaneously, already crowned with an Oscar and accompanied by glowing comments. Back home, in the time it took me to shower a dozen people with my recent learning, it was already running on Broadway, thus frustrating my sense of superiority, at least over Parisians. As for the rest of the country, let me be clear: in Châteauroux, in Ribérac, in Merlin-sur-Cloche,[3] demand a screening of *Gerald McBoing-Boing*. Beseech your local film exhibitor, create, sign, and circulate petitions.

You will see one of the very few animated films that breaks

Signed: C.M.

Source: *Esprit*, n.s., no. 185 (December 1951): 826–27.

completely with Mr. Disney's cheap delights.* All things being equal, I see there a reaction comparable to that of the Mighty Five against Wagnerism.[4] It's the revenge of the clear-cut over the vague, color over hue, stress over purring, a mechanical pigeon over a steam elephant, action over morality, sinew over blubber. All that's short-lived, ruthless, flawless, encompassed, in the drawn line, in the music, in color, in even the story, forms a projectile, like a cold and dense snowball, in the figure of Cinderella's father with his sunsets in moleskin and chorus of *Houris*.[5] No moral mechanism, reward or punishment in the screenplay. There aren't even any surprises, plot twists, or ingenuity that is the opposite of genius, whereby the ingenious René Clair murders the great Faust:[6] Gerald says "boing boing" at birth and he'll say it all his life.

Several years ago, Mr. Disney presented us with a similar story about a child prodigy.[7] But then came the final gag, and thanks to it the return to normal, which is the obligatory ending in all his films, following a code as rigorous as Mr. Jhdanov's edicts.[8] In this handling of a character it might be possible to identify a filmic principle, according to which he returns to normality, or chooses the abnormal or moves away. As when spectators gather in a cinema, like someone at a train station expecting a friend's arrival to take them home, only to lose touch after some time together and are left with nothing but a memory. We would find Disney and Capra, in the first category, Robert Cannon (Gerald McBoing-Boing), Walter Lantz (Woody Woodpecker), and Sturges and Welles in the second. And while Snow White, Mr. Deeds, and the Dalai Lama are tainted for us (living with them reveals their wrinkles, embonpoint, and tics)—Gerald, Woody, the hero of *The Magnificent Ambersons,* and the heroine of *Brief Encounter* remain

---

* We had a similar revelation fifteen years ago with Anthony Gross's *La Joie de vivre*. But it was ahead of its time and the public wasn't interested. In contrast, *Gerald McBoing-Boing* was elevated to Broadway, probably an unprecedented event in the history of commercial film.

as pure and unchanging as our memories. Is it any wonder to find in the cinema—the art of secrets and the invisible par excellence—this mystical proposition: we really only possess that which we've lost?—Or by looking for proof among our film masters, first and foremost in the greatest and most elusive of all, the little tramp who wanders off, Charlie Chaplin?

AN ORNAMENTAL FORM

TRNKA SAYS: "I'M NOT A FILMMAKER, JUST AN ILLUSTRA-
tor." As if one of cinema's fundamental powers was not the gift of
time that it alone can confer at will on drawing, painting, and imagery. As if the act of cinema that prunes time of its false starts
to give us an exemplary life in two hours, stripped down yet filled
with all that it lacks, as if the stylistic act did not find its counterpart and equilibrium in its opposite, where drawing, painting, and
imagery in general are pure style, but where time is missing. And
in so doing, they affect us in a new way, creating another common
denominator that is no longer contemplation but participation.
Never was the word *spectator* less apt than in cinema. No more
false distinctions between theatre and cinema, painting and cinema. So, too, with cinema, the art of movement. It's not because
the camera is mobile (on the contrary, the less it moves, the better) that Resnais's films on painters are first and foremost cinema.[1]
It's because in his films painting finally regains its own time. It's
because the duration of its action is no longer determined by the

---

Review of *Prince Bayaya,* film in Agfacolor by Jiří Trnka. Screenplay based
on a story by B. Nemcova. Poems by B. Nezval. Music by V. Trojan. Production:
Czechoslovak State, 1950. Distribution: Procinex. Signed: Christian Marker.
Source: *Cahiers du cinéma: Revue mensuelle du cinéma et du télécinéma,* no. 8
(January 1952): 66–68.

spectator's time, which is suspended, but instead by the running time of the projections, which is a journey. And charm occurs to the extent that, thanks to cinema, painter, artwork, and spectator share for the first time a common element, experience a dynamic relationship, and are temporarily sewn into the same skin.

Trnka's *illustrations* emanate from the same charm. The story's simplicity and the temporal slowness seem to confirm that cinema is a matter of essence and not of means. It seems that in fact the gift of walking freely within magical imagery, exploring the other world, suffices on its own and excludes this cunning, this checkerboard of special effects and *suspense* to which Mr. Disney resorts (perfectly convinced—and rightly so—that just exploring his universe against painted backgrounds is insufficient in itself to enchant the paying spectator). But the comparison with Disney is

Prince Bayaya (1950), Czech filmmaker and puppeteer Jiří Trnka's stop-motion animated feature about a peasant farmer who disguises himself as a knight, vanquishes a dragon, and saves three princesses, one of whom he marries.

too easily overwhelming for Trnka, and doesn't do him justice. Setting the rich browns, deep reds, grays, and bistres of *Prince Bayaya* against *Fantasia*'s lyrical bruises, for example, is insufficient to celebrate Trnka's redemption of all the sacrificed hues in Disney, the order and pleasure of this luxury.

Comparing Trojan's music with that of Churchill to a victory of a folk theme over a hit tune fails to express the nobility of the former's music (and these harsh voices carried by a skillful orchestration like cathedral angels). The ingenious efforts by which Disney's special effects try to make us believe in the story he's telling contrast with Trnka's simplicity, equally at ease in the limits of his "illustration" as a picture inside its frame. All of which highlights the paradox by which Disney's universe remains closed on itself, while Trnka's world opens onto ours. And on this point, let's be fair, Trnka has an additional advantage: the third dimension. A puppet will beat a drawing every time in this business of the marvelous, because in 1951 the first condition of the marvelous is the concrete. It's no longer possible to walk in gauze and apparition, and, even more than *Miracle in Milan* and *Gerald McBoing-Boing*, *Prince Bayaya*'s puppets approach poetry to the extent that they resemble an object.

What we think about when we leave *Bayaya* is an almost-forgotten *ornamental* form. An ornament that is no longer, like what we know by this name since the Dark Ages as an inferior realm of art, a currency of beauty—but what is in enlightened periods, in the Middle Ages or in primitive societies, a value of civilization, a constant homage given to creation through imitation. The breadth and precision of history's progress remind us of medieval novels, where wonder arises as much from a description, the concrete grasp of a setting, an armor, or a body, as from narrative surprises. (Both refer elsewhere, through symbolism, to the same absolute.) This investigative concern for beauty—whether in the form of brown-reds or chords from Beethoven's Ninth—returns us to the pleasures of decorating, to the pleasures of illuminating, and pleasures often called gratuitous because so obvious.

And it's sad if while acknowledging all its charms, *Prince Bayaya* is reproached by some for its supposed "slowness." But this is also an acknowledgment. Human beings of the twentieth century dislike wasting time under the spell of a charm. They want to assess things quickly—and we know only too well to what extent they are disadvantaged in their temporal relations in comparison to the cow for contemplation and the frog for lust.

THE PASSION OF JOAN OF ARC

IN AN UNUSUAL ANALOGY OF FATE WITH ITS SUBJECT, THE negative of Carl Theodor Dreyer's *The Passion of Joan of Arc*—long thought to have been destroyed in a fire in 1937—was recently rediscovered. It's a little as if one morning the Chartres cathedral appeared pristine white. While we might miss its former patina, the original film fulfills us. It brings us, along with an increase in image clarity and detail of this unique work, a corresponding increase in both our emotion and our questions, previously raised by the mutilated and faded copies that we had seen.

We must therefore offer a laurel wreath to Lo Duca, the lucky discoverer of the lost negative.[1] We owe him much more than the simple "scholarly" joy that we would have, for example, in discovering a manuscript by Racine. We know that Dreyer sought to focus his attention on the *close-up,* so that the entire drama, with the exception of some establishing shots of the tribunal and the torture at the end, unfolds on the actors' faces. Dreyer was helped in his endeavors by two things: first, by the recent fine-tuning of panchromatic film stock, which finally made possible nuances of gray on the screen, and second, by the absence of makeup on

Review of Carl Theodor Dreyer's *The Passion of Joan of Arc*. Signed: C.M.
Source: *Esprit*, n.s., no. 190 (May 1952): 840–43.

the actors, which allowed him to push the dramatization of the human face further than anyone before him (a challenge that no one has since taken up).

The chance to present a "new" copy of these images in which skin texture, tears, drool, whites of the eyes *perform*, and where the human figure is no longer rendered a black and white ideogram by orthochromatic film, which brilliantly showed off Chaplin, but the equivalent, in relation to the screen, of a crowd or of a landscape—this possibility is much more than just a film historian's satisfaction. It's a gift to the spectator. And spectators make no mistake, since this silent film from 1928 has been showing continuously for several weeks in a cinema usually reserved for short runs (true, it does have a soundtrack, but it's just discreet enough so that in 1952, the audience, accustomed to muttering in their seats, stays quiet and doesn't hear the silence). Moral of the story: adding a soundtrack is the only way to make a truly silent film.

Among all the problems that this film raises, one of the most fascinating is doubtless the response that it brings to this conflict, challenge, never-ending exchange of space and time that the cinema alone among the arts confronts. "Space is the measure of our power, time the measure of our powerlessness" (Jules Lagneau).[2] Between American trickery, whose crudest example is the unavoidable calendar where the days are plucked off, the commonplace image of a dissolve, time-lapse, that elides time as soon as it becomes significant, that is painful (experiencing a time that is not one's own weighs as much as inhabiting another body) and the Italian-style faithfulness that goes to the limits of what's tolerable, the cinema seems to have cleared a vague opening of these two *measures,* which compensate for each other. I'm thinking here of Racine's preface to *Bajazet,* which states that spatial distance redeems temporal proximity.[3] In cinema, it can be said that the viewer's rapprochement or estrangement in relation to the character or the action (a rapprochement or estrangement determined by the choice of shots, the close-up corresponding to the greatest rapprochement and the establishing shot to the most estrangement) results in a visual proximity or retreat similar to grammatical tenses. Thus, an establishing shot matches the past and a close-up, the present. If in an action, the most "demanding" passage, the one that requires us to fully engage, a maximum of complicity and identification, generally relies on a multiplication of nearby shots, we were too quickly told that it was to sensitize us to details. For a doorknob or a fired gun, a thousand cases fail to achieve this justification. In reality, it's a question of situating the action *in the present*. And in the example of a historical film, destined almost inevitably to the picturesque and to an action reserved for fable, this use of the historical present enables human contact by making the viewer sensitive to the story and deflecting it from a reassuring historical framework. That is why it may not suffice to see in Dreyer's predilection for close-ups only an analysis of a psychological and realistic order, and even less a stylistic performance. Here again, the technical bias is the result of a much larger idea. The use of close-ups, lack of makeup, and neutral settings and costumes all contribute toward the same goal, which is to compose a film, if I may say, in eternity's present.

Another gift of this restored copy is the confirmation of this superficial but satisfying understanding that every beautiful soul is matched by its physical expression. Falconetti's face resembling a young mutinous sailor becomes here more feminine. Her beautiful gaze (which always betrays the body ever so slightly, is a signal made by the soul behind her prison-cell window) is embodied by the rest of her face, and particularly in the admirable texture of her mouth. We might thank the Protestant Dreyer for having bestowed such beauty on one of our saints, if Joan's saintliness played any role here. But aside from the historic cry "You have burned a saint," the emphasis is on an entirely different aspect of Joan of Arc: the accused witch.

What dominates this chronicle of her trial is neither the miscarriage of justice, nor the political betrayal, nor even the ecclesiastical myopia. The coercion of the English and the legal tricks are not developed here, as they are in so many plays or films on the same subject. The drama here focuses instead on a human being walking toward her soul's salvation, through the false directions of a church that unfairly claims for itself the right to govern her (with or without cynicism: the scene where the "good" judges, who are Joan's friends, beg her to recant, proves that Dreyer blames not only the corrupt and fanatical priests) going so far as to receive in her ordeal a paradoxical reward. This is very much a Protestant Joan, and her appeal to the "pope of Rome" over her judges is, in fact, the very height of Lutheranism. But in this, too, she joins the witch's myth so dear to Dreyer, which continues in *Vampyr* with an even clearer concern to identify everyone.[4] More than a saint— that is to say a privileged being—Joan appears as the personification of each being alone between Satan and God. The accusation of witchcraft is a confession that everyone can make, of having encountered evil. The divine paradox is that in these trials innocence is purified in unworthy hands, and that those who believe they are condemning are those who save by bringing suffering.

Dreyer is obsessed with the Christian sentiment of suffering. As long as the world turns, Christ on the cross never stops bleeding. And suffering remains the only means for humankind to join Christ, to be HIM a little. It's the imitation and the projection of the Calvary: the film is called *The Passion of Joan of Arc*. Which also explains Dreyer's predilection for physical suffering in torture. The torments of the inquisitors in *Leaves from Satan's Book* (1921), Joan at the stake, the burying of the doctor in *Vampyr* (1932), the burning of the witch in *Day of Wrath* (1943), the confrontation of the shattered couple in *Two People* (1945) all come from this same miserable and cruel fascination when faced with evil. He suggests domestic hell in *Master of the House* (1925), which at a distance appears unrelated, but still conforms to this conception of evil. So much so that you could say that the protagonist in Dreyer's work is evil's incarnation, invisible and present like God in *Athalie*, the

Devil.[5] Not always Invisible: in *Leaves from Satan's Book* he's an honest devil with a goatee, bribing souls in his unexpected disguises as the evil Jew, the Inquisitor, the *sans-culotte*, and the Bolshevik. In *Vampyr* he is only suggested. In *Two People*, a film with two characters in a single decor, an enclosed bedroom, he is completely disintegrated. We see the road traveled and the rigor of his itinerary that makes Dreyer pass, from 1919 to 1945, from Mephistopheles to the Hell of *No Exit*. For a long time now, Dreyer has broken with the alleged incompatibilities so often emphasized between the cinema and non-cinema: theatre, painting, and the novel. He does so by establishing a metaphysics on the screen, and in restoring to the image a power of *revelation* that cannot be taken too broadly. Useless to look for other filmmakers who show both such an ambition and a made-to-order language: if Dreyer is the equal of the greatest in film language, he surpasses them in purpose. And if it's futile and no doubt impossible to choose the second masterpiece in the history of film, it is equally impossible to hesitate in naming its first: *The Passion of Joan of Arc* is the most beautiful film in the world.

LETTER FROM MEXICO CITY

MEXICO CITY, APRIL 1953

If we can believe a recent news item in *Cahiers du cinéma*, the announcement in France regarding developments in Mexican film was premature (assuming of course an interest remains in this sort of thing). The near coincidence of the *Ley de la Cinematografía* [Film Law] with the election of the new president, whose politics are openly progressive, made this law appear as the manifestation of the cleanup this country so badly needs.[1] The reality, however, is more complicated: first, the law is one of the previous administration's last acts, a parting gift whose motives everyone can rationalize according to their mood—a real concern for improvement or a reflection of the demagogic halo of the final days of Alemán's government. (This excellent man has inaugurated more public places in his last month in office than President Lebrun ever did.[2]) Or in the fact that Miguel Alemán's son owns an independent production company. After all, a president is still a father. The government's area of jurisdiction was as follows:

Signed: Chris Marker

Source: *Cahiers du cinéma: Revue mensuelle du cinéma et du télécinéma*, no. 22 (April 1953): 33–35.

—Authorize or ban the showing of films;—Authorize their import and export;—Establish a 50 percent exhibition quota for
Mexican films in programming;—Authorize the construction and
operation of new studios;—Regulate distribution and crack down
on infractions;—Apply import and export taxation to the financing
of the film industry;—Establish a National Council of Film Art, as arbiter for all problems.

I say "was" because it's fairly certain that the law will never be
enforced. Since current production is unable to supply the 50 percent needed for exhibition, a policy for production should therefore be added, which, in order to be valid, immediately raises the
problem of quality and thus the need for a "Cinema Subsidy." But
the slogan of Ruiz Cortines's government is "Spend more." The
billions Alemán devoted to Mexico City's university campus have
served, for the time being, only to build a dead city. So there's little chance that the construction of studios and a subsidy policy
will now be considered. But the strongest reason the law won't be
enforced is because doing so would endanger the only real film
power in this country: the Jenkins "Monopoly."
   It's said that [William O.] Jenkins was the American Consul in
Puebla during the Mexican Revolution. Taken prisoner and incarcerated by the revolutionaries, he later demanded, out of esteem
for his own person, exorbitant compensation from the government. Those funds provided the basis of his prodigious fortune.
At the time, film exhibition was just beginning to be organized.
There was a "Film Bank" that had created a distribution circuit,
the *Operadora de Teatro* [Film Exhibitors], and it seemed promising. In retaliation, Jenkins began buying up cinemas. In short
order and relying on the tried-and-true methods of racketeers to
convince those who were reluctant, he soon controlled practically
all film distribution in Mexico, having taken over the *Operadora*.
The Film Bank still exists, but it has become silent and paralyzed.
On subjects as serious as the Film Law, its director avoids taking

a position, and when the Monopoly is mentioned, he changes the subject. Jenkins's power is such that when some newspapers recently wanted to raise advertising rates, the Monopoly forced them to surrender by canceling advertising. And that's not all. To manage the trust, the earnings of his profitable speculations were invested in production, so that Jenkins presently controls Mexican production almost as much as exhibition. Which leads us to consider said production.

It's dreadful. Ever since *María Candelaria* we harbor a vague suspicion: are we really seeing the best of Mexican production? Aren't we overlooking masterpieces? But this suspicion doesn't survive some explorations of Mexico City's cinemas (and the fact that brats under sixteen are allowed admission has no influence on my judgment, I swear). I'm not a great fan of *María Candelaria,* and aside from the visuals of *Río Escondido* I've never placed the Mexican cinema that we know in high esteem.[3] But just as Fernández and Figueroa tolerably and tirelessly make the same film, others, those without their talent, always make—in a mediocre or abominable vein—the same film, with the same story. There's a lot of buzz at the moment around *Soledad's Shawl,* an apoplectic melodrama that not even Grenier and Hussenot could salvage.[4] It features a raped girl, a bastard child, tears, and redemption, and similar characters in a dramatic (see *Soledad's Shawl*) or comical vein. The latter showcases the relatively more original character of the *macho.* The hero's aggressive virility appears here as an aspect of public welfare, as the just man in *Sodom.*[5] Regardless the film, advertising often emphasizes the existential details: a girl on her knees, a bottle in her hand, a placemat on her head, a lewd and loud laugh—in other words, the Mexican Way of Life. This image is only superficially unpleasant. In fact, it's rather tragic. It hides this country's deep sadness, its constant need for intoxication that drowns itself in tequila, in the radio at all hours, or in other imported substitutes. And in this respect, it's clearly no accident that *María Candelaria* and other films manage to touch us.

It's an absolute rule: every time here that the old Indian culture is evoked, a finesse and a culture commanding respect reappears. But the fashionable Mexican retreats from it, when they are not ashamed, replacing it with a kind of United States subculture (insofar as that exists). And the conspicuous anti-Yankee demonstrations don't change anything.

This situation disheartens many Mexicans who are perfectly aware of the betrayal and harm that these films represent, without mentioning their ongoing noxious effect on the Mexican people. But the all-powerful Monopoly, whose motto is "My audience likes this," leaves no room for an authentically Mexican creation. Whereas from time to time Americans like Huston, Ford, Steinbeck, Hackenschmied, and Paul Strand—or a Russian like Eisenstein—or a Spaniard like Buñuel appear to give Mexico its chance to linger in our memory.[6] Still, Buñuel had to endure a certain number of surprises—such as *Gran Casino,* with Jorge Negrete and Libertad Lamarque—(I understand that in Paris you've just seen *Susana* who is not pricked by iguanas)—to finally be able to make *Los Olvidados,* which no one wanted to finance and which was saved by a courageous producer.[7] Anyway, good or bad, Buñuel's Mexican films have had no success. Let's wait for his *Robinson Crusoe* and for the strange project that will result from his remake of *Wuthering Heights* with Jorge Mistral.

Recently, a Mexican weekly sadly announced: "There is no Mexican cinema. There is only cinema made in Mexico." We should add that the atmosphere in which this cinema is made continues to astonish Europeans. Thus, the big film event at the start of the year was the contention between the crooner Jorge Negrete and the actress Leticia Palma.[8] Following complicated events that included a contract matter, a car crash, stolen documents where each party involved produced contradictory but steadfast witnesses willing to have their throats slit, these two characters daily published in the evening newspapers reflections of the following sort: "This woman should be locked up." "This man is a monster."

"If she were a man *(macho!)*, I would smash her face in." "He thinks he's the boss of Mexico City with his *pistoleros.*" Finally, the issue was brought before the Actors' Guild. Negrete declared: "I never wanted to hit Leticia. I believe that a man who raises his hand against a woman deserves to have it (his hand) cut off." And again: "I have no hatred, I'm only expressing my feelings with the nobility at my disposal" *(sic*—but in Spanish it sounds much better and is less surprising). Between these two wildcats, the good Cantinflas tried to restore peace in "our big family" when a female union member declared for all to hear that "under Cantinflas (he used to be secretary of the Actors' Guild) we were living in a pigsty!" Insulted, Cantinflas withdrew from the dispute. Then Leticia was finally expelled and Negrete triumphed, while the foreign assistants remained in the dark about the trade union nature of the matter.

Cantinflas, since we're talking about him, is definitely a character.[9] It's hard to know if he has real talent as an actor. The abysmal stupidity of his screenplays precludes all judgment. And he's hardly blameless since he's his own producer, in association with Santiago de Reachi. He's enormously popular and since he's talented, he puts it to good use. Still, he's just had some major problems. Didn't the Communist painter Diego Rivera just undertake to depict him as Juan Diego with the Virgin of Guadalupe on his overcoat?[10] Uproar from the so-called Nationalist Mexican Party: "The Virgin has been insulted!" The newspapers explained that Cantinflas didn't carry the Virgin on his back, but in his "Mexicanissime" heart *(mexicanisimo corazón).* The incident seems now to be closed, but it nearly came to an auto-da-fé.

All this is very cinematic. As is the following news item: a thousand people living in barracks on a no-man's land have just been expelled. The new owner of this deserted property was able to get the police to toss them into the street without any kind of compensation. Doesn't that remind you of something? But there's no miracle in Mexico City, where the cinema is so present in the streets that it forgets to return to the screen.

LETTER FROM HOLLYWOOD
ON THREE DIMENSIONS AND A FOURTH

HOLLYWOOD, JULY 1953

We used to think it was the atomic age. But no. It's the stereoscopic age. Just now along Hollywood Boulevard, I saw a restaurant advertising "*3-D Dinners.*" I really wonder.... When introduced to a buxom young lady on his television show, Bob Hope dons a pair of Polaroid glasses. 3-D encourages lots of Jane Russell jokes. Finally, all Los Angeles is abuzz with the story of a man who enters into a 3-D film after the screening has begun and is bothered by the expansive back of the person seated in front of him. "Could you move a little," he asks politely, while tapping the man on the shoulder. "You're blocking my view." And the other responds: "I can't. I'm in the film." Such good humor is laudable in a city ravaged by famine and unemployment. The city anxiously awaits the results of its new secret weapon to learn if it will survive, while TV antennas, perched on roofs like vultures, attest to the threat and the promise of a bloodbath.

Los Angeles has become a ghost town. Right now there are just

Signed: Chris Marker

Source: *Cahiers du cinéma: Revue du cinéma et du télécinéma*, no. 25 (July 1953): 26–34.

twenty-six films being shot in Hollywood (including coproductions and films shot overseas). Warner Bros. studio has closed. MGM is producing two films, 20th Century–Fox also two, Paramount one, RKO one. Industry-wide unemployment is estimated at 80 percent, partially compensated by television (which thus bears the brunt of all its evils by also being the remedy). Nevertheless, as far as one can tell, it seems that the desertion of cinemas had touched . . . bottom, and that it was possible to hope, after the public's honeymoon with television, for a profitable saturation followed by a rebound. But Hollywood didn't want to wait or couldn't when faced with the figures: out of 23,344 cinemas in the United States, 5,038 have closed since the end of the war. And things are only getting worse: by the end of this year that number may double. Although automatically relying now on compensatory practices such as the high-volume sale of candy, 33 percent of ordinary cinemas and 28 percent of drive-ins (screening spaces for cars) lost money in 1952 (which proves, incidentally, that despite what was thought, at least 28 percent of couples attending drive-ins were paying attention to the film). Finally, the Council of Motion Picture Organizations brought our attention to this pithy equation: when the sale of television sets goes up 2 percent, cinema ticket sales drop by 1 percent.

To which you'll find people here and everywhere say in a condescending tone: "If only Hollywood understood that what they need to do is make good films." But this argument strikes me as weak. The most recent B-film seems like Bresson when compared to the average television fare. All things considered, Hollywood would perhaps have done better to fight the battle over form rather than content. American television shows are at best a bland pudding. Their stupidity and laziness are immeasurable and the psychological toll of this insidious monster, which brings the appearance of intimacy while destroying the essential, is incalculable. In short, Hollywood decided that lacking something satisfactory, something new was needed, and that something new was 3-D.

And since it's numbers that count, the numbers seem to say that Hollywood wasn't wrong. In its opening three days in New York, *House of Wax*, Warner's Trojan horse, took in $75,000—26 and a quarter million French francs.[1] Ever since, in every new city where it appears, 3-D submits its victory reports.

A significant increase in novelties followed suit. When technique falters, vocabulary is enlisted. Such as the theatre that replaced its screen with a newer one to suggest, with the term "magic screen" or "the latest thing in screening," that this refurbishment has something to do with 3-D. The anaglyphs of 1935 are resurrected and presented as state-of-the-art.[2] Programs are designed with ten minutes of 3-D and two cheap features so that the advertising suggests that the entire program is in 3-D (one of these films is generally a jungle story, in order to remind viewers of *Bwana Devil*, etc.).[3] Among the truly new techniques, Natural Vision and Paravision emphasize that they possess real depth, while Cinemascope possesses it for the psychological dimension and brags about skipping the glasses. Then there's Audioscope, Tri-opticon, Polarama, Triorama. And the best of all, Cinerama, which continues to sell its seats three weeks in advance and has just planted its flag in Hollywood. (We would like to know what has become of the technique of another Frenchman, Sinibaldi, which was announced two or three years ago like a great wonder.[4]) Of course the most astute exhibitors are dialectically employing this hullabaloo to distribute flat films. The distributor Albert Margolies considered it the right moment to re-release the silent film *The Freshman* (1925) with Harold Lloyd. And he introduces it thus:

> This revolutionary film relegates actors and spectators to their proper places, the former to the screen, the latter to their seats. Technical experts, employing the latest methods of calibration, declared the screen of the Paris cinema particularly well-suited to screening this film. Faced with the problem of finding a screen that isn't more convex than concave and vice-versa, experts noticed in tests that the

Paris screen, completely flat, lent itself perfectly to the 2-D technique used in *The Freshman.* Which means that there is no need to reconstruct the theatre. That means there'll be no lions on your knees, loud-speakers in corners, inside chandeliers, under your seat or in the sinks. You can comfortably enjoy the film in all safety.... And by the way, it's a good film.

We can't say the same for the first films of the new age that we watched through 3-D glasses. We're shocked that, in this city where everything is possible, no one thought it might actually be worthwhile to make a good film in 3-D. The risk wasn't great. Success, due to the technique's novelty, was all but guaranteed. The public came to try on the glasses and see people in space; the rest barely mattered—anything was possible, even a story, a dialogue, what do I know, even talent, no one would have raised an eyebrow. But undoubtedly talented people are prudent and allow others to do the dry run. It is striking to see Hollywood abandoned by first-rate directors and noteworthy that the only two important men currently working, Fred Zinnemann and John Huston, are in fact shooting outside Hollywood, the first in Hawaii and the other in London.[5] No major director has yet committed to 3-D. The sole exception, Henry Hathaway, who is going to direct for 20th Century–Fox, *Prince Valiant* in Cinemascope.[6] But ever since *Niagara,* we know that Hathaway has decided to make fun of everyone, which he does with a lot of brio.

Lacking a man of genius, it's André DeToth who has the honor of delivering the first blow to flat films with his *House of Wax.*[*] Chronologically the honor actually belongs to Arch Oboler and to this thing that you saw in Paris, called *Bwana Devil.* Despite (or rather, if the amount of time saved is taken into account, and therefore, money, thanks to) its great contempt for the photographic implications of the new technique, *Bwana Devil* was

---

[*] It should be noted that André DeToth, who is one-eyed, is the only man in Hollywood who remains excluded from the perception of stereoscopic relief.

something special. But the stereoscopic age's *Jazz Singer* is *House of Wax*.[7] Before closing its doors, Warner Bros. carefully covered its risks to maximize its chances: satisfactory technique, terrific advertising campaign, and a subject that's a perfect match. The idea of unearthing a German horror classic, *Waxworks,* only seems anachronistic.[8] Horror is what is most thriving in the United States right now. This is evident in scanning comic books, which are veritable X-rays of the American unconscious, on any magazine rack. They're very different from the comic books of our youth: Li'l Abner, Dick Tracy, Dagwood, and Blondie have retreated to a corner, Terry and Steve Canyon are mobilized in Korea. There's the usual contingent of love stories to warm your heart. But what's really selling, which is displayed on at least two shelves, are horror stories, nightmares, and the Living Dead, where the covers and screenplays increase in the only field where censorship thinks it needs to intervene. This raises questions about what's going on in the mind of the reader (and I'm thinking not only of children: far more dangerous is the frustrated adult) that one meets in every bus station, in every restaurant, close-up of a man buried to his eyes and surrounded by enormous red ants, or by a zombie with dripping flesh who stretches his claws toward a screaming girl. Dozens of faces deformed by fear, scalped, blinded, and tortured. (And it's hardly surprising to find in one of these publications an anthology of torture methods through the ages, accompanied by detailed drawings.) The key to all this is perhaps precisely in this fear and this need to gaze at it. And in order to understand its appearance at this particular moment, all you need to do is go down a shelf to find the same agitated faces of the war comics, devoted in part to the Korean War and partially to the "next world war" (with the usual warning, as in the infamous special issue of *Collier's:* it's in preparing for it that we will avoid it). The most striking thing is it's not only the enemy that adopts these monstrous heads. *Combat Casey* is the American hero of 1953: he certainly has a hint of the red-bearded Prussian seen in World War One caricatures. He skewers the Chinese with a loud barbaric laugh, wipes the blood on his bayonet with a haunted look, and sticks a razor blade between his primate jaws when he heads off on patrol. Because in contemporary American imagery, a man with a knife between his teeth is a G.I.

I think that this forms a coherent picture of the climate in which *House of Wax* was released. And as timid as are the excesses of the screen alongside those of the printed page or the imagination, you couldn't dream of anything more appropriate. Certainly, we're getting our money's worth: fistfight amidst a fire, slow disfigurement of melting mannequins, dead people who stand up in the morgue, the strangulation of a black man, evil genius, idiot genius, and other surprises you've seen. For weeks now, small stereoscopes in boxes, hung at the entrance of cinemas, offered the public a foretaste of the film's bloodiest scenes. The big premiere took place at midnight, in Hollywood and Los Angeles, with greenish floodlights that decomposed the spectator in advance. At 1:30 a.m. we returned home, vaguely looking for ectoplasm under the bed, wondering if we had experienced a historic evening. Sadism had a hand in it. But what about cinema?

Well, the meticulous work should be recognized, practically without a fault. More special effects of gigantism and distortions in the style of *Bwana Devil,* a satisfactory picture resolution, and an effective color process (Warnercolor). All that might have been significant. But the stakes were higher. It was a matter of winning a total victory, and consequently, following a tried and tested method in Hollywood, to strike at the highest level. The screenplay addresses the spectator's sadism and the film their stupidity.

Because we wouldn't know how to compare the spectator before and after 3-D, to the spectator before and after sound, and even less to the spectator before and after the cinema itself. For a long time, just the sight of moving images on a screen was enough to amaze. To hear them speak provided an incredible upheaval. Seeing them in three dimensions. . . . Here, the effect is much weaker, since our mind reconstructs depth all by itself, and at best, 3-D relieves it of a constant operation, rather than offering it a revelation. It's enough to close an eye under the Polaroid glasses to be convinced. In itself the relief is nothing; it's much less than sound and less than color. It can begin to be only by the use made of it. It will or won't be aesthetic (but for the time being, it tends to be convulsive).[9] And the only problem will be to give the feeling of space, of playing with space. To convey the feeling of a vase of flowers, there are two methods: to highlight its forms and colors by artistic means—or smash it over your head.

Without hesitating, DeToth headed straight for simplicity. And 3-D's basic function, for the moment, seems to be to throw the greatest variety of objects in front of the spectator's face. It's a shooting gallery in reverse. In *House of Wax*, we catch one mannequin after another, a dead person, a halberd, balls on a racket (inherited from an anaglyph act that has nothing to do with this story), a skeleton, punches, the feet of Con-Con dancers, some furniture. Is it useful to say that we tire more quickly of this repeated surprise than of everything else, and that in the end it's exactly there where an effect is not sought that it is most productive? Let's acknowledge one effect that does pay off, when the surprise works this time back and forth, and that a character appears unexpectedly in the foreground, rising from under the frame: there, he really stands up in front of you and you jump. But we'll get used to that, too. Of the two films in 3-D so far presented, the only promising moment for the future of the technique is a shot from *Man in the Dark*.[10] There the following are thrown at the spectator's face: a bird, a flowerpot, a roller-coaster carriage, and several detectives, but where nothing happens: a woman walks in the street, leaving a store and carrying two packages. And suddenly in a moment of respite in this beatdown of images, we notice that we *feel* the wall pull away from her, we *feel* the physical volume of the packages, we *feel* the shape of her face and her shoulders. It doesn't last. Two minutes later things are still being tossed at our heads, but we have finally had the feeling of space, and we know that this can be of use in the movies, when directors will have stopped playing with fire.

After all, this feeling of space is certainly in the natural order of things. In its current form and caricatures, isn't 3-D simply the culmination of our beloved depth of field?[11] Isn't research into representational depth an expression of an impatience and a troubling phenomenon? Creators, who think they are pursuing a particular goal, participate in the living and collective development of an art form, following laws they think they've invented. Is *Citizen Kane* to 3-D what *The Passion of Joan of Arc* was for sound film—the crowning of all present techniques and impatience for what's to come? It hardly matters that it is by this or that technique that the metamorphosis occurs, if it should be done. I have little confidence in the glasses except as—it should be said—a kind of reactionary prejudice: this would be the first time that an art form stipulates the adoption of a stranger's body. But let's count on science to resolve this problem, if only by creating babies with naturally polarized eyes. There will be many others, starting with the size of screens and the layout of cinemas. The way things stand, the spectator seated up close to the screen loses considerable definition and partakes in a fuzzy world—while positioned far away, the screen is like a kind of aquarium, where from time to time lights flash and get lost in a no-man's land.[12] Because a two-dimensional film has its limits, those of the screen, recognized and admitted. But the third dimension *is without limits.* No frame in front or in back. For the first time, in a representational medium, the infinite appears. The tennis ball that escapes the screen, or that hits you in the eye, is lost, ceases to be. A world in three dimensions without tactility is a world of ghosts in which we are as foreign there as Sartre's dead, more foreign than in the world, admittedly, of flat images.[13] One day no doubt we'll accept the realism of 3-D, but a period of incubation will always be needed. Realism doesn't necessarily go hand in hand with improved representation. It doesn't come from the imitation of reality, but from the reference to a representation. The "newsreel" aspect of Italian films illustrates this quite well, and it's easy to think of a film like *The Quiet One,* where its enlargement from 16mm to 35mm results in a more visible grain and equates the image to a newspaper photo.[14] From its technical imperfection, the film thus acquires an increase in credibility. This is perhaps why every technical advance is accompanied first of all by an aesthetic step backward.

But things move quickly in the film world, and the margins intersect. Despite its pretensions, 3-D turns its back on realism, and the flat film manages finally to establish itself in its natural domain. As a last chance, an American film here succeeds. And the real event of this last month could well be, despite *House of Wax* and its trumpeting of depth, the discrete showing of Irving Lerner's *Man Crazy.* A producer of this latest passing success is said to have declared: "I've found a fourth dimension: I have a story." Lerner may have had only two dimensions, but he did have a story.

Some years ago, in a small American city, a doctor went out one evening, leaving his house to three babysitters, high schoolers aged 16 to 18. With him gone, they decide to play dress-up, and in the course of their ransacking discover a box containing $17,000. Immediately, they lose all interest in the baby and they're off to New York City for an escapade of banal debauchery. They indulge in beautiful dresses, nightclubs where they can show them off and some young men to remove them. But the hotel becomes suspicious. One of the young men flees with the key to the safe-deposit box where the babes had deposited the money, and the police arrest everyone. The worst off is the unfortunate doctor, who didn't press charges. The money came mostly from abortions, and he was hiding it to avoid paying taxes. Scandal. Suicide of the doctor and the imprisonment of the young girls, guilty of having believed what was said to them every day in different ways: money is the key to everything, and if it is commendable to pick up a fallen comb, it is even more so to scoop up $17,000 when one stumbles on it.

Philip Yordan and Sidney Harmon were inspired by this true story to write *Man Crazy,* which they financed themselves in order to do it without compromises. They hired Irving Lerner to oversee directorial duties. Lerner is a documentary filmmaker. He was the cameraman on Flaherty's *The Land* and the editor of Van Dyke's *Valley Town*. During the war, together with Robert Riskin and Phillip Dunne, he made the O.W.I. Overseas Branch one of the top producers of short films. We owe him such films as *A Place to Live* (1941), the film on Toscanini and a hymn of nations at the end of the war, and the clever and ironic *Muscle Beach*.[15] He was looking for an opportunity to handle a "story" as a documentarian when *Man Crazy* was offered to him. With limited funds (less than $200,000) and just sixteen days for shooting (eleven for the essential action, five for the rest, including an excellent "introduction to Hollywood" in pure cine-eye), all in real locations (forty or so different places) and with only one experienced actor among a group of beginners or amateurs. Lerner was aided by Floyd Crosby, another documentary veteran, but whose dazzling reentry in *High Noon* made him the most in-demand cameraman in Hollywood (he directed the photography of *Man in the Dark*).[16] Irving Lerner found himself in the same conditions as "neorealism" and has made a film worthy of all the virtues normally tied to this label.

Of course, it's not enough to shoot outside of studios to be realistic, and Jules Dassin has proved to us that it's possible to make expressionism in real locations.[17] But that's not the only reason that the use here of a real drugstore, real apartments, and real streets in Hollywood was particularly decisive. The key was the free hand given to the director. In contrast, all that I've seen of American films on my visit leave an impression of amphibious works. A film developed by the director is mixed with the producer's versions and with alterations made by different individuals or

corporations. Each of these films briefly dominates the others before falling back into the fray. Lillian Ross enlightened us on these
matters with her account of the making of *The Red Badge of Courage*.[18] And these different points of view explode in the profiling of
the characters. I won't say that the actors of *Man Crazy* are "better" than those of the average American film: quite simply, there
are no better. And the fact that they are second-tier actors only
reinforces their achievement. In Hollywood it's a law that there
are no bad supporting roles. Mediocrity is a privilege of the stars.
Moreover, for a Lana Turner or a Marilyn Monroe, the vast majority of stars are extraordinary creatures of cinema who become
one with their character to the point that after becoming used
to American films, and feeling nostalgic for French fare during a
screening of *Justice Is Done*, I remain gobsmacked before the sheer
number of these men and women *reciting their roles*.[19] But this
elite group of actors is helpless against all the taboos that under-
mine their characters from within and inflict on them such psychological upheavals that in the end, the edifice collapses. What
is striking in *Man Crazy* is the perfect conformity of the characters' words and actions with what they are, socially and physically.
It's probably best not to overanalyze the film before its release in
France that we heartily wish.[20] But we'll remember this astonishing handful of youngsters for a long time: Colleen Miller, Irene
Anders with her flabby sensuality, Joseph Turkal, a kind of nasty
Gérard Philipe. Neville Brand who provides a salubrious note to
this story, without ever having to right wrongs. And in the role
of the robbed pharmacist, the actor John Brown. And especially,
Christine White. They are to American teenagers what the children of *Shoeshine* were to Italy.

And this is where the film runs into trouble. As soon as we talk
about realism, we expect more or less consciously to see people
who behave like Italians. All that American reality encompasses
that is superficial, unfinished, or lazy risks being attributed to the
film to the extent to which it will be the most faithful. It's highly

likely that America refuses to recognize itself in this overly dull reflection. This lack of style and emphasis, which prevents most American teenagers from radiating their vitality, is part of an observed asceticism. A little more madness in how the three girls spend their money would perhaps make this sequence more "agreeable." But it would betray the truth and even the plausibility of their cold enthusiasm. It's remarkable that in order not to despair of their characters, in order to keep at least from the bottom of this anecdote a momentum toward life, two shreds in the form of hope, the authors were forced to invent, to add a role, to leave at the end (and in a manner too clever for me to reveal) a chance for purity. The true story, however, left no hope; it was simply sordid. I don't think Yordan and Harmon are any less honest and Lerner less "realistic" in thus having refused to make naturalism an alibi for the contagion of despair.

It's because in realism, love of life plays as big a role as its representation. Just as with the choice of language, there is a mental attitude, an intention. This intention is exactly what is missing in Hollywood, amid the competition for the most appropriate means to give it an expression at the first sign. A patient and ingenious investigation of all the means of representing reality, from forest fires to the uncertainties of the human heart, has been in the works for years in this large refinery, under less hardly ascetic pretexts. Hence, almost every Hollywood film—no matter how stupid or despicable it may seem—impresses, in passing, by the inclusion of a discovery or new material carefully recorded to be better exploited one day. Just the noise of the horn that pins José Greco to the *barrera,* in the pretentious large machine *Sombrero,* is worth eighty-two minutes of frustration. And failing to find enough food for its capacity of translation, Hollywood has come one day, like Lili's fox, which, in order to offer a fur stole promises its own hide, and tears itself apart, displaying on its own dead body its style of dissection. Such was *Sunset Boulevard.*

If the 3-D operation was meant to fail, or if it condemned cinema to sink more and more into the *House of Wax* genre, if Hollywood was really condemned to death, it would be ethical for this extinction to coincide with all the signs of a promised flowering. The very existence of *Man Crazy* and *Salt of the Earth*—a C.I.O.-backed film on miners that was sabotaged by the anti-Communist brigade and finished, despite the odds, in Mexico—as well as the work of Wyler, Wilder, George Stevens (whose *Shane,* which merits an article all to itself, is the first realist Western) attest to an incredible possibility for great cinema.[21] A current theory says that if television is victorious, so much the better. TV will become a *mass medium,* and cinema will take over from the theatre in a more elevated sector of entertainment.[22] Besides the price of a film and the fact of imagining success only by the yardstick of popular success, there is something incredibly unpleasant in this idea of the "hoi polloi" happily abandoned to lowbrow fare while the elite ring the bell of cinema. In any case, we will learn in the coming months if Hollywood, which does not make the best cinema in the world, will at least have been the place where the best cinema was possible, but only that—and if America is once and for all the land of squandered wealth and unfulfilled expectations.

CINERAMA

DESCRIPTION: YOU ENTER A TRAPEZOID-SHAPED ROOM
of theatrical proportions where the stage is occupied by a concave screen similar to panoramic backgrounds imitating the sky.
It's about three times wider than the usual screen in relation to
its height. This screen, which gives us an impression of continu-
ity, is made up of hundreds of thin parallel strips, opened obliquely
like the slats in a vertical Venetian blind. This is in order to elimi-
nate the distortions of light reflected on its concave surface. In the
same cinema, three enclosed booths converge in crossfire on the
screen. Each of the projection booths is large enough to house an
anti-tank cannon.

Total darkness. On the central screen (slightly narrower it seems
than a standard screen) the well-known radio broadcaster Lowell Thomas appears in his office crammed with travel souvenirs,

---

Review of Mike Todd's documentary *This Is Cinerama*, which premiered in
the United States on September 30, 1952. Signed: Chris Marker.
  Source: *Cahiers du cinéma: Revue mensuelle du cinéma et du télécinéma,*
no. 27 (October 1953): 34–37. One year later Marker republished this article
(with only a minor change) in *Cinéma 53: À travers le monde* under the title
"And Now This Is Cinerama." In the anthology's Table of Contents, this article
is cosigned with British film critic Gavin Lambert, who contributed a second
part to the essay, probably translated by Marker.

including a portrait of Colonel Lawrence.[1] It takes him just five minutes to outline the history of cinema, nay, the history of the efforts to capture movement in art ever since the prehistoric cave paintings. Starting with the cinematograph, which he calls an American invention conceived and perfected by American brains (let's be fair, a German after all is mentioned) for humanity's greatest good.[2] Along the way, we learn that the goal of Muybridge's experiments was to prove that a horse holds its four hooves simultaneously in the air. Alright. A long clip from *The Great Train Robbery* is shown, which is always a pleasure, and then in a matter of seconds silent film and talkies are disposed of *and now: This Is Cinerama!*

On this cue the image fills the entire screen. In a loud din, the open cars of a roller coaster start to move and the entire audience lurches forward on the tracks at Rockaway Beach. Fifty years of American invention here flows into roller coasters.

There follow several investigations (dangerous word to use in these times) into the technique's possibilities: a ballet from *Aida* danced in Milan's La Scala (a very pretty girl in the center to give you the first clear idea of psychological depth), Niagara Falls seen from an airplane, a moment of art and mysticism.[3] Then the "Hallelujah Chorus" from Händel's *Messiah* sung by two lines of insipid Buddhist monks filing on the screen accompanied by their stereophonic voices, faithful like sound shadows.[4] (This scene is really convincing from a realist perspective: we get bored almost as much as at a concert.) Then we see the world as Americans dream of it at a distance and close-up: Venice in pigeons and gondolas, Scotland in kilts and bagpipes, Spain in bullfighters and castanets, nothing more and nothing less. A moment of horror, more unbearable than Buñuel or Boris Karloff: "The Blue Danube" wailed by the Vienna Boys' Choir. Finally, the *climax* of the first part, the finale of the second act of *Aida,* with trumpets and everything, some matches on a misstep, some cutaway shots of the audience in evening dress (the two spaces face each other, it seems, with satisfaction). As if we were there. . . . Intermission.

In the second half, we see palm trees, speedboats, legs, and America. This last is presented from the perspective of a touristic good Lord, photographer and collector, with commentary and music implying that this corner of the world gave rise to a particular providential concern, for undisclosed reasons. This hierarchy of angles that reveals America in God's eyes and the rest of the world as seen by an American is undoubtedly unconscious. But precisely, the unconscious. . . .

In short, not a single cliché is spared: the presentation is nonchalant and the effect crude. The imagery stops at postcards, art with opera, and the universe with America. In addition, there is the technical imperfection, although the sound is certainly perfect. But apart from the roller-coaster scene that sweeps everything along in its movement, the separation of the three screens is almost constantly noticeable. Occasionally, the edges overlap. Variations in density change the color from one screen to another, the absence of the image's customary steadiness is multiplied threefold, and rises from one to the next. . . . The fact remains that we have just witnessed the first screening of what will henceforth be cinema, Cinerama, or whatever its name, the spectacle of our time.

It's obvious. A vague obviousness that is already impatient about not being able to study the future forms of this spectacle more closely. Undoubtedly, expensive, heavy, cumbersome, and imperfect as it is, Cinerama is only the phenakistoscope (or rather the Optical Theatre) of the cinema to come.[5] This one will perhaps be Cinerama simplified, cinemascope perfected, or it is the Popov technique.[6] No matter. The conviction is immediate and stays with us as we exit the theatre. The rest is simply extrapolation, optimism, and tea leaves.

Naturally, the theatre is included. The ballet of *Aida,* with its life-size characters (there is a girl who . . .—but I've already said that) demonstrates that the problem of *a theatrical impression* is ultimately resolved. But it would be rude to stop there: from the moment when the two sides of the mirror are identical, each one can preexist the other. And the faithful reproduction of a given theatre responds to a transfiguration with the possibility of an almost infinite expression of volumes and sounds. The old and already lamentable tale of filmed theatre vanishes there in dust in the novel idea of a theatrical cinema. A theatre, yes, but enormous, the only theatre where a playwright can decide, without condemning themselves to the library, like Claudel at the beginning of *The Satin Slipper:* "The stage of this drama is the world."[7] Artaud's Theatre of Cruelty also comes to mind when we see the performance space curve and expand, as if headed toward this total surrounding of spectacle where, strictly speaking, there will be no more *emergency exits.*[8] And even more, we think of a theatre freed of its intimate and middle-class apparatus, as magical as it is, a theatre equipped for great collective emotions. Doubtless this "religious" hypothesis will be contrasted with the realist and figurative nature of the technique. But it is certainly possible that the religion of the twenty-first century will at last be that of the world.

Theatre but also fresco. In Mexico City, I saw Diego Rivera's *murales.*[9] Chairs are placed in front, you sit down, and you *watch* this painting-spectacle for an hour. In spatial terms what comes to mind is Greek theatre or revolutionary painters.[10] Cinerama is much more in synch with a great collective spectacle than with this "rare spectacle, expensive and thus constrained to quality" described by Mr. Cartier in *Paris-Match* (it being understood that there may be other "constraints on quality" besides financing by the ruling classes). It's even possible that the Cinerama's inventors unwittingly contributed an instrument to future celebrations of the Popular American Republic. It's a matter of optimism, as I've said.

With regard to what the "theatre" gains (but the two terms will have to disappear), what does "cinema" lose? Rapid editing certainly. Excessively jerky camera movements with a tightened margin of justification. Close-ups other than an occasional, exceptional one (although a face filling a Cinerama screen shouldn't be unpleasant). Filmmakers will have to learn to cut in long shots, using wide angles (with the proviso that almost *nothing* forces the director to use the entire surface of the screen: the very shock of the roller coaster's appearance following the words "This Is Cinerama" proves the point)—but it's what the best are already doing. Actors will have to learn to perform a scene instead of rehearsing a phrase dictated by the director. But that's how the best are already recognized. We must no longer confuse the sometimes brilliant ransom with the appalling spatial limits of cinema that we have known, with its nature. Editing and camera movements were the form given to the momentary impossibility of embracing the visual field. And after all, silent cinema also had its privileges. A certain art of montage can disappear as easily as a stylistic signature, without leaving us more than a superficial regret, less and less vivid as we become interested less in the sign and more in the meaning—and perhaps we notice the existence of an infantile sickness among critics, where handwriting is mistaken for style. Finally it is not impossible that through the technocratic crisis that seems to threaten us, Cinerama (or its offspring) will bring new value to the authors themselves. Once assimilated and absorbed until it is invisible, technique—like that of printing, page layout, or theatrical staging—becomes again what it is supposed to be: that is, a servant of reflection. Undoubtedly this would already be clearer and better developed if cinema had been able to advance on the basis of the invention rather than commerce. Efforts to modify and integrate theatrical space punctuate it. (A little belatedly Abel Gance receives his due![11]) With all its laziness and lack of imagination, there is standardization and crystallization in Hollywood whose best recipes, seemingly set in stone, television is now challenging. It's a strange world that perfects its airplanes in wars and its cameras in crises, a world that seems able

to give birth only out of fear. . . . It is symbolic that Cinerama was
also invented during the war from a panoramic screen seemingly
destined to train aerial machine-gunners.

   Because in the end, after so many reprimands and praises, perhaps it is suitable to acknowledge those responsible for this undertaking. For example, the inventor Fred Waller, a man of the cinema
with a machine gun (the Waller Gunnery Trainer).[12] He also invented a template for waterskiing, an anemometer, a camera with
a 360-degree aperture, and another that gives clients' measure-
ments to tailors in one-fiftieth of a second. Then there's Merian C.
Cooper, John Ford's producer and collaborator, and coauthor with
Ernest Schoedsack of *Grass: A Nation's Battle for Life* and *Chang:
A Drama of the Wilderness*. Rather incredibly, the program fails to
mention their masterpiece, *King Kong*. Apparently *Chang* is very
good (it's Colpi who says so and he can be trusted).[13] All the same,
King Kong includes one of the most beautiful love scenes in world
cinema. Moreover, it's said that Cooper is going to do a remake in
Cinerama. Last but certainly not the least: Louis B. Mayer himself,
after having left MGM, like the old walrus Walt Disney, under attack by the young walrus Dore Schary, has become president of
the Office of Cinerama Productions. The presence of this clever
man is new proof of Cinerama's future, if not of its improvement.
Concerning *Kiss of Death*, Mayer told Lillian Ross: "*They* fling an
American mother down a staircase, *they* stomp on her, and *they*
pretend it's art. . . ." We shudder thinking of the offspring that this
maternal advocate has in store for us.

   The program also includes the name of Robert Flaherty. "Flaherty was chosen to direct the first Cinerama production. But
unfortunately Flaherty died before production details of the production were resolved." This isn't exactly true. Flaherty had already
severed ties with Cinerama when he died, and in a way, it's also because of this that he died. Not that he was mistreated: it seems that
the break was mutual. But he had just come to understand that
cinema was passing through a stage where a unique creator, more

wizard than technician, no longer had and still didn't have their proper place. A difficult and symbolic situation that summarizes an era, and all reasons for doubt and fear caused by Cinerama's appearance. We are the children of a pivotal moment. The time for telling stories about makers of monsters and robots is over. The monsters and robots are here: the future of science henceforth is no longer a matter of perfecting them, but of giving them a soul. It will be neither easy nor certain. But we must consider them, Cinerama in the lead, with confidence. Film energy, like atomic energy, can change signs.

THE FRENCH AVANT-GARDE
RENÉ CLAIR'S *Entr'acte* (1924)
LUIS BUÑUEL'S *Un chien andalou* (1929)
JEAN COCTEAU'S *The Blood of a Poet* (1930)

BEFORE ADDRESSING THESE THREE FILMS, IT'S WORTH quickly reviewing the time and the conditions in which they were made. In contrast to most important works in film history, those associated with the so-called avant-garde are linked with a movement or more generally with personalities. They are inseparable from the history of ideas, literature, and the arts.

The Avant-Garde Climate

Between 1925 and 1930 the so-called intelligentsia made known their attitude toward the cinema, which oscillated between condescending curiosity and pure and simple contempt, if not outright horror. ("The cinema? A disturbing return to barbarity," opined the Académie française's Permanent Secretary.) In contrast, young people were entranced by it. These two opposing attitudes resulted in: on the one hand, a "commercial" cinema dangerously cut off

Signed: Chris Marker

Source: *Regards neufs sur le cinéma (New Perspectives on Film),* collection Peuple et culture, ed. Jacques Chevallier (Paris: Seuil, 1953), 249–55. Marker's essay was not reprinted in the abridged edition of *Regards neufs sur le cinéma* (1963), which was reduced from 510 to 352 pages.

from culture, and on the other, an experimental or literary use of cinema that baffled the public and isolated their *auteurs* in an underground ghetto.

Generally speaking, the avant-garde in those years—whether in painting or literature—expressed a backlash against a deadly and absurd war that forced the most lucid to challenge the worldly "values" surrounding them. The ensuing revolt was fed by other rebellions in the means for self-expression. Traditional forms of language and representation were attacked. *Futurism* sought a rhythmic and artistic foundation of a new art in a mechanical universe. *Dadaism,* born during the war, mobilized an anarchic liberation of words and fought absurdity with the absurd. *Surrealism,* which succeeded it, organized this destructive frenzy by investigating the world, which relied on forces hitherto intentionally fettered in human beings: dreams, the unconscious, love freed from moral and social obstacles, revolutionary fervor, flamboyant atheism, etc. Finally, individual experimenters, unattached to any school, like *Jean Cocteau,* pursued a methodical exploration of expressive means, turned toward this same obscure part of the unconscious, irreconcilable with logic, that seems to give birth to humankind's deepest commitments.

Behind the apparent or real disparities separating these tendencies, we find a common background. Besides a vestige of the last war and a premonition of the one to come (this premonition often assumes a truly prophetic character, and we're surprised— confronted with surrealist texts and images—by their perfect conformity to the events and actual pictures of the war), there is the Soviet revolutionary experiment and the promise it seems to provide (this is particularly true for the surrealists, some of whom— with Louis Aragon in the lead—will join the Communist Party); Freud's theories on dreams and the unconscious that lead to a greater attention to sleep images and to random acts, as well as to a new importance ascribed to childhood and sexuality. And then there's also, whatever one's opinion of it, the new phenomenon of

unusual literary and artistic activities removed from and sometimes hostile to the middle class that for the previous century
monopolized them. These activities are fed by scientific and sociological discoveries that reflect and illustrate the disorder, ambiguity, and violence of a world less simple than it seems.[1]

An interest in film is the natural result of such a climate. A certain mystique surrounding machines, combined with a disen-
chantment with the forms of classical narration that are forced
on it, leads some to dream of a "pure" cinema, that is, a cinema
of pure movement, pure form, with no anecdotal ballast whatsoever. At the same time, the dreamlike nature of the filmic image
will seem to make it the ideal representation of dreams, while its
shock power will give it an explosive value, from an erotic or revolutionary point of view, infinitely greater than that of the novel
or painting.

A Word of Caution

It is only natural that films whose conception is completely alien
to the usual film environment surprise the uninformed public and
on occasion completely bewilder it. Such films must therefore be
presented with some precautions to dispel the idea—ever-present
in the spectator's mind—that they are being mocked. Otherwise,
there are the accusations of mental disorders, morbidity, and even
hermeticism.

In such circumstances it is worthwhile to stress film's basic nature. Impoverished on a psychological level in relation to the novel,
which is equipped with language to render moods, film compen-
sates with the image. One good way to encourage the spectator

Top: Slow-motion sequence in René Clair's avant-garde short feature
Entr'acte (1924). *Middle:* Crawling ants signal sexual arousal in Luis Buñuel
and Salvador Dalí's *Un chien andalou (An Andalusian Dog)* (1929). *Bottom:*
Protagonist poet (Enrique Rivero) contemplating his hand in *The Blood of
a Poet (Le Sang d'un poète,* 1930), the first in Jean Cocteau's avant-garde
trilogy marked by the mythic poet Orpheus's obsession with life and death.

to accept these avant-garde films is to make them aware of the importance of images in their own thinking and the fact that an *association of ideas* is very often a simple *association of images.*[2] Images set in motion by a song, a memory, or any excitement willingly assume the form of a surrealist film, without recourse to mental disorder. Only a sclerosis of habit makes the spectator inaccessible to an order of sequence that is deep down more familiar to them than sacrosanct logic.

On the other hand, the spectator must be warned against an obsession with "understanding" at any cost. As if for each film there was only one response and as if the exact solution should warrant a prize. A film—even one without motive or the most symbolic—is above all a succession of events presented on a screen. These events, like all events and all beings, can be interpreted from various perspectives: logical, psychoanalytical, visual, and even entertainment-value. The *auteur*'s own intentions and the fact we attribute others to him *is unimportant.* In the same vein we can discuss the true meaning of Greek tragedy, Hieronymus Bosch's paintings, and Jules Verne's novels. And that in no way prevents anyone from enjoying them and finding them to their liking.

Even so, it's worth emphasizing that the three *auteurs* did have an intention, to avoid the accusation of "made without beginning or end to make fun of everyone." The following notes will be able to guide the presenter.[3]

Entr'acte

Director: René Clair. Screenplay: Francis Picabia. Photography: Man Ray. Actors: Jean Borlin, Francis Picabia, Erik Satie, Marcel Duchamp.

Entr'acte was intended as the intermission for Picabia's dadaist ballet *Relâche* (1924). A score by Erik Satie accompanied it. According to director René Clair, it was intended to drive the audience out of the theatre between the two ballets by playing on the disorienting power of images. Initially random, using typical special effects, linked only by their magnetism, they are organized little by little like a thought or a dream taking shape. "The madman is the man who has lost everything except his reason" (G. K. Chesterton). *Entr'acte*'s funeral is crazy only insofar as it lacks everything except logic.

The virtuosity of Clair's montage and the film's musical rhythm are striking. The apparent disorder of these images and the rigor of their visual and rhythmic relationships make us follow this narrative without a story with the same intensity as a dramatic construction. We also note the appearance of a familiar leitmotif in all of René Clair's work: the chase.

Un chien andalou

Director: Luis Buñuel. Screenplay: Salvador Dalí. Actor: Pierre Batcheff. Photography: Albert Duverger, Jimmy Berliet [uncredited].

After dadaism came surrealism. After the free outpouring and the concrete use of dream images for a cinematic ballet, here are dreams at the service of reality. To describe this simple and classic situation—a young man's pursuit of a woman—Buñuel and Dalí resort to surrealist shock devices consisting above all in the *encounter*. It's not a question of "symbolizing," but of introducing objects or signs on the neutral field of the film, much as a dream reveals us to ourselves by placing end to end memories and signs separated by our conscience. It is thus after the shock of the birth identified with the severed eye that the film's hero appears. He is restrained in his pursuit by the full weight of his childhood: these white capes are similar to a child's smock; lines on a tie and a box are clearly a Freudian motif; harnessed priests, donkeys, and pianos restrain him; and a school desk covered in dust. The hero intensifies his efforts to forbid and punish himself, but ultimately fails in his quest. He becomes a prisoner in his closed room while the woman rejoins a free man in the open space of the wind and the sea. This plausible exegesis, which moreover psychoanalyzes the *auteurs* perhaps more than the film itself, should not however be taken literally.

If the direction is less than perfect, it has at least a singular capacity for bewitchment. Pierre Batcheff's extraordinary performance has a lot to do with it.[4] The relationship between images is much more unified and distorted than in *Entr'acte*. But that's the price for the desire to *tell a story*. This tension between an oneiric freedom and narrational demands creates a certain ambiguity. It is interesting to note that this ambiguity will be resolved three years later in the documentary *Land without Bread* (1933), in which the simple depiction of the living conditions of a miserable Spanish people, the Hurdanos, will integrate indisputably the cruelest of surrealist images. In particular, a donkey eaten alive by bees echoes the dead donkeys on the pianos. This itinerary is meaningful to the extent that it summarizes surrealism's every direction, benefiting from the foreknowledge at work in the images and events reproduced by reality. In 1951, newsreels and scientific films constitute the true surrealist cinema.[5] (Examples: Painlevé's *Freshwater Assassins,* the Soviet film *Experiments in the Revival of Organisms,* Grémillon's *Sixth of June at Dawn,* and war footage.)[6]

The Blood of a Poet

Director: Jean Cocteau. Photography: Georges Périnal. Music: Georges Auric. Actors: Lee Miller (the statue), Enrique Rivero (the poet), Pauline Carton, Odette Talazac, Jean Desbordes, Féral Benga, Barbette.

The Blood of a Poet has incorrectly been called a surrealist film. There should be a caveat against such misuses of language, as indefensible as "communism" for the early Christians, or the current connotation of "existentialism," which has become a fashion style. Surrealism as a school and the surrealist apprehension of the world are one thing. And everything that belongs to the resources of dreams or of a specific logic isn't necessarily related to surrealism. With regard to Cocteau, who didn't know Buñuel's films and who had violent arguments with the surrealists, this label is particularly inappropriate.[7]

"The poet must pass through several deaths in order to be re-born in immortality." Such is the guiding principle of this filmic poem, deeply tied to Cocteau's personal mythology. Once again, it's not a question of symbols, but of signs. The chimney that comes crashing down at the film's beginning and end does not "symbol-ize" an abolishment of time. Rather, it concretely *says* a poet's life is contained in any temporal fragment, that its time isn't that of calendars. Likewise, this mysterious mouth that opens in his hand—which he *caught* like leprosy—translates, in poor language, a carnal refraction of this mysterious evil of beauty. *Talking about* the poet's wound or *showing* this wound amounts to the same thing. We see once again the work identified with death. The poet gets lost on the path of damned poetry. He surprises this coagu-lated and ambiguous world of hotel rooms at dawn and explores the temptations of drugs and narcissism. Later, he steals the heart from the child he was (and the snowball fight is a childhood mem-ory for Cocteau and a leitmotif in his work, like his physical con-tact with poetry). He sacrifices himself to the public, this worldly public with neither heart nor brain that applauds his suicide. He finally reaches the paradise of immortality paid for with his *blood*. Of course on this theme (and the author has often specified it) ev-eryone is free to find the personal extension that occurs to them. The essential point is not misjudging the seriousness of the under-taking, obscured in part by a certain awkwardness.

The only criticism that we can make of Cocteau in 1931 (he says so himself) is his lack of a true film language. An association of ideas, allusions, and visual puns is infinitely more cumbersome on screen than on the page. And it's a kind of assembly line that makes this film—intended to represent the poet's struggle with his expression—exit the screen and testify to this struggle (and, it must be said, to a certain failure). The main themes of *The Blood of a Poet* will be taken up again in *Orpheus* (1950) with a total mastery of language that will make it a kind of masterpiece.[8]

These three films, each in its own way, have had few offspring. They were tied too closely to their time and their *auteurs*. René Clair applied his virtuosity to the exploitation of something marvelous and popular. Buñuel after *L'Âge d'or* (1930), closely related to *Un chien andalou*, and *Land without Bread*, made realist films in Mexico that remained unknown to us until the admirable *The Young and the Damned* (1950), with mixed success.

Cocteau has followed his trajectory without disciples, having only (in America above all) mediocre imitators like Kenneth Anger.[9] Only the dream sequences in commercial American films *(Dr. Jekyll and Mr. Hyde; Murder, My Sweet;* and *Spellbound)* refer to these attempts.[10]

AN *AUTEUR*'S FILM

CARL THEODOR DREYER'S
The Passion of Joan of Arc (1928)

Credits

Screenplay: Dreyer based on Joseph Delteil's study of Joan of Arc.[1] Cinematography: Rudolf Maté (who later worked as a d.p. in Hollywood, e.g., *Gilda*. Today he is a filmmaker). Art decoration: Hermann Warm (set designer for *The Cabinet of Dr. Caligari*). Costumes: Jean and Valentine Hugo. Actors: Falconetti (Joan)—Sylvain (Cauchon)—Maurice Schutz (Inquisitor)–Michel Simon, Antonin Artaud (Judges). Production: Société Générale des Films, France, 1928.

The negative, which for a long time was thought destroyed, was rediscovered in 1951. A new dubbed copy with religious music has been made.

Synopsis

Dreyer condenses episodes from Joan of Arc's trial and her execution into a single long day. Joan appears before her judges. She is

Signed: Chris Marker

Source: *Regards neufs sur le cinéma* (New Perspectives on Film), Collection Peuple et culture, ed. Jacques Chevallier (Paris: Seuil, 1953), 256–61. Marker's essay was not reprinted in the abridged edition of *Regards neufs sur le cinéma* (1963).

Joan receives water from a compassionate woman as soldiers lead her to the pyre at the conclusion of Carl Theodor Dreyer's *The Passion of Joan of Arc* (1928).

questioned. Her answers bewilder her questioners, irritating those who wish for her downfall. Her answers convince one of the most honorable among them, who is expelled. Cauchon, the presiding judge, attempts an underhanded move with a forged letter from King Charles VII. Other judges attack Joan on religious grounds. But these maneuvers and nuances are no match for Joan's innocence. An attempt is made to intimidate her by presenting her with instruments of torture. She is ready to concede, but then pulls herself together and faints. She is carried to the cemetery. Between the threats, the pleas, the grim spectacle of the cemetery, and her own exhaustion, Joan ultimately signs her retraction. The judges are satisfied. Joan is led to her execution, after having received communion. The crowd in attendance breaks out in a riot. The English occupiers organize a police intervention and disperse the crowd by force, before retreating to their fortified castle. Joan remains alone on the stake and disappears in the smoke like the approaching night.

Key Images

The film's first visual impression is obviously tied to the almost constant use of *close-ups*. The entire drama occurs on the faces, except for the final scene. In light of such a rigorous bias, an examination of its precise meaning is in order. Here, as in every important film work, form and content are linked to such an extent that it would be childish—under the pretext of *formalism* or *concern for the subject matter*—to separate one from the other or to ignore one for the other.

Sartre once said that "all novelistic art refers back to metaphysics."[2] Similarly, every film style refers to a conception of narrative *time*. Because in film, time is the number-one problem. Requirements of screening duration and the image's *retrospective* nature almost always lead the director to cheat time. The crassest and best-known example are superimpositions of calendar pages to evoke a passage of time, there where the novelist could easily have made its passing noticeable.

In the case of a historical film, a "costume" film as they are called, the problem is more complicated. Confronted with history, viewers have a preordained attitude that makes them lose, for the benefit of the picturesque, the suspension of disbelief that they grant to their contemporaries. A historical adventure affects us more on the level of legend than on a human level, even if all the reconstructed events are authentic. To reconnect with the public, the problem is thus no longer the subject, but the style.

Film syntax has introduced a stylistic notion all its own, making up for time with space. Similarly, Racine, in his preface to *Bajazet*, believed he was authorized to handle a current topic, on the condition that the geographical distance granted the audience the same *disorientation* as a historical one.[3] We can say that the spectator's rapprochement or distancing in relation to the character or the action entails a *method* or visual *step backward* that belongs to grammatical time. The rapprochement or distancing is determined by the choice of shots: the CU (close-up) corresponding to rapprochement and the LS (long shot) to distancing. The long shot corresponds to the past (he *arrived* in this city; he *did* this); the close-up to the present (Joan *listens* to the judge, she *says* this).

Dreyer's manner of probing faces and the absence of makeup result from his need to place Joan's story in the present, *that is, in eternity,* in order to make it noticeable to the audience by distracting it from the reassuring framework of the past. The stylized sets with their bland costumes and their complete lack of anything picturesque correspond to this idea of eternity. We mustn't reverse the movement and look for Dreyer's biases only in terms of technical performance. *Joan of Arc*'s close-ups are no more an end in themselves than the ceilings in *Citizen Kane*. Both are the results of a style and a conception of narrative.

Dreyer and the Devil

This aesthetic bias clarifies Dreyer's intentions. This great Danish director (one of the four or five greatest male directors of our time) is obsessed with the Christian sense of suffering. For a Christian, Christ on the cross never stops suffering for humankind as long as the world lasts. And suffering is the only means of partaking in Christ, being Him a little. Whence this need to make Joan's suffering felt in the present, to make the spectator in a way participate in it. This is also the source of Dreyer's fascination in all his work for suffering, and particularly physical suffering in torture. Torture at the hands of the inquisitors, in *Leaves from Satan's Book* (1921), Joan's pyre, the doctor buried alive (*Vampyr,* 1932), the witch's stake in *Day of Wrath* (1943), or the couple torn apart in *Two People* (1945) falls under this same pitiful and cruel fascination in the face of evil.

This doloristic perspective affects even *Master of the House* (1925), a distant relation. So much so that we could say that the main character in Dreyer's work is Evil's very embodiment, invisible and present as God in Athalie[4]: the Devil, not always invisible, since implied in *Vampyr,* and openly (and naïvely) depicted in Dreyer's second film, *Leaves from Satan's Book.* On this topic it is significant to note how this depiction evolves. From 1919 to 1945, Dreyer goes from the most traditional imagery of a Devil with a goatee bribing souls, to a devil inside the protagonists of *Two People,* a film with *two* characters on *one* set—an enclosed room, isolated from the world, which is exactly the Hell of *No Exit.*[5]

Another leitmotif: a fascination with the character of the witch, the human being who pushes to the extreme ties with the Devil, Death, and to whom suffering is delivered like a kind of paradoxical grace. It's understandable that this fascination led Dreyer to address the witch of witches, Joan of Arc. And it's hardly a paradox to say that she is offered as an object of pity more as a witch than as a saint.

Leaves from Satan's Book also encompasses Christ's Passion. Dreyer reconnects today with his first weapons, since he now wants to film a *Passion* on the holy sites in Israel.

Situation and Comparisons

The Passion of Joan of Arc's very date situates it as the culmination of silent film. Its lengthy intertitles attest to this impatience. We might dream (if such an undertaking weren't so expensive) of a sound version of it, as the Russians did with *Battleship Potemkin.* On the other hand, the composition of images and the rigorous editing equal the very best of silent cinema with all its expressive means. It is in this sense that we can see in *The Passion of Joan of Arc* an expressionist masterpiece, in contrast to both the nonsensical realism and puerile stylization of Fritz Lang's *Metropolis.* We can, for example, compare the crowd movements in both films. In Dreyer, the crowd seems to be filmed on the fly, and the expression is in the angle or the camera movement. (One meaningful example: when the crossbows are thrown from a window to the English soldiers, they are taken one at a time by a hand that disappears below the frame. And it's the camera itself, in retreating from a setting where nothing is happening, that suggests the movement of the crossbows from hand to hand in making a chain.) In Lang, faced with a listless camera, the crowd engages in a horribly composed unrealistic ballet "to express" despondency or anger.

We can likewise indulge in formal comparison with a film like Robert Bresson's *Diary of a Country Priest,* where everything also takes place on the faces, but where, in accordance with the aforementioned temporal law, the necessary distance is kept.

Finally, from the perspective of the subject, we can compare this *Joan of Arc* with the myriad of other film versions, more or less successful. It is nonetheless advisable to excuse the most recent. Taking into account the laws of genre, the lack of a historical film's *contemporaneity,* and the fact that Dreyer's genius risks making us harshly judge those who are merely good craftsmen, *Joan of Arc* is a high-quality film.[6]

Other than that, we can have some fun discovering a distant echo of a Dreyerian rigor in shots from *Gilda,* the work of Rudi Maté.[7] But *The Passion of Joan of Arc* has no filmic posterity. Masterpieces are more often culminations than starting points.

CINEMA, ART OF THE TWENTY-FIRST CENTURY?

AT THE MOMENT WE'RE SENDING THIS BOOK TO THE PRINTER, it is perhaps worthwhile to say a word about the extraordinary changes occurring in the very nature of filmmaking in the year 1953.

These changes are first of all technical. But as is customary in a world that produces only when frightened, it is a profound economic crisis that triggered them. Once again it is Hollywood that has jump-started the technical and aesthetic revolution (as it did with the Talkies). But once again, Hollywood simply uses, profits financially from, and very often debases ideas and inventions that are foreign to it. Everything begins with Hollywood because Hollywood alone has the necessary financial means to provide the scale of methods that elsewhere remain at the stage of experimentation. But let's not be fooled.

Competition from television has triggered a questioning of film industry norms. Considering the dramatic drop in moviegoing, the

Signed: C.M.

Source: "Afterword," in *Regards neufs sur le cinéma,* Collection Peuple et culture, ed. Jacques Chevallier (Paris: Seuil, 1953), 499–502. Marker's essay was not reprinted in the abridged edition of *Regards neufs sur le cinéma* (1963).

closing of a large number of cinemas, and the well-documented equation (a 2 percent increase in the sale of TV sets means a 1 percent decrease in box-office receipts), American production houses began *looking for something new.* At least this strictly commercial reflex had the happy result of tearing film away from its entrenched standardization (imposed precisely by the Hollywood diktat on most markets) and to reconnect it with a normal, technical evolution, in which many researchers (Abel Gance in France with his three screens, Spottiswoode in England with 3-D film) anticipated the forms without, however, being able to go beyond their individual efforts.[1] On the one hand, the idea of 3-D—without being as decisive as sound or color—could be expected as a new and normal step in the history of representation. On the other hand, screen dimensions—standardized for convenience—were completely arbitrary, and maintained a vision of a "mask" or of a picture rather incompatible with the realistic tendency of modern film. It is thus on these two points regarding a change in filmic space—in depth and in width—that the battle for renewal has been waged. It is perhaps interesting to note that both tendencies appear together in this "staging in depth" about which so much has been said since Orson Welles's *Citizen Kane* (1941). That film broke precisely with a grammar of montage based on a rapid shot analysis in order to reintroduce a complete value of the filmed universe in which the spectator exercised (relatively speaking) their own analysis, the one that they exercise in reality. Thus, once again, aesthetics outstripped technique, showed it the way, and demanded an answer.

Technique had its answers all prepared. Everyone remembers the static stereoscopes known to photographers, those *anaglyphs* introduced as a curiosity around 1933, in which by the mediation of a bezel in different colored glass—green and red—two images superimposed with a certain difference (one green, the other red) conveyed an illusion of three dimensions to the spectator. The principle is quite simple: the human eye, *recognizing* an image, works to match it. Each eye is blind to the image of the other eye because of a chromatic complementarity. As a result, the eye's focus occurs at the intersection of two beams; that is, the images are staggered in front or behind the ideal surface of the screen where they appear when the two images coincide. As the discrepancy varies depending on the shots, the elements of the final image are organized in the same relationship as in reality (all this in an ideal perspective, the perfect representation of reality being, as in ordinary photography, a borderline case occurring below all optical deformations). The key premise of this process—the independent vision of the two eyes—was picked up by what we now call 3-dimensional films (and of which some rather poor examples have been shown in Paris: *House of Wax, Man in the Dark,* and the over-the-top *Bwana Devil.* But several specialized cinemas earlier had offered a much better illustration with several British shorts for the 1951 festival) with a significant improvement: the basic differentiation of bicolor glasses is replaced by light *polarization.*[2] (The possibility, by means of a filter, to stratify, so to speak, the luminous beams alongside and depending on the chosen diagonal. Thus, when two images are polarized—depending on the diagonals in opposition to 90 degrees—the spectator equipped with filtered glasses perceives only one image with each eye.) But after an initial infatuation with the technique, the need to wear glasses and the lack of renewed effects have apparently disconnected the public from 3-D.

In contrast, the "wide screen" technique seems to open a more promising path. The most spectacular technique is that of *Cinerama,* screened by three projectors on a concave screen that approximately triples the field of vision. This width of field is more in line with our natural vision, due to the fact that when our interest is centered on an image, we continue to surround it with the idea of a universe that extends it, combined with the effect of the depth that a curved screen provides. Together, this creates the conditions for a *psychological dimension* (as opposed to a mechanical one). It's a purely mental operation, as much and all the more convincing than 3-D, without the inconvenience of glasses or of tunnel vision. *Cinemascope*, invented by the French engineer Chrétien and purchased by 20th Century–Fox, achieves a similar effect by the use of a wide (but not as wide as Cinerama) and curved screen.[3] It replaces the three-projector system—which would require reconstructing all the theatres and presents serious inconveniences due to weight, high cost, bulkiness, and imperfect technique—with a special lens, the Hypergonar, which compresses the image in the filming and then restores its width during screening, thus allowing—with the exception of the lens and the screen—the use of standard material. Finally, while waiting for better, cautious production houses like MGM make do by using masks to alter the screen proportions. We'll have a better idea knowing that while normal screen proportions are 1.33:I, the MGM screen carries them at 1.75:I, Cinemascope at 2.55:I, and Cinerama approximately at 2.80:I.*

These novelties, whatever their fate, will be only as good as the use made of them. That they are for the most part rather ridiculous is an unfortunately normal phenomenon insofar as it's a matter above all of a war of big production houses (against television, as well as against each other) and consequently of an appeal to the lowest levels of entertainment. Nevertheless, it would appear that through this commercial operation a prodigious means of representation is in the process of being mastered. More perfect both in the reproduction of the world and in its abilities to create a universe of its own, it integrates—perhaps even definitively—the theatre while it extends cinema's conquests, pushing its technical perfection to the point where it becomes a matter for specialized

---

* The "Panoramic Screen" announced by several French cities is a deceptive ploy that consists, in order to modify the image proportions, in subtracting from the top and the bottom.

engineers and, in turn, enhances the sole *auteur*. The spectacle taking shape amidst so many upheavals might be an instrument of the twenty-first century's great collective celebration: the culmination of film, theatre, and mural painting, the veritable new vision of an entire people.

FAREWELL TO GERMAN CINEMA?

An Assessment

The German Film Clubs conference, which is held annually in a small city away from any fanfare, is unique in its genre. First by its international nature: it's much more than just a meeting of German film-club discussion leaders. Film professionals also attend and participate. Flaherty attended before he died, as did Paul Rotha, Jacques Becker, Le Chanois, Staudte, Rouquier, Käutner, and this year Tati. Stars come not to be seen, but to contribute to an inquiry: we saw Gérard Philipe introduce *Beauty and the Devil* and Howard Vernon defend *The Silence of the Sea,* two films whose meaning and significance are greatly altered in a German context.[1] And here is the second characteristic of this conference: publicity plays scarcely a role and social niceties none at all. Disagreements can frequently occur, but one thing is certain: people attend because they truly love films. A good film emits waves of joy to the audience, while a controversial film incites rows on

---

Signed: Chris Marker

Source: *Positif: Revue de cinéma,* no. 12, special on American cinema (November–December 1954): 65–71. A German translation of this article, "Deutscher Film Adieu?" in *Der Film—Manifeste, Gespräche,* was published in *Dokumente,* ed. Theodor Kotulla (Munich: Piper Verlag, 1964), 2: 132–38.

the way out. There's no role-playing. We're not at a festival. There are no prizes, no bargaining, no influences, and very little diplomacy. Moreover, it takes place in a country that hardly attends to such things. In short, it's a little island of freedom. By supporting this initiative and facilitating the annual participation of French filmmakers and critics, those in charge of Cultural Affairs and the Mainz Film Bureau deserve much more than just the usual pat on the back. Albert Tanguy who runs this office is a recognized cinephile. It's a real delight to see a man in whom function and authority coincide so precisely. Will I misrepresent the intentions of them all if I write that Bad Ems this year, like Titissee, Bacharach, Lindau in previous years, was one of the rare places where the cinema is neither a pure instrument of commerce, nor its exact opposite, a hearth around which one swoons, but above all a wonderful toy—like Orson Welles's electric train—frivolous and serious as only a toy can be, and that responds to the "childish" side of us all, which is certainly neither the best nor the worst of us.

The foregoing is not a preamble designed to soften what's to follow. It is rather offered specifically in the name of this friendship that allows us to gather along the Rhine periodically in the name of the often admirable work that the German film-clubs are doing. Above all, we must, in the name of a generation of young filmmakers and critics who breathe the same air as we do and share our concerns and anxieties, sound an alarm without illusion or hesitation.

West German cinema finds itself bogged down in a dead end. This is perhaps the result of the narrow-minded ostracism in which German production in general has been held hostage since the war. The truth is West German cinema has withdrawn into a kind of moral and aesthetic ghetto from which we see no escape. In East Germany, in contrast, a style is sought and sometimes found. But for reasons of lofty foreign policy, our access to these films is barred (I repeat: are we waiting for Staudte to die in order to screen *Rotation* and *The Kaiser's Lackey* in France?).[2] It is obvious that films from the West are banned, and the regular applause they receive in festivals illustrates the sad joke of a national production incapable of crossing its own boundaries, worn down in itself, and whose symbol, in the credits, could be a lens fastened to a navel!

It's been said a hundred times: it was to be expected that in 1945 German cinema reconnected with expressionism. This attested to the Hitlerian sterilization and the need to start from somewhere. But after ten years, there's no longer an excuse. Everyone knows that since German musicians have emerged from Wagnerism, Wagner has become popular in the cinema, and that fog, storm, and chiaroscuro, Tristan's horn, and Banquo's ghost (wait a moment, that's no longer Wagner, but the intelligent reader[3] ...) constitute the German filmmaker's arsenal. Tradition? Let's be clear: all national cinemas are on the one hand theoretically heirs to world cinema. And on the other a certain German cinema can lead to *Shane, The Crimson Curtain,* or *The Fall of Berlin.*[4] Hence reciprocity doesn't really work. A supposedly German cinema of quality is heir only to itself. (Because there exists of course, underneath, a banal production owing nothing to anyone.)

It's well known that intermarriage begets stupidity. But it is abnormal that in 1954 the "beautiful photography" of German film still relies on this *kunstlerisch* [arty] style that is situated in a backlit, geometric postcard setting, with black lace lingerie, and a torchlight procession. It is abnormal that a television director introduces as an "experimental film" a version of "The Sorcerer's Apprentice" that could easily fit between two reels of the *Nibelungen.*[5] And abnormal that an important German producer declares *Hoheit lassen bitten* [Your Highness, Please Leave] "the best fantasy film of the year." Judge for yourselves: in a great duchy of Central Europe circa 1900, the grand duchess has an operetta singer doppelgänger. ... In short, the aforementioned UFA operetta has just been released, spanking new from its cans as it might have been in 1935. What is problematic isn't the fact that the film is bad. After all, we've seen others of its ilk. It's because it's bad like a bad film of 1935, and not like a bad film of 1954. It's because the director, Paul Verhoeven, demonstrated in directing *Heart of Stone* for DEFA that he was capable of making a captivating, original, and lively film. There's something absurd and outrageous in this return to moribund forms, whether it's a question of sub-Erik Charrel in a "commercial" vein or of a sub-Caligari in an "artistic" vein.

A small, educational film illustrates this regression. The same Paul Verhoeven has the praiseworthy ambition of initiating the viewer to "film techniques" by presenting the same scene shot in different ways. Excellent premise, but à propos: while in its first example—perfectly sober and bare—the scene occurs without difficulty, incrementally as the "film techniques" appear, it becomes heavier, more embarrassing, and less convincing. Shadows exaggerate the stairwell, strange and unmotivated shot angles dwarf and deform the characters, and an intrusive music inflates everything. (Oh, and there's also a faulty reverse-shot: it's hard to think of everything!) In short, we are more and more in the cinema, but one that is completely passé. And as always, we tend to forget about the film and to wonder if this Germany that is rebuilding around us, with admirable efficiency and dynamism, isn't also—in its concern for being more and more German—an outdated Germany.

Within this dismaying production, three films warrant our attention, partially because of their unique style, but especially because of their careful approach to contemporary and serious topics. These are Victor Vicas's *No Way Back*, Heinz Paul's [sic] *08/15*, and Helmut Käutner's *The Last Bridge*.[6] We note, incidentally, that Vicas is Russian and that *The Last Bridge* is an Austro-Yugoslav production where only the director is German. Obviously, these exceptions dangerously risk confirming the rule.

In the eyes of some Germans, the fact that *No Way Back* is anti-Soviet is a wholehearted recommendation. Its true merits, however, lie elsewhere. Because an objective review of the screenplay leads to the conclusion that to accumulate so many implausibilities, the subject matter need not be credible. But what is striking is the quality of images and the mise-en-scène to which American productions of the same caliber have not accustomed us. Perhaps because in Hollywood this task is left to underlings. (Kazan is the only great director to venture to do it, with *Man on a Tightrope,* which didn't exactly shine by its realism.[7]) Still, Vicas clearly profited from his wartime stay in the United States. And if his style is more skillful than personal, it makes us want to see him tackle a subject to his liking, if such a thing exists. (Let's wait to see his adaptation of *Siegfried.*[8]) But how strange it is that a film—aimed at granting Westerners the monopoly of humankind—is utterly lacking therein and that this plea for the human person has the appearance of an exercise in a cold and almost abstract style! There's even a joke: the head of the Soviet police—a character whose screenplay function is intended to provoke a general anti-Russian sentiment—is at this point the embodiment of his boss. His portrait is displayed on the desk for the spectator to see. Rotten luck: it's Beria![9]

08/15 is undoubtedly this year's most talked-about film. Based on Hans Hellmut Kirst's novel, which is strangely similar to *From Here to Eternity* (I prefer not to repeat the nonsensical title of the book and film's French versions), adapted for the screen by Ernst von Salomon.[10] It is first of all a fairly realistic and impressive chronicle of army life under the Wehrmacht. And as such, it has an undeniable first effect of being soundly antimilitarist. We won't soon forget the scene of the NCO's drinking bout, collectively removing their trousers on the mess tables. But the book and the film's advertising campaign emphasizes *wie es wirklich war,* as it really was. The expression's ambiguity is obvious and encompasses both denunciation and nostalgia. Of course it was appalling and brutal, but *that's* what I, me a German soldier, experienced, and on whom a veil of forgetfulness or condemnation was subsequently drawn. Now I *receive my due justice* in showing "how it really was."

It is on this point that the antimilitarist contents of the film are balanced by a more subtle and dangerous complacency. The men who recognize themselves in the characters, and who laugh at seeing the NCOs ridiculed much as the Revenge generation could laugh about Courteline, cannot forget that this period they spurn, or feign to spurn, was that of their youth.[11] It must be difficult to make a man disown his twenty-year-old self. If *08/15* makes the army repulsive to the youngest spectators, so much the better. But it's not impossible that their parents attend this anti-Wehrmacht spectacle much in the way that Hamburg residents go to the Lili Marleen Brewery to hear the widely advertised Afrika-Corps and to play popular tunes.

But it is the film's ending that reaches the height of ambiguity. Following the same progression as *From Here to Eternity* (although the Deborah Kerr–Burt Lancaster couple is reversed: the NCO's wife offers herself to the lieutenant. In the German army, adultery focuses on hierarchic ascension), the screenplay results in a confusion of nasty NCOs, in the promotion of good soldiers, by the machination of an omniscient, above-suspicion, and generous High Command. Then everyone meets for a military parade in the barracks courtyard, with not a gaiter button missing, as the radio announces the impending war. The colonel and the ex-corporal Asch, a likable figure, exchange a half-smile. And when the screen is enveloped in darkness with the word "End," a bombardment explodes. Thus, three tricks in just a few feet of film: the reversal that causes the sympathetic victims of the military atrocities to find themselves in the position of Europe's conquerors, in an army purged of its bad elements and directed by wise men; the smile of complicity that can be selectively connected to the two men's personal situation or to the global situation; and the discreet evocation of the war about which it's possible to say whatever one wants. And undoubtedly the official intention is this: these poor young people were destined for slaughter. But this mental reservation carries little weight when faced with the totally absurd character of this war that falls from the sky. Here the comparison with *From Here to Eternity* becomes compelling and sheds a more favorable light on Zinnemann's film.

In the latter, indeed, the war is indicted by the absurdity with which it retrospectively destroys the best conceived plans of mice and men. Likewise, *dixit* Malraux, just as death transforms life into fate, here the war transforms peace into a failed game. "The hazards of the army led me here, where a Japanese plane or a sentinel's bullet can send me into eternity, and nothing of what I try to build my life on will have any meaning." It is thus not as a fatality, because of its immanent absurdity, that the war is denounced, but for its power of transformation and scorn. War has no proper existence of its own: it is only the malady of peace. In contrast, in the German film, we pass from one world to another, war is another planet. Going to war is making this leap into the absurd, into irresponsibility—we noticed it in Nuremberg.[12] Through their *esprit de corps,* Zinnemann's American soldiers have the feeling that an abhorrent war has been imposed on them. On the other hand, Heinz Paul's [sic] German soldiers subscribe to this "timeless military wisdom" epitomized by the recently published *Calendar of the German Soldier* (1955), with the following words: "No questions. Forward. March!"

Helmut Käutner and his screenwriter Norbert Kunze's greatest virtues are to show us a war in which questions are asked. And after the picture I've just drawn of contemporary German cinema, we understand that a film that exalts human brotherhood through and against war, which offers a valid depiction both of soldiers' lives in occupation and those of partisans, and in addition despises effects and draws its language from *Paisà,* is worthy first of all of our sympathy. The theme itself was ingenious and rich. A German nurse is captured by Yugoslav partisans to care for a wounded man. She remains with them against her will, and ends up understanding the meaning of their resistance. Unfortunately, all praise stops there. First, because of the screenplay. The screenwriters couldn't resist the easy option of a dual love story, with a

German soldier on one side and a partisan on the other, which results in melodramatic reunions and weighs down the entire story
with a fictional poor taste. Then, because of its mise-en-scène.

Rarely does such a clear opportunity reveal to what extent neorealism—before being an ensemble of formal biases—is in fact a
state of mind. The ingredients are all here: location shooting in real
settings, the use of local characters and nonprofessionals except
for the protagonists. They extend to situations that leave the characters their disconcerting and invisible share, without conveying
the feeling "it happens as in the cinema." But inside, something's
still missing. This is explicitly clear in the overwrought dialogue,
but more subtly in a perpetual lag between the action and the
means of the mise-en-scène—a little as if, in the manner of *Hellzapoppin'*, Käutner had the wrong film in mind. And if there's an
error of real firmness in the handling, a technique he dominates
fails to master a subject that gets lost in obscurity.* This is how
we don't escape human sacrifice. Between her German fiancé and
her Yugoslav lover who call to her from opposite sides of the "last
bridge" (even Maria Schell can't save this scene from ridicule), the
poor nurse expires, struck by an unforeseen bullet. What can real
bushes, real stones, a real bridge, real soldiers do when confronted
with such a theatrical situation?[13] Conversely, a coinciding of the
action and the depiction gives us, for example, a battle on the river,
with German boats and a typhoid convoy, which is a part of a wartime anthology. Thus, what is missing in *The Last Bridge* is the
courage to push its intentions to the end, to renounce screenwrit-
ing trickery that ultimately makes it fall between two styles, like its
heroine between enemy camps. We can't avoid thinking of Käutner's first postwar film. *In Those Days* likewise finishes on a river-
bank, as the hero cries *"Illigenborg!"* [sic] while he makes his way
across the river.[14] That was a cry of hope, the first that was heard

---

* One criticism, nevertheless, for Käutner: he doesn't know how to use cats. In
The Last Bridge and *In Those Days*, cats fall completely unnaturally from the
sky, tossed by the props person.

in a Germany in disarray. What new disarray, what anxiety, what disappointments prevent a German filmmaker from reviving it today? In a country so enamored of symbols, what demon leads to this dangerous one of a deceased young woman between two worlds? What is this frontier on which—deprived of all options—a crucified Germany agonizes? Is it the demarcation line, the Oder–Neisse line, the East–West line, a fate line, or a lifeline?[15]

HOLLYWOOD ON LOCATION

1

When I arrived in Hollywood in the spring of 1953, sundry stories were appearing in the newspapers: Charlie Chaplin had just announced his intention of settling in Europe (the local press was outraged at his ingratitude); the tax law that exempted taxpayers living overseas was going to be rescinded because of actors' misconduct; Louis B. Mayer was to be named president of Cinerama Productions in New York, while Samuel Goldwyn was embarking for England on a study trip. I asked about my favorite directors: Ford was filming in Africa, Huston in Italy, and Zinnemann in Hawaii; George Stevens, after finishing *Shane,* claimed to be without work and had left for New York. The only common denominator in all this news was its centrifugal nature: Hollywood was a sinking ship. And when I later read that Roz Russell was conquering Broadway and Esther Williams was adding restaurateur to her prowess in swimsuits, I understood that they, too, were in the process of jumping ship.

These were the first signs, or at least the most apparent, of a

Signed: Chris Marker

Source: chapter 3 in *Cinéma 53: À Travers le monde,* Collection "7e art" (Paris: Le Cerf, 1954), 27–48. Other authors in this 194-page volume include André Bazin, Jacques Doniol-Valcroze, Gavin Lambert, and Jean Queval.

"crisis" that would soon fill magazine pages, astonish the world, and exhaust more than one critic. The statistics published by *Compo* were rehashed and discussed ad nauseam: since the war's end, 5,038 cinemas have closed in the United States; 33 percent of regular cinemas and 38 percent of the drive-ins were experiencing deficits. In areas "saturated" by television, there was a 40 percent decline in revenue, with 22 percent on the "skids." In short: whenever the sale of TV sets rises by 2 percent, box-office revenue decreases by 1 percent.

As a result, exhibitors began relying on compensatory businesses like the sale of popcorn and chocolates, not to mention launching lotteries and giveaways of crockery to female audience members (overheard conversation: "What are you going to do with your prize money?—I'm going to buy a TV set."). Production companies began looking for new tried-and-true success formulas, but in the meantime fired 80 percent of its technicians and closed all or part of its studios. Faced with this internal betrayal, help was sought abroad. Mr. Darryl Zanuck would explain to General Eisenhower the crucial impact of American film on public opinion in Asia and Europe. Zanuck complained about the lack of collaboration between Washington and Hollywood, going so far as to recommend the insertion—in films relevant to "difficult" countries—"of a scene here and there that wouldn't detract from the film's entertainment value, but still might do a lot of good." The first result of this appeal for clemency would be the nomination of Cecil B. DeMille to the position of Dr. Johnson's film advisor for the "psychological preparation of the Cold War." In retrospect, this gave a truly prophetic clairvoyance to the Oscar jury.

So was this the death of Hollywood? The idea can be entertained when you're here because it flatters a certain fondness for daydreaming about the demise of empires. The symbolic wall separating the Paramount studios from the Hollywood cemetery was headed for collapse. And nothing is more mausoleum-like than these immense empty buildings—useless like train stations before the railroad's invention—that most of the studios have become. The MGM–Irving Thalberg wing and all the recently closed Warner studios weigh on you deep into a California May, like the cold of dead planets. Far more funereal anyway than the safe-deposit room where Valentino's ashes still bloom, or the structure—only a little smaller than the Palais de Chaillot—that preserves Douglas Fairbanks's memory. Obviously, once you're on this slope, the signs of illness jump out at you.

First of all, there are the layers of dead glory on which we tread, but where nothing grows. The soil is sterile. The aftertaste of ashes, which rereading a ten-year-old film magazine gives you, is felt perhaps more acutely in the United States than anywhere else. Films here have a short lifespan. Aside from some specialized cinemas in New York and college towns, film revivals are practically nonexistent. Consumption is instantaneous, greedy, and final. This is hardly surprising in a country where books are usually discarded once read. Hollywood, like America, wants to be without a past. Memory's sole sanctuary is perhaps—apart from the tombs—an astonishing little cinema on Fairfax Avenue, the Movie, that screens only silent films.[1] At dusk, cinema's bygone veterans gather there to relive their youth, almost furtively, as in a house filled with memories.

And, when all is said and done, the famous footprints and handprints at Sid Grauman's Chinese Theatre, designed for immortality, confer about as much of that as an armchair at the Académie française. Marion Davies and Bebe Daniels, calendar saints for us, are powerless over the young American crossing Hollywood Boulevard. All that remains of Jean Harlow are her hands and the impressions of her (tiny) shoes in the cement. Hollywood is not haunted. The total ruin of the demigods here doesn't even allow one to purchase a ghost. The sight of living demigods is hardly more reassuring. During the evening premieres, enormous floodlights pivot on the sidewalks, as one by one the stars ascend the stage amidst a shrill cheering. The ritual never changes, nor do the cries, the smiles, or the canned dialogue before the mikes. There's an expression for every situation, as young girls are taught. But their hearts are not in it. It's a loveless confrontation; the demigods are interchangeable. This very odd young man with painted lips and made-up eyes sitting next to me continually swoons at the sight of the actresses: "Isn't she wonderful? Isn't she beautiful?" The tone is set for the myth of a star who has reached the stage of cold obsession. Like the war. The fragility of this superficial world, the audience's versatility, its methodical elimination of everything that could offer warmth or generosity (and of which the Chaplin affair was the culminating point), sly persons' maneuvers, the opposition's exile, shortsightedness, and laziness render all sudden deaths likely.

It turns out that all-conquering television had for a long time, perhaps unknowingly, been this fifth column in the heart of the enemy city. And dreaming of the Los Angeles suburbs resettled by other industries, with turbines and fireplaces proliferating on the studio sites like figs in a jungle surrounding temples, grasping some spared ruins (those of the Chinese Theatre, for example, with its paving stones) where Hollywood has prudently enclosed its fossils in advance.

All this of course is a manner of speaking and we apologize for having dreamt out loud. Hollywood has been in business for a long time and is controlled by the New York financial industry, so that the subdivision no longer occurs between rival companies, but between different types of financial groups. You can be sure that if Hollywood hadn't seen the crisis coming, New York certainly knew what to expect. Reports about the cinema-television conflict are a little too simplistic and poorly done to really satisfy and inform us. The fundamental mixing of industries (the big studios have interests in TV or contemplate producing for it) is necessarily more intimate at the level of real financing. The real conflict lies with the banks in order to preserve or acquire control of the two industries.

Still in the midst of all this, the crisis of film exhibition is undeniable: 270 cinemas closed during the first three months of 1953, with 357 more between April and July. But from a production standpoint, we wonder if Hollywood and its *mahouts* haven't intentionally pushed things to the utmost in order to take advantage of the situation's gravity.

Slogans like "The Death of Hollywood" and better still "Is cinema going to disappear?" are troubling. But they are out of touch with reality. Congress passed the tax reduction on tickets sold, but then ran up against a White House veto. Other entertainment industries are demanding the same thing, by complacently painting the gloomiest picture of their situation. The presidential veto was perhaps a convenient way of delaying the choice, but perhaps also a clue that the dismal outlook began with the producers. Pressure on the government, as well as on public opinion ("If you're going to the movies less, soon you won't be going at all."), the forceful introduction of new techniques and formats—are beneficial for their buyers—and the profits of a doomsday policy are clear. In any event it's possible to remember the hypothesis of the rigging of a crisis in a rigged world (it is no more unbelievable to rig an economic retirement than a strategic one), even if for once, naïvety consists in lacking it.

2

In contrast, the political crisis has provided little fodder for slogans and special magazine issues. Whence the need to address it in greater depth here.

At first glance, the Hollywood "purge" seems like a joke. When you read articles about the *communist infiltration* in Hollywood, you fall into a far more troubling kind of hallucination than its purported deaths and metamorphoses. It seems that before 1947—the blessed year when the witch hunters came to practice their (anonymous) social talents on Sunset Boulevard—American cinema fell prey to the Bolsheviks. It was hardly noticeable in the films themselves, but that was a diversionary tactic. For more information, I

refer the reader to the *American Legion* newspaper, in whose pages
you will learn that Michel Eisenstein, a Soviet commissioner in
a major industry, came to San Francisco on business in 1934. He
had planned to infiltrate the film industry together with his consul
Galkovitch and a group of "liberal" American intellectuals.[2] This
conspiracy (that strangely echoes the screenplays from the anti-
Red series) aimed "at the complete domination of cinema for thirteen years." We can wonder why, notwithstanding this complete
domination, there is so little difference in the output of films produced before, during, and after these thirteen years. But the *American Legion* doesn't beat about the bush: "Only this last goal—the
complete domination of American film—wasn't achieved." Why?
Because of the House Un-American Activities Committee in 1947.
After thirteen years. It seems that the average American finds this
kind of demonstration very convincing.

In truth, these thirteen years certainly do correspond to something: namely, the period of Hollywood history when the Roosevelt
administration and the appearance of fascisms in Europe forced
movie financiers to tone down their fundamental antiprogressiv-
ism. The Hollywood milieu, especially actors and screenwriters,
was certainly more liberal and anarchist than communist, and
firmly progressive, like all artistic and intellectual milieus on the
eve of World War II. Antifascism played a decisive role in the crystallization of this environment, and led a fair number of cinema
people to unite with the communists, and sometimes to join the
party. The trade unions, besides IATSE, the technicians' union—a
very strange union—quickly ratified, short of the physical elimination of those in charge, the three guilds of screenwriters, directors,
and producers. The three guilds meant principally the Screenwriters Guild, this "Hollywood left" that self-identified in advance for
the attacks coming from the New York bosses at the first good
moment.

1934 . . . Instead of making a time stamp of the conspiracies
with the Russians in the film world, the motivated journalist with

whom I spoke might have seen a watershed of Hollywood politics. Upton Sinclair, the Democratic candidate for governor of California, was defeated by a reactionary coalition. Increasingly enslaved to financial powers, Hollywood attained a total subjection with the transition to the Talkies (the Morgan Bank was in control of Western Electric and Rockefeller RCA). The situation became so intolerable that the following years would see film artists totally devoted to regaining a certain independence. In that respect, it wasn't film content (which was always more or less hobbled by the tyranny of being "commercial") that was challenged. Instead, it was the existence of a liberal hotbed demanding labor and professional freedoms, which triggered massive efforts to implement destruction.

Although the times weren't right, the threat was too big for the powerful not to try to subdue the revolt prematurely. Starting in 1937, the Dies investigation was a brilliant precedent to McCarthyism.[3] *Confessions of a Nazi Spy* was accused of being a communist film and Shirley Temple of being a Red (she was about eleven years old, poor tyke). But once again, progressivism in Hollywood was on the right side of history. Until the war's end, it only gained in strength and cohesion. We imagine with what sigh of relief the financiers welcomed the turning point of 1946, when the progressive–communist–Russian spy commingling would become not only possible, but desirable and patriotic. Thirteen years of conspiracy? No, thirteen years of a prepared and long-simmering revenge. But it wasn't a matter of an internal dictatorial purge: everything was going to happen democratically, out in the open, from denunciation to investigation then the purge. There was no lack of willing participants wanting to make a name for themselves, providing records in playing the role of investigator. Once again, the American Legion was there for the occasion. Legions are always present for sweep operations.

The Tenney Investigation opened fire in 1947 (poor Martin Dies had an advance of only ten years). The cauldron had been coming to a boil since 1944, an election year when Dewey's supporters had consolidated in Hollywood an Alliance for the Preservation of American Ideals (among its noteworthy members: Cecil B. De-Mille, Sam Wood, Walt Disney, Cedric Gibbons, King Vidor). The principal American ideal, in closely examining the operation of this Alliance, seemed to be establishing blacklists. It was thus the Trojan horse in place to provoke the start of the Hollywood witch hunt. Jack Tenney was its spokesperson alongside the famous Thomas–Rankin Committee. One of the presidents of this committee was inadvertently sent to prison, for reasons that had nothing to do with ideology. Mr. Eric Johnston, the MPAA president, initially declared, "As long as I live, I will never participate in something as un-American as a blacklist." But by the end of 1947, the so-called Waldorf Declaration was published with the blessing of the still-living Mr. Eric Johnston. It was committed to: (1) eliminating all "identified and unrepentant" communists and (2) "getting rid of anyone who would not testify openly on the topic of communism when heard as a sworn witness by the committees." Translation into basic French: anyone who would refuse to hand over friends.

Impossible here to retrace all the episodes of this inquisition. It would be even difficult to make an accurate assessment of it, since this special committee decided to delete from its archives "everything that could harm its prestige." Consequently, the published chronicles introduce only the prosecution's case. Nothing more harmful for the committee's prestige than a witness's statements proving its president's errors and falsehoods. But the committee also earned itself a solid reputation for imbecility (Congressman Starnes, stumbling several times on the name of Marlowe in an incriminating article, sternly asked the witness if this "Marlowe" was a communist ...). The committee achieved fruitful results, including the imprisonment of the "Hollywood Ten" as its crowning achievement.

The American Legion, for its part, wasted no time. Its system of denunciation deserves analysis, because it is one of the most villainous ever conceived. The principle was "to help film industry members, placed in the position of suspects, and yet innocent, to prove their innocence." As a result, the Legion kindly provided the studios with a list of all the gossip, denunciations, and extrapolations regarding their employees, and invited them to provide clarification for the benefit of all those involved. Never has such a typically fascist situation ever been so hypocritically disguised where the innocent must prove their innocence. This hypocrisy is noticeable in other declarations also—for example, defending itself for having organized pickets against *Limelight* by specifying in writing that the Legion has too much respect for the freedom of its regional offices to prevent them from organizing pickets, if that seemed to them advisable. (In letters to the editor, readers respond to the Legion's question: "What can we do about this bastard Chaplin?": "His last film, *Limelight,* is likely to be screened in your city.") Hypocrisy, too, in this appeal to public opinion: instead of saying that studios must sack individuals suspected of communism, it says "the studios are not obligated to employ individuals spurned by the public for their communist sympathies" (*American Legion Magazine,* May 1953). Hypocrisy, too, in the outrageous claim in which money earned by pro-communist filmmakers would go to fill Russian coffers, therefore transforming *Limelight*'s spectators into Soviet taxpayers. Having the gall to compare Leni Riefenstahl's Hollywood visit to Chaplin's stay, the *American Legion Magazine* goes on to write: "The difference in principle between the boycott of an artist who filled Hitler's coffers with the American box-office, and the boycott of those whom we're not certain don't similarly fill those of Russia, was never clearly articulated." Indeed, what a shame.

Believe me, I take no pleasure in reporting such nonsense. The problem is that stupidity here is terror's bailiff. Because what completely enabled the destruction of the Left in Hollywood is the work on public opinion whose agitation and disorientation always finds refuge in a democratic alibi. A public opinion hostile to progressivism is thus forged. Then progressives are persecuted in the name of public opinion. It's both a caricature and sham of democracy.

In 1953 Hollywood, the guilds shifted to the political right. The famous thirteen years of efforts in the name of the film-worker freedom and dignity have been annulled. The most vigorous protesters have been either imprisoned or exiled. Others, broken by blackmail. The only deed that the investigative committee takes into account is denouncing the largest number of possible suspects. The accused thus found themselves caught between an insidious debasement and the loss of all career prospects, if not of their very way of life and their country. I was struck by the moderation with which some filmmakers, beyond reproach, talk about those who have caved under pressure. And it's easy to imagine the tricks and traps, the seeming harmlessness of first disclosures, the ensuing spiral, and the false confessions triggering real confessions. In short, an ignoble political mishmash in which some of the best people have been caught. The results are nonetheless appalling. Dmytryk's case is unfortunately typical, but how many filmmakers with a respected and courageous body of work owe their apparent impunity to giving into this threat?[4] Kazan, the first name of some importance to participate in a vulgar film of anti-Red propaganda *(Man on a Tightrope)*. Or Huston, who dug through the list of his technicians in Italy in order not to include any communists and who expressed solidarity with the American Legion to prevent one of his films from being picketed. . . . And writers like Budd Schulberg or Clifford Odets, whose play on trade-union struggle was recently performed. Both were thanked for their "invaluable help" by the HUAC commission. . . . Schulberg told us all about it in his novel *What Makes Sammy Run?* Now Sammy, a.k.a. the producer Jerry Wald, is Harry Cohn's right-hand man at Columbia. Perhaps one of these days we'll see his name alongside Schulberg's in the same credits.

But not everyone has this chameleon-like adaptability. John Garfield is an example of a man completely broken by blackmail. It seems he, too, was driven to "talk." And he died not long after. Another actor, J. Edward Bromberg, placed on the blacklists and exiled to England, died in 1951, of a heart ailment aggravated by persecution.[5] These were supposedly natural deaths and as such went practically unnoticed. But we think about them here in Hollywood.

The screenwriters have been hit the hardest. Either they have more character, or, were considered as less redeemable and generally unknown to the public, so they were offered less assistance than the filmmakers, and especially the stars. "Lucille Ball Is a Red" was worth a *New York Times* front page. But it would be better for public order were she not. In contrast, the screenwriters' guild includes people it was a pleasure to get rid of. With the result that the Screenwriters Guild has been, for all intents and purposes, decapitated: around 10 percent of its members have been charged with communism. Out of the 114 accused, only 17 appeared "cooperative," while 32 refused pure and simple to respond. This purge was done with the producers' tacit consent. Not yet being targeted, they remained prudent. Which rendered them all the more vulnerable and "cooperative" when their tumbril came.

At present, the operation can be considered over and done. Everyone who couldn't be intimidated has been liquidated. And everyone who hasn't been is held in check. The "repentant" communists are supposedly the most docile. Those in charge of the witch hunt are pleased. There remain the extreme reactionaries, the clumsy ones, the agitated like the unspeakable Jimmie Tarantino who pursued Dore Schary, MGM's production head, with his denunciations (Schary, comfortably ensconced in Louis B. Mayer's slippers, is careful not to answer), as well as the Schwab's drugstore waitress ("Have you ever been served by a Communist waitress?"—*Hollywood Life,* October 5, 1951). With horror Tarantino discovers books by Stalin in a bookstore whose address he obligingly distributes. He invites his readers to write accusatory letters to Washington, adding, "It doesn't matter if you sign. You will be doing your country a favor." He advocates a law that forbids any member of the American Bar Association from defending a communist, and finishes a film review by requesting that the a-bomb be immediately dropped on Moscow. A grotesque individual to be sure. Unfortunately, the current atmosphere in Hollywood confers a dangerous power on this sort of person.

Curiously, film content has hardly changed. But let's be clear: it's hard to imagine in a film today an answer like "Young man, a Red is a fellow who wants 30 cents an hour when I'm paying him 25" *(The Grapes of Wrath)*. And as it was necessary to justify the accusation of communist corruption in film, a certain number of works have been blacklisted: *The Best Years of Our Lives, The North Star, Mission to Moscow,* and even *Pride of the Marines*. It's hard to take these mind-boggling accusations seriously. In fact, if progressive screenwriters and filmmakers occasionally took advantage of expressing themselves in their material, this margin was always extraordinarily limited. Sooner or later we will have to address the spectre of American taboos, classifying them into major and minor ones. Minor offenses are sometimes tolerated, while major offenses are routinely questioned. A typical example: the racial problem. We remember Elia Kazan's *Pinky* and a white man's love for a black woman.[6] They break up at the end with all our sympathy. Love, sympathy, justice, it's already a lot for a southerner to stomach. Minor taboo to be overlooked. What counts is that, whether they like it or not, they won't sleep together. A major taboo. Something will always happen. We feel sorry for them and think of what they could have been. We will be with them in our hearts, regardless in the end. Doing it—the real thing and not its promise or its regret—will not have been committed. Similarly at the end of *The Grapes of Wrath,* Tom Joad will start to organize the resistance against the exploiters. But we won't see it and even less its victory. (For that, there are Capra's films: the millionaires who come to play the harmonica in the poor man's cottage.) Hope doesn't prevent the wealthy from sleeping. Were these hopeful films due to a surge in generosity? I hesitate to assume responsibility for the disillusioned comment of a Hollywood insider with whom I discussed *The Grapes of Wrath:* "It's clear to see which way the wind is blowing at this moment. Zanuck who boasted about having produced *The Grapes of Wrath* is today prostrate before Eisenhower." And seeing my surprised reaction, adds: "My friend, there is no virtue in Hollywood."

3

Furthermore, it's obvious that Hollywood consumes talent. And that knowledge and filmmaking expertise reach greater perfection here than anywhere else. And we'd like to add, given the means put at its disposal, it would be ironic if that weren't the case. The technical marvel—and by technical I mean a graceful dialogue, an ambiguous atmosphere, a plausible character or inspiration in framing, tempo and direction—is an attitude of a booklover, not just a reader. And for the last sixty years we have had the time to become accustomed to the fact that pages move. There is a perfectibility in machines, but not in the arts. The confusion created between cinema's two distinct poles makes us treat the maturity of the machine at the expense of art and gets its unseemly benefit like a dollar that changes its exchange-rate.

But the time is no longer far off when an equally divided perfection will force us to look for other criteria. And when we will be in raptures before the discoveries that punctuate 80 percent of the images and sounds of American films. When we will still hear the sound of the horn that pins José Greco to the fence in *Sombrero,* or the clang of pots and pans that gives us, in *Ivanhoe,* the first realistic depiction of a remarkable, medieval battle. When we will still imagine the burning forests of *Red Skies of Montana,* the falls and bells of *Niagara,* the luxurious smoking in the first reel of *Moulin Rouge,* or Australia inhabited by the blue marsupials seen in

Kangaroo, a stricter haul will bring us a fairly poor catch. By over-looking, perhaps wrongly, the formal virtuosity of certain young filmmakers who play in the infrared of production, the division of what counts (in satisfaction as well as in disappointment) will be established as follows. On the rise: Fred Zinnemann, George Stevens, and the meteoric *Lili.* Stable or on borrowed time: Gene Kelly, Vincente Minnelli, and William Wyler. And declining or plummeting: Ford, Huston, Hathaway, Mankiewicz, Hitchcock, and Kazan.

But this manner of citing directors is a European foible. My Hollywood stay taught me that the distance between filmmaker and film is generally greater here than in France or in England, and infinitely greater than in the USSR. That a director like Huston is unable to edit his own film strikes us as outrageous. On the other hand, the producer's creative input is constant, for better or for worse. There we have a delicate system to assess, and which only becomes really familiar to us when the filmmaker is also his own producer, as in the case of George Stevens (and as a result gives us his best films. Coincidence?). Generally the producer adds or subtracts (and from there these zones, these stylistic and psychological restitutions that convey the impression of seeing three films all at once). Occasionally, he fits right in.

This is obviously the case for Stanley Kramer, whose production system is founded on intelligence. Within this system Zinnemann's talent developed. But if at the time of *High Noon* praise could be divvied up between Kramer, Zinnemann, Tiomkin's music, and Floyd Crosby's images that made a sensational film, the direction of *The Member of the Wedding*—and if the recent news from New York can be believed, *From Here to Eternity*—seems to prove that Fred Zinnemann has earned his place among the top directors. Against the general tendency to break the dramatic mold and to restore the ambiguities of reality with more or less cunning, Zinnemann plays the game of dramatic space and time with a sort of classical purity. Whether he is provided with a screenplay as sharp and taut as that of Carl Foreman's in *High Noon,* or with a

George Stevens's Western *Shane* (1953) about a gunfighter (Alan Ladd) whose friendship with a homesteader family involves him in a local range war.

nuanced text like Carson McCullers's play, the basis for *The Member of the Wedding*, Zinnemann always finds the same starting point in his screenplays. The part is sacrificed to the whole and each formal experiment—lord knows they exist—combines with others until invisible, like a text uniformly underlined, instead of standing out in grandiose set pieces. Zinnemann perhaps draws this equilibrium, this rigor, this luxurious austerity from his experience as an editor. At the same time by his indifference to the plot's geography, and his almost abstract taste for rhythms and volumes, he places himself for the moment (but perhaps it's only a phase) diametrically opposed to realism, that is, from Stevens.

I regret not meeting Stevens in Hollywood. Because I would have liked to ask him to what extent he was conscious of being Orson Welles's heir. Everyone I asked assured me that Welles's time in Hollywood was little more than an inconsequential flash in the pan, devoid of any real influence on the history of American film style. It seems to me, however, that there's a lineage from *The Magnificent Ambersons* to *Something to Live For* (absurdly renamed in France *L'Ivresse et l'amour [Drunkenness and Love]*) to *Sunset Boulevard*. Because despite a weaker screenplay and in any case less accessible to a European audience than *A Place in the Sun*, *Something to Live For* will have been Stevens's most revelatory work prior to *Shane*. We sometimes wonder if Stevens isn't first of all someone who knows how to marvelously place his characters beyond door frames, curtains, furniture, companions crossing the screen and blocking our vision with a nonchalance as studied as that of flâneurs who cross the stage for no apparent reason in Agnes de Mille's choreography. Unbelievably, he also dares to film an exchange between two persons in a static shot in almost complete darkness. (This obscurity can convey a feeling of censorship, for example, in the erotic bedroom scene in *A Place in the Sun*.) We can well wonder if all that makes a style, as we might wonder if with Welles we weren't fooled by a banal text . . . wonderfully punctuated. But there is something more in *Something to Live For:* the meticulous description of characters in their milieu, the use of time restored until being perceptible (that is to say intolerable), and the camera's intrusion as it jostles among obstacles, which gives our viewing a pleasantly ambiguous nature—that's not far from turning the spectator into a voyeur. Despite an impressive Oscar, it is perhaps in *A Place in the Sun* that Stevens was the least at ease—because of the fragmentation and the temporal strides required by the abridgement (unfaithful, otherwise) of Dreiser's novel.[7] In *Something to Live For* as in *Shane,* the action is divided into very long continuous periods, where dramatic time gets under the spectator's skin and destroys them like napalm. The same fastidious concern for the layout of places, for the weight of objects and things, that can be confused with simple craftsmanship in *A Place in the Sun* and *Something to Live For,* but that assumes its full import in *Shane.*

In the latter, for the first time, the most glorified genre, the Western, finds itself exorcized. For the first time, the misery of the landscape, the depth of the mud, the cramped saloon where the chairs have to be pulled back for two men to have enough space to fight. And for the first time, too, the degeneration of a character and a soul to the traditional "bad guy": the first enemy occupant of the good farmer, who in a plea of singular greatness recalls what life was like for the pioneers. *High Noon* remains the Western's chef-d'œuvre, but *Shane* is something else. Their only point

Studio publicity photo of Leslie Caron as lead character in *Lili* (1953), a lighthearted U.S. musical comedy about a naïve sixteen-year-old whose infatuation with a group of itinerant carnival performers is staged through puppet theater.

in common is the mythological subject of man alone. Man alone is by definition defeated: this is the lesson of *To Have and Have Not*. But man alone and winner is consequently the world's most powerful myth that moreover knows no fellowship. Alan Ladd in *Shane*, freeing the country of its oppressors and starting afresh in abandoning an unrequited love, is *Parsifal*'s final chapter. About Charles Walters's *Lili* I won't say much: everyone will agree about it, or not. That it is possible that so many heavy and complicated things—giraffes, projectors, cameras, foot-operated cranes, hydraulic trolleys, what do I know, with their bespectacled Martian crews, switchgears, helmets, their armchairs on wheels, and their enemy ears—all lean forward as Leslie Caron whispers her dialogue without disturbing it seems nothing short of a miracle. Unless it's Leslie Caron, if we reverse this proposition, who is herself akin to a miracle. This seems not to have been the opinion of most critics. But then miracles aren't usually recognized by doctors, but by the healed.

Leaving Wyler and Hitchcock to their experts, we quickly arrive at various stalemates and disappointments. The unfulfilled promise of a dazzling *American* like Gene Kelly is not to be expected in *Singin' in the Rain*—alas disappointing in its trite screenplay, excessive references to *On the Town* and *An American in Paris*, as well as its unwillingness to tenderly mock Hollywood's awkward age—but rather in this *Invitation to the Dance*. Vincente Minnelli, responsible for the intelligent direction of this last film, gave us with *The Bad and the Beautiful* a little Hollywood chronicle at once too faithful to the frivolity of its subject ("the characters are superficial, but the people that they depict are even more so," a producer told me) and too subtle in its game of hide-and-seek with the censors to be appreciated at its true value. Regarding John Ford, we're familiar with his adage: "Subject or not, what counts is being on set at 8 a.m. every day." This solid, workmanlike ethic explains his directing films as incredible as *The Sun Shines Bright* and *What Price Glory*. In the latter film—which probably won't be released

in France since it's set in the command post of an American pla-
toon during World War I—surrounded by a uniformly ridiculous
and venal French population (with the exception of a young lady
who sings and Corinne Calvet who tries to), we would like to be
sure that Ford intentionally chose colors from the front covers of
the *Saturday Evening Post* of the period—as Becker adopted the
style of the *Petit Journal illustré* for *Casque d'or.* But with this incredible fellow we're always left wondering.[8] That said, the scenes
between a gout-stricken James Cagney and Dan Dailey are wonderfully executed. At the very least Ford remains a director who
knows how to push a situation to the extreme and exploit all its
dramatic possibilities. *The Quiet Man,* which preceded these two
films, had all these qualities and the additional virtue of an entertaining screenplay and the beauty of Maureen O'Hara. These of-
ferings from a man who knows his profession better than anyone
give us predictable pleasure. By dint of being at the studio every
morning at 8 o'clock, John Ford may still (while laughing about it)
surprise us.

Huston's case, on the other hand, is more serious.[9] Few filmmakers have consistently demonstrated so resolute a unity of concerns. Interestingly, the young French critics responded more to
his screenplays' shortcomings in character development than to
this fundamental virtue whose failure merely highlights profound
sobriety. This is particularly true in a country like America where
luck, secular Providence, always tends to diminish virtue by rewarding it: energy in the Stendhalian sense. A screenwriter before becoming a filmmaker, which isn't necessarily a bad thing,
Huston can claim to be the champion of a very special category
of "literary" cinema (nothing pejorative about that either). Both of
his ambitious projects were beautiful stories of pure energy: *Moby
Dick* and *The Red Badge of Courage,* the latter an adaptation of Stephen Crane's Civil War novel. I advise the reader to consult Lillian
Ross's remarkable book, *Picture,* for details on the machinations
by which *The Red Badge of Courage*—accepted by MGM against

Louis B. Mayer's will—was sabotaged, perverted, and then, almost not released. The tampering that was supposed to transform (fortunately without success) this hymn to man into a soldier's eulogy, nevertheless failed to mask a mise-en-scène that hits a bull's-eye. The mise-en-scène eliminating the era's consciousness reproduces war's reality—its courage and fear—and in its "Fabrice in Waterloo" aspect suddenly and fully justifies the Stendhalian reference.

But *The Red Badge* was a trying experience for everyone. After Huston's departure, its producer Gottfried Reinhardt was left all alone to defend the film. Having understood the lesson, Reinhardt became a filmmaker, and his film, *The Story of Three Loves,* completely acquiesces to public tastes. Dore Schary, who had supported Reinhardt at MGM, and was kept on only because the head honchos in New York had an interest in substituting him for the less malleable Louis B. Mayer, also understood. It's ironic to see that Schary, once Mayer's *bête noire* because of his daring ideas, is today producing—form follows function—exactly the same kind of virtuous and conformist films *(Plymouth Adventure, The Next Voice You Hear)* as his former boss. It seems that Huston also got the message. Add to that the personal misfortune of seeing *The Red Badge of Courage* massacred, together with the aforementioned political climate and the enormous funding requirements: clearly, it was no longer time to take risks. Although perfectly well made, *The African Queen* redistributed all Huston's creative gifts, exchanging exploration and toughness into tints of facility and seduction. He confided to Reinhardt that "I'll never be embarrassed to make a lot of money." This can serve as an epigraph to *The African Queen* as well as to *Moulin Rouge.* Here, we can admire the fine work of Eliot Elisofon and be bowled over by Colette Marchand. But as far as Huston is concerned, we can only wish that he make a lot of money, for damages and interest.

As for Henry Hathaway, he had his own *Red Badge* with *Fourteen Hours.* The weak spot of this excellent film, where the void below the hero becomes almost a parable for the world of tragedy, was a mediocre screenplay, weighed down by a dime-store psycho-analysis. I learned that the original screenplay was censored and diluted until this fine result (with the added luxury of two endings, one optimistic and the other pessimistic, depending on the au-diences). Hathaway thus decided to have some fun. *Niagara,* the result of this amusement, is an anthology piece. Rarely has a di-rector attached himself so fiercely to reinforce the absurdity of his screenplay and his actress. With the caveat that we're left wonder-ing if Miss Monroe doesn't pass herself off as more idiotic than she really is for obscure advertising purposes. What prevents me from fully enjoying these operations is that with Hathaway we're losing another Stevens. But I'm guessing that Charles Einfeld, the man who invented Marilyn Monroe, must be enjoying the demonic glee of alchemists.

Joseph L. Mankiewicz's *Julius Caesar* delivered a particular kind of disappointment. It is unusual to see a Hollywood adapta-tion of Shakespeare and Roman history err by excessive respect. Nevertheless, the film's constant inhibition, rigidity, and narrow-mindedness are ultimately fatal. A comparison with Olivier's films would be unbearable.[10] But at least it would demonstrate the dif-ference between the likeness of a play and its kitsch counterpart. A fake fidelity—the height of treason—is served however by a won-derful cast, where the Hollywood cohort (Marlon Brando, Louis Calhern, Edmond O'Brien) hold their own opposite the classic, British element (James Mason, John Gielgud). The very concep-tion of the roles of Mark Antony and Caesar (oddly heightened in our eyes by Louis Calhern's resemblance to General de Gaulle) is interesting. Unfortunately, all these performances are for naught, due to a bland mise-en-scène whose textual hyperfidelity para-doxically leads us to the same infantile Romans as Cecil B. DeMi-lle in his follies.

But these satisfactions and disappointments play on a very thin surface production. Dean Martin and Jerry Lewis, Ma and Pa Kettle (more or less, Hardy family heirs), a great many musical comedies of consistent perfection of acts, and even Fred C. Brannon's episodic worldwide *(King of the Rocket Men)*—which are to Feuillade what the *Pieds Nickelés* are to Töpffer but whose works don't lack charm—finally play a more important sociological role than anything we have said here. We would like to believe, as the critics do, that cinema's crisis is above all a crisis of subject matter and that the American public smolders in the expectation of good films. But it's a pity that a film like *Bwana Devil,* simply by virtue of a poorly used optical trick, can find an audience.

The purely commercial reflex of "looking for novelty" had at least the happy result of tearing cinema from its entrenchment in standardization, thus reconnecting it with a normal technical evolution. Many researchers (Abel Gance in France with his three screens, Spottiswoode in England with relief film) had foreseen the forms without however being able to advance beyond their personal endeavors. On the one hand, the idea of relief, without being as decisive as sound or color, could be expected as a new and normal stage in the history of representation. On the other hand, absolutely arbitrary screen proportions standardized by convenience have become a vision of "mask" or picture rather incompatible with the realist tendency of modern cinema. It is thus on these two points of change in filmic space in depth and in width that the battle for renewal is played out. It is obviously the wide screen that opens a more fertile path than 3-D. But these things are considered by another critic, in another chapter.

Thus, Hollywood—which has invented nothing but consistently found in Europe, explored or imported, sources for renewal—will continue leading cinema's evolution by brute force of Phynance.[11] In the shadow of this carnival of abstract marvels, it is just as important to witness the birth of a production infinitely more humble in its means while focused on a less glamorous image of America. The important films of 1953 for me are *Little Fugitive,* made by Joe Burstyn's crew who made *The Quiet One,* and *Man Crazy* by Irving Lerner, who also did *Muscle Beach.*[12] And above all it is important that producer Paul Jarrico, screenwriter Michael Wilson (both blacklisted), and director Herbert Biberman, one of the former "Hollywood Ten," managed by sheer willpower to finish their film, *Salt of the Earth,* in Mexico, a film on New Mexican miners' plight, whose shoot began in Silver City, New Mexico.[13]

The real homage to this film's modest undertaking, seemingly nonexistent opposite the behemoths of 3-D and wide-screen (albeit by a preliminary shrinkage, as in the so-called panoramic cinemas where the top of a normal image is cut off in order to give it new proportions) is seen in the relentlessness with which the vilest means were used in order to destroy it. From the arrest of the Mexican star by the immigration authorities to the organized street fights, including a producer who said he held the rights to the film (no, not Rouquier) and other antics, everything was done to keep the film from being finished.[14] Today, it is finished. It is only natural that the body and soul of American cinema will at times evolve in very strange directions. May they one day coincide.

ANIMATION FILM
UPA

DURING THE LAST CANNES FESTIVAL, WALT DISNEY REPORT-
edly said: "I pride myself on having developed a nearly perfect
technique for animation. It's now up to others to pursue creative
advances." If this quotation is accurate, it suggests more modesty
and lucidity than we would have expected from Mickey's father. It
is certainly true that until recently, Disney represented technical
perfection. And it would be absurd—given his overwhelming bad
taste, megalomania, and production methods that have little to
do with an enlightened democracy—to deny the sort of genius he
has invested in his work. The complete conquest of animation's expressive potential (even false and betrayed ones like Fischinger's in
Fantasia) was necessary and undoubtedly demanded this concen-
tration, this dictatorship from the sole studio capable of achieving it.[1]

Still, everything has a price. And this triumph over technique
has caused animation's current impasse. Animation is triply constrained to scorn its sources and childish imagery. First, by a

Signed: Chris Marker

Source: chapter 11 in *Cinéma 53: À Travers le monde,* Collection "7e art" (Paris:
Le Cerf, 1954), 137–43. Other authors in this 194-page volume include André
Bazin, Jacques Doniol-Valcroze, Gavin Lambert, and Jean Queval.

"plumpish" figurative style that prevailed until those who wanted
to reject its style (Grimault, unfortunately[2]); second, by the submission of this imagery to a simplistic morality, a sadism for a
clear conscience (the wolf's torture by the pigs), and a basic an-
thropomorphism; and finally by a stalemate of all fantasy and true
poetry weighed down by a verisimilitude that pairs nicely with
the characters' moral constraints. Felix the Cat's enormous visual
freedom—making a banjo of the setting sun behind a palm tree,
replacing his tail by a question mark—is unthinkable in a Disney
world of obedient cats, weeping does, well-behaved rabbits, and
chastened bad guys.* The fact remains that the Disney dialectic,
if it isn't made for dogs, operates on mice. Walt Disney's principal merit will have been—thanks to his technical superiority—
the training of young talents endowed with a taste superior to his
own. His management and the ensuing conflicts forced the aforementioned talents into a freedom with which they had to make do.

The great strike of 1941 in the Walt Disney studios would give
rise to a team that, in 1953, succeeded in opposing him on production grounds. During that strike, any individuals suspected of
progressivism or union steadfastness were eliminated. As it happened, they were the most aesthetically advanced. Reunited under

---

* Cannes screened Disney's *Peter Pan* (1953), a film situated in its progeni-
tor's impassive and endless career end, with the same certainty of pencil
and the same confiseries. Let's call it an intermezzo aesthetic. Cannes also
screened Disney's medium-length film with live action—the studio has recently increased its output—from the series "That's Life" (aquatic birds). It is
composed of shots filmed by a good many directors (amateurs and professionals, ornithologists and laymen) purchased at great cost. The Disney studios
adroitly edited the footage, ultimately creating a kind of ballet. This fare de-
lighted several audiences. Still, we must protest against the vulgarity and the
misdirection of an undertaking that subjects the bird, a royal creature, to the
filmmaker's amusement, instead of the other way around. A screening of this
clever, more shameless than indecent film should be followed by the wonderful *Vadvízország* (*Kingdom on the Waters,* Hungary, 1952) in order to allow its
fans to appreciate the pleasant fraud.—J.Q. [The byline J.Q. refers to the critic
Jean Queval, the author of five articles in *Cinéma 53.* —Translator.]

the title United Productions of America, or UPA, they first worked for the army. Under the leadership of Stephen Bosustow, who went from Hollywood to the Bureau of Army Newsreels, they quickly established themselves as a political and artistic avant-garde.[3] Their first major success was a cartoon for the United Automobile Workers' Union (UAW), made to counter racial prejudices: *Brotherhood of Man.*

This short film broke with all Disneyesque practices. It offers an adult subject matter, human characters, a purposefully unrealistic style (moreover employing figurative techniques that could be mistaken for Saul Steinberg, the greatest American cartoonist). For the first time since Berthold Bartosch's *Idea* and Gross and Hoppin's *La Joie de vivre,* the cartoon asserts itself qua drawing. It finds its path in an internal logic—synonymous with its nature, and not to any angelic filtering of the real—and with a heightened credibility and power of conviction.[4]

But it is Robert Cannon who first brought the discussion to public attention. In 1950 he adapted a story by writer and cartoonist Ted Geisel, better known in the United States as Dr. Seuss. It told the story of a young boy with a mechanical voice. Although unable to speak, he is gifted with an ability to reproduce all kinds of sounds—automobile horns, advancing tanks, whistles, and bagpipes. This idiosyncrasy, which initially concerned his parents and got him kicked out of school, later earned him fame with a radio audience more attuned to noises than words. This story, and its makers' willingness to treat it with the proper analysis and stylization, might have frightened the Columbia studio that now oversees UPA. But the year has been good, and the most conventional films made after the contract with Columbia *(Robin Hoodlum* and *The Magic Fluke)* both won Oscars. Cannon was thus allowed to pursue his "artistic adventure." The result was *Gerald McBoing-Boing,* the most successful cartoon short to date (including Disney's).[5] The drawings by Cannon's team (still very Steinbergian, especially the sets), Geisel's text, and Gail Kubik's music made not the slightest concession to what the producers purported to be the public's preferences. Nevertheless, the public made such a triumph of *Gerald* that the producers, while despising this "artistic adventure," were embarrassed by their error and rushed to fix it. In so doing they committed a second error by commissioning a sequel from UPA: *Gerald McBoing-Boing's Symphony* (1953).

UPA was now no longer just a group of avant-garde researchers getting by on official commissions. The studio enjoyed public popularity and could hire the technicians and artists it wanted. By carefully choosing his collaborators and granting them a productive freedom in their work, Bosustow transformed UPA into the world's most advanced center for cartoon production, with the exception of the Trnka studio in Czechoslovakia. Regular commissions from the army, technical agencies, and television (no less aesthetically interesting than commercial films) with interventions in films like *Dreamboat,* with its false TV ads, *The Girl Next Door,* or the intermissions of Stanley Kramer's film *The Four Poster,* were at once the cause and fruit of this success.[6] Meanwhile, simple cartoons continued to provide the genre its newest and most refreshing elements by introducing dialogue (before UPA, no one seriously discussed an animated film's dialogue) and the characters' transformation. The animals themselves, still hindered in early efforts by Disneyism, were eventually set free. Take, for example, the wonderful blue horse taking the stage to save his dairy boss from ruin and Mr. Magoo's dog. Magoo himself, an honest, nearsighted fellow, was initially invented as a secondary role in an earlier production, but quickly became a UPA star.

The hero's break with the world—which Mickey's kindness prevented him from finding, and that made Pluto's cowardice, Donald's bitterness, and Goofy's stupidity the effective star—that Woody Woodpecker finds in madness and Tom and Jerry in their mutual hatred—Mr. Magoo finds in his myopia. It is characteristic of the UPA spirit that it is a physical handicap (but one never perceived as a disability, thanks to Mr. Magoo's ever victorious dynamism and self-assurance) and not a moral defect that is the source of the hero's adventures. Perhaps. In any case, we can also believe in Mr. Magoo's existence, a filmic creation, and see in him a new creation of importance: W. C. Fields's unexpected on-screen heir.

Today UPA is all-powerful. It can give life and credibility, psychology, and consistency to an animation. It can also appropriate a visual system and convert it into movement. *Madeline,* adapted from Ludwig Bemelmans's famous children's book, is one of the most disturbing experiences there is. We've often seen an animation drawing inspired by still images with greater or less fidelity. Here, Bemelmans's own drawings come alive, as strictly faithful to each image as if the author, suddenly now a technician, had drawn each of them himself. A UPA representative in New York told me that "We can animate anything." And this height of freedom that is submission without deviation to a style opens cartoons to still more perspective. It's worth recalling that *The Blood of a Poet* was initially to have been an animated film.[7] Currently, the metamorphosis is occurring in James Thurber. We are already ecstatic at the thought of soon seeing animated the prodigious creation of characters begotten by the most firmly idle pencil possible.

It was unfortunately logical that in gaining importance and money, UPA also won respectability. Not on a moral or aesthetic level, where you're most left alone these days in the United States, but on a political level. The group's left wing already broke free and the shift seemingly continues, since John Hubley, UPA's vice-president and personally responsible for its best work, has just resigned. I am sorry for Hubley, UPA, animated films, and America.

The bedazzlement inspired by the UPA cartoons make us judge unfairly the rest of production, which is much less revolutionary, but still far ahead of the Disney aesthetic. I already mentioned Walter Lantz's creation, Woody Woodpecker, which for a year won the contest in the realm of a goofy temper over Donald Duck. As free in his relationship with forms as the late Felix—lowering a window in

Frame grabs from *Madeline* (1952), Robert Cannon's Oscar-nominated animated short about a young girl's misadventures at a boarding school in Paris.

a wall or curtain shutters until they disappear and blend into the wall, learning how to chop up his enemy by discovering sausage-cutting machines on a desert island, further gifted with top-notch musical scores—Woody, a myth of free enterprise, seems now to slow down. As far as we can judge (but distribution for animated film is done in such a way that happenstance alone determines our investigations), Fred Quimby's productions are second in quality after UPA. In particular his *Tom and Jerry* cartoons, which although loathsome in their abstract violence, are still exceptionally paced, ever effective in their jokes, and are sometimes endowed with—as in *Johann Mouse* where Tom plays the piano and Jerry dances in the Austrian court—an original poetry.

On the American continent, there is another, widely known production center: Canada's National Film Board, where Norman

McLaren has created animated films directly onto filmstock. At the time of the Festival of Great Britain, his abstract fantasies incidentally led him to animated film in relief and thus to the proof that 3-D lends itself much more to abstraction than to realism. *Around Is Around* and *Now Is the Time* will remain the real landmarks of 3-D film, not *Bwana Devil*.

Unfortunately, McLaren now devotes a large part of his time to a different abstraction, that of UNESCO, and has abandoned his research in directly drawn images, 3-D, and synthetic etching. But at least there is in Ottawa an excellent team of animators headed by Colin Low whose *The Romance of Transportation* we saw at Cannes (afflicted, alas, with a questionable title in French).[8] It is a kind of minor masterpiece, employing a modern drawing style with almost as much grace as UPA. A style that we find in most of the NFB's technical films, as in those produced in Hollywood by admirable small teams (Churchill–Wexler, among others). But medical, educational, and scientific films still remain outside the purview of critics. May 1983 come quickly and may the cinémathèques open up.

ON THE WATERFRONT

IT'S WELL KNOWN THAT CINEMA HAS MORE TALENT THAN filmmakers. Here's a film that testifies once again to the maturity of the machine and the puerility of men. Or at least to their duplicity. It is sheathed in a formal perfection that American cinema still monopolizes; its different themes (whether explicit, implicit, hidden, or alibi) play a brilliant game of hide-and-seek, and set all kinds of traps. Since the film is about longshoremen, enthusiasts of that world will discover here, via the subject, a technical quality otherwise invisible to them in a film about cowboys or motorcyclists.

And as the subject in question is incredibly confused, others will be blinded to it to the point of denying said quality. But what quality? And what subject? Well, then, we can try to define this visual quality common to most great works of American cinema by the concurrence of a photographic aesthetic that we can rightfully call today the "New York School," without forgetting that it is the Frenchman Cartier-Bresson who activated its crystallization.[1] This is a photo that turns its back on "beautiful photography" to exploit its own resources—the grain, contrasts, cropped

Review of Elia Kazan's *On the Waterfront*, released July 28, 1954, in the United States and September 1954 in France. Signed: C.M.

Source: *Esprit*, n.s., no. 224 (March 1955): 440–43.

framing, the white that burns, the black that smothers, the gray that dissolves—in short by using for "realistic" ends what least "resembles" it. Thereby undoing its curse of having been born of an apparatus of imitation, by meeting *art* in its willingness to destroy appearances to recover meaning—with (it's a question of the concurrence) a dramaturgy hostile to balance that contains a twist that seeks to break the dramatic mold, by preserving in the filmed event its possibilities of obliqueness, escape, surprise or the unexplained, while also loading each of these elements, freed from the plot, with a tension as strong as the filmmaker's imagination matched by the technicians' instinct to realize it.

Insofar as *On the Waterfront* plays a part in this school, it offers us its best moments: the walk in the square, the trial, the fight, and above all the *roof,* with its pigeons, its television antennae, and the Hudson River in the background—we think of the *roof* in *On the Waterfront* much as we think of the *mud* in *Shane* or the *studio* in *Sunset Boulevard:* special circumstances in which the dramatic space far exceeds its function as a "set" and fits into the action that inhabits it like syntax in a story. Similarly, this willingness not to *develop,* not to force the *climax* (by comparison the best European cinema, except for Clément and Becker, is out-of-date): a man gives evidence in a trial; everything rests on his testimony. Traditionally, our attention would be gradually centered on him, until he lets out his crucial answer and "resolves" the scene. But here we have brief shots and brief questions. In a skillful mismatch Brando, conveying to the viewer his "impression of being elsewhere," answers off to the side until the moment when the scene cuts to a television screen, only to be switched off right before the crucial answer. . . . Still, even that, which could be an "effect," isn't one: we cut back to the *attorney* whose commentary immediately clarifies what this answer was.[2] Thus, no dramatic climax, no surprise effect, no high point—achieving in just a few seconds all the psychological insight that we would have thought only a first-rate novelist would be able to express, and in words.

Similarly, this fight devoid of sadistic and theatrical insistence: just a few huffing blows depicted with verisimilitude, naturalness, and at the same time, if you will, originality—and all of a sudden the framing hides what is most important—a head suddenly blocks the silhouette of two men in the background. After years of exhibitionism, the image has finally discovered the value of understatement.

But not everything is of this quality. And unfortunately it's precisely when the screenwriter or the director shows their true colors, one by his hypocrisy and guilty conscience, the other by his excessive fondness for the theatre, that things go awry. Everything happens as if, in the American cinema of today, routine was brilliant and intention abnormal.

Intentions are certainly not lacking here, from the excessive allusions to the McCarthyist climate, to Brando's metamorphosis into a proletarian Christ. How to explain that every time intentions like these become explicit the film grows dull and ridiculous? It's hard to imagine, for example, that a longshoreman whose crew wants to get rid of him plays along by remaining all alone in the middle of the hold, just when a shipment, deliberately unbalanced, comes along to crush him. Or that a scene between two men in a taxi having an incriminating conversation continues until one of them remains alone—and that at that moment, while it becomes clear that the cab driver is a spy, fate would have it that he finds himself exactly where the killers are going to grab him. Poetic license, shortcut, or aesthetic concern? No, because what would have been acceptable in 1930 isn't any longer, and in 1954 plausibility has become an aesthetic value. Such facile solutions don't seriously affect the plot's credibility, but are inimical to its overall style. And this is why the famous "passion" scene at the end of the film—Brando's stumbling among the dockers until he reaches the indifferent and completely implausible boss—along with the teetering, subjective camerawork, is absolutely unbearable: it's theatre of the worst kind, despite all the technical skill. This theatrical impulse often ruins Elia Kazan's art (similar to George Stevens because in many ways their styles are comparable), but here he is not the only one to reproach, and it seems that the screenwriter Budd Schulberg has his fair share of blame.

It is known that Schulberg's behavior before the [HUAC] *Investigators* was far from exemplary.[3] It would be unseemly to dwell on it if there weren't in the screenplay an ambiguity that can only be the fruit of a guilty conscience. One example: at one point the policeman says to Brando: "I remind you that you have the right not to answer questions that could incriminate you." There is some reason to see in this allusion to the Fifth Amendment an intentional response, perhaps a cue for applause ("We live under a prince who is an enemy to conspiracy."[4]). But at the same time this reply is addressed to the accomplice of dangerous criminals, who can make only the worst use of this right conceded to him. What then? A reminder or a travesty of democratic freedoms? Take your pick. Perhaps both. We can imagine how, in this fairly dehumanized and inhuman Hollywood, that self-loathing has reached the point where nostalgia and ridicule are indistinguishable. The two form a smoky black fire, caught in the blades of the best-oiled machine ever, yielding the best cinema in the world. But let's not delude ourselves that this backdrop of priest, gangsters, and longshoremen prevents us from seeing that this film is the story of a whistleblower trading *omertà,* even friendship, for a state policy based on snitching. All this derives infinitely more from McCarthyism than from the holier-than-thou lesson of a working-class morality that it supposedly imparts.

But is this really the film's subject, this morality lesson, this "moral awakening," as is pompously said? As tough as American trade unionism may be, it's hard to find in this world of sheeplike, passive dockers, where labor solidarity has been replaced by the underworld's unwritten rules, any hint of "social" values. Maybe this wasn't how it really happened, since *Waterfront* is based on a true story, but it certainly isn't in the film.[5] Neither at the end nor

in the beginning. At no point does Marlon Brando's trajectory resemble an awakening concerning class issues.

The film's setting may pass it off as a "social" film, just as the
presence of the priest passes it off as a "religious" film, and too
bad for those who fall for it. But this double fraud doesn't explain
everything. From certain signs we can guess another subject, another itinerary—parallel but secret—hiding behind these crude
and convenient screens. Another consciousness. . . . And in my
opinion: the consciousness of the woman.

Brando's character in fact helps us detect this hidden gem, this
pullout subject.[6] This extraordinary actor, despite his tics, is undoubtedly the most astonishing cinema creature that we've seen
in recent years. His profile gives him away; this profile that Cocteau in *The White Book* claims to recognize wherever it hides. And
to see between him and the gang leader the same ambiguous relationship that he made palpable in the 1953 Mankiewicz film, between Mark Antony and Caesar, sets us on the right track. Let us
look more closely at this gang, their café, these meetings where no
woman's face ever appears. . . . Now compare that to *Touchez pas
au Grisbi [Don't Touch the Loot]* where immediately we see appear,
whether harried or ignored, a bevy of girlfriends. Let's also consider, on the one hand, the protagonist's relations with the gang
leader: this sham aggressivity, these schoolboy pokes, this taste
for physical contact. (The homosexual significance of fighting is
well known.) And on the other hand, his relations with the young
men of the boxing club, their jealousy, their stubborn misogyny
(the rooftop scene with the pigeons). We're in a virile environment,
and Brando's story is his escape from this universe in favor of the
woman. Ultimately, it is for her and through her that he *betrays*.
We can see here the Nazi mythology hovering in the background.
In any event censorship made it difficult to handle the subject
more candidly. A theme infinitely more compelling than the other.
But how not to see it surface at every moment? And as far as awak-
enings go, Eva Marie Saint is, my God, highly recommended.

However, it is nonetheless true that this story of a converted homosexual, burdened by his conscience as a penitent whistleblower,
has been camouflaged as a Christian allegory, for which it even
won the Catholic Organization's Grand Prize at the Venice Film
Festival. Forgive us for not elaborating on this particular topic.[7]
Except for a high-powered priest, an Alain Resnais lookalike, and
his virtuous (but ineffective) outcries, I challenge the coolheaded
viewer to find anything Christian in all this.[8] Remove the priest,
the story remains essentially the same, to a metaphor, and moves
in a world as foreign to Christianity as that of the *Pieds-Nickelés*.[9]
But no matter: the priest is there, the words are pronounced, the
signs are made, nominalism prevails, and Rome gives its blessing.
All that was needed was a priestly collar—the poor man's halo. It's
been a long time, in Christendom, since we've been offered a world
where clothes make the man.

TRANSLATOR'S NOTES

Henry V's White Horse

1. Besides Malraux, Marker's ideas here also suggest his familiarity with André Bazin's seminal essay "The Ontology of the Photographic Image," first published in Gaston Diehl's edited volume *Les Problèmes de la peinture* (Lyon: Confluences, 1945).

2. From the anonymous play *The Mystery of the Passion,* first performed in Paris by the Confraternity of the Passion in 1402.

3. *Ivan the Terrible* (1944) is Sergei Eisenstein's two-part epic historical drama.

4. From the Chorus's Prologue in the Oxford Shakespeare, *Henry V.*

5. In English in the original.

6. The film's mise-en-scène reproduces pages from the *Très Riches Heures du duc de Berry* (1412–16), the most famous example of late Gothic manuscript illumination.

7. The French painter Jean or Jehan Fouquet (ca. 1420–1481) was a noted master of manuscript illumination and apparent inventor of the portrait miniature.

8. The writer and political activist Francis Jeanson (1922–2009) was introduced to the *Esprit* group by Emmanuel Mounier in 1948. At Seuil, Jeanson oversaw the series "Écrivains de toujours," to which he contributed a volume on Montaigne (1951) and Marker his volume on Giraudoux (1952).

9. The English kings, including Henry V, were descendants of the Norman warrior William the Conqueror, who became monarch of England in 1066 after winning the Battle of Hastings. William never mastered the English language, and for several hundred years French was the language of the English court. Henry IV, Henry V's father, was the first English king since William the Conqueror whose first language was English.

10. Signed on May 21, 1420, the Treaty of Troyes was an agreement that King Henry V and his heirs would inherit the French throne after the death of the French King Charles VI. The treaty was signed following Henry's successful military campaign in France during which 40 percent of French nobility perished. Following the decisive intervention of Joan of Arc in support of the French Dauphin, Charles VII, the French ultimately won the war at the Battle of Castillon in 1453.

11. *Holinshed's Chronicles* (1577) was an extensive collaborative work that provided historical source material during the English Renaissance to writers including Marlowe and Spencer. Shakespeare used the *Chronicles* for more than a third of his plays.

12. In *The Jungle Book* (1894), Rudyard Kipling uses the term *Bandar-Logs* to refer to monkeys in Seeonee Jungle.

13. Roger Boutet de Monvel (1879–1951) was a French writer of historical studies.

14. *The Most Dangerous Game* (1932) is a film by Ernest B. Schoedsack and Irving Pichel, based on Richard Connell's eponymous novella (1924).

15. Olivier's production was budgeted at £475,708 or $1,311,051 USD. Marker's reference to *Ben-Hur* is presumably to the 1925 version, budgeted at $4 million. Closer in time to *Henry V* is the epic blockbuster *Quo Vadis* (1951), budgeted at $7.6 million.

The Imperfect of the Subjective

1. In 1930 André Malraux published his novel *The Royal Way,* a tale of two nonconformist adventurers Vannec and the older Perken, who travel on the "Royal Way" to Angkor in the Cambodian jungle. The novel is often regarded as a companion to Conrad's *Heart of Darkness* (1899).

2. A year after adapting and starring in a radio broadcast version of *Heart of Darkness* on November 6, 1938, Welles offered RKO Pictures a 174-page adaptation of it.

3. Montgomery participated in the decisive Battle of Normandy, a.k.a. Operation Overlord, in June 1944.

4. At the urging of John Rankin, Congress created the House Committee for the Investigation of Un-American Activities (subsequently and forever after mislabeled HUAC) a standing committee. Under Rankin's unofficial leadership, HUAC investigated the Communist Party in the United States. In 1947 actor Robert Montgomery was among a group of so-called friendly witnesses who testified before the committee.

5. Boris Vian's first wife, Michelle Léglise, introduced him to various Anglo-Saxon authors and collaborated with him on several translations.

Corneille at the Movies

1. In English in the text.

2. Founded in 1920 in the western Paris suburb, the Sèvres High School was established as a feeder school for female students for the Sèvres École Normale Supérieure. German forces occupied the high school during World War II. In 1945 it reopened as the International Center of Pedagogical Studies.

3. Corneille's 1640 play drew on the fratricidal battle between the Horatii and the Curatii described by the Roman historian Livy. Corneille wrote it in response to criticism of his 1636 play *Le Cid* and dedicated it to Cardinal Richelieu. Considered one of Corneille's greatest tragedies and a resounding success at its premiere in 1640, *Horace* helped inaugurate French classical tragedy.

4. The term *bobby soxer* first appeared in a 1943 *Time* article referring to teenage girls who were fans of popular music, particularly Frank Sinatra, and wore ankle socks called bobby socks.

5. Cocteau did indeed write the screenplay of *Ruy Blas,* based on Victor Hugo's eponymous play, for the 1948 film adaptation directed by Pierre Billon and starring Marais, Danielle Darrieux, and Marcel Herrand.

6. Marker refers here to *L'Écran français,* a weekly with Communist leanings published from 1943 until 1952.

7. *The Eternal Return* (1943): Jean Delannoy's romantic retelling of the Tristan and Isolde legend.

8. Pierre Corneille, *Horace,* trans. Alan Brownjohn, introduction and notes by David Clarke (London: Angel Books, 1996), 32–33.

9. Giuseppe De Santis was a major contributor to Italian Neorealism. Marker refers to his *Tragic Hunt* (1947).

10. The Marshall Plan, also known as the European Recovery Plan, was a U.S. recovery plan to aid Western Europe following World War II. Enacted in 1948, it brought $15 billion to the continent. Michèle C. might also have made the slip in reference to Michèle Morgan's first husband, the American William Marshall, whom Morgan married during her wartime exile in Hollywood.

11. Camilla is young Horatius's sister and Curiatius's prospective wife. Camilla is killed by her brother when she repudiates Rome over the death of her beloved. Andrée Clément (1918–1954) is a French actor whose husband died in the Battle of France. Among her most notable acting credits are Bresson's *Angels of Sin* (1943) and Delannoy's *Pastoral Symphony* (1946).

12. Sabina is Horatius's wife and Curiatius's sister.

13. H. C. Potter's 1941 musical comedy was distributed in France in 1947.

One Hundred Masterpieces of Film

1. Jean Kanapa (1921–1978): writer and leading member of the French Communist Party. Under the pseudonym Vernon Sullivan, Boris Vian published four crime novels, most infamously *I Shall Spit on Your Graves* (1946). A habitué of the St. Germain des Prés jazz clubs where he met legendary African American jazz musicians, Vian was a fan of the American hard-boiled fiction that in France would be called *romans noirs* or *polars* that Marcel Duhamel helped popularize with Gallimard's "Série noire."

2. *Dangerous Liaisons* was Pierre Choderlos de Laclos's epistolary novel, published in 1782. *Andromache* was Racine's third play, first performed in 1667.

3. In 1950 the average cost of a movie ticket in the United States was 46 cents.

4. Gance's *Blind Venus* (1941), starring Viviane Romance, was one of the very first French films undertaken during the German Occupation.

5. French historical film directed by Charles le Bargy and André Calmettes.

6. Marker refers to the Mexican director of photography, Gabriel Figueroa. *Brute Force* (1947) is an American film noir by Jules Dassin. *The Stranger* (1946), Welles's third feature, stars Welles as a Nazi fugitive in a New England town.

Orpheus

1. Cocteau was likely reflecting on the premature death of his young friend Raymond Radiguet, who died from tuberculosis on December 12, 1923, after a trip with Cocteau. Two years later, Cocteau wrote his play *Orpheus*.

2. Jean Cocteau, *La Difficulté d'être* (Paris: Éditions Paul Morihien, 1947); *The Difficulty of Being*, trans. Elizabeth Sprigge (Brooklyn: Melville House, 2013).

3. The repetition of the adjective *vrai* (real) here and subsequently in this review foreshadows its usage in *La Jetée*. See, too, the essay "Farewell to German Cinema?" and Marker's comments on Käutner's *The Last Bridge*.

4. *Combat* (1941–74) was a French newspaper whose publication was clandestine during the war.

5. Diaghilev's advice to Cocteau when the latter began writing the screenplay for the ballet *Parade* (1917).

6. Cocteau, *Plain-Chant* (Paris: Éditions Stock, 1923); *Plain Song*, trans. Ian Burton (Paris: Garden Press, 1979).

7. Cocteau, *Les Mariés de la tour Eiffel* (1921), a ballet with libretto. Agnès Varda's film-within-a-film in *Cléo from 5 to 7*, starring Godard and Anna Karina, is a clever nod to Cocteau's title: "Les Mariés du Pont Mac-Donald, ou méfiez-vous des lunettes noires" ("The Newlyweds of the MacDonald Bridge, or Be Wary of Sunglasses").

8. Cocteau here reworks the closing lines of Apollinaire's poem "1909" (*Alcools*, 1913): "That woman was so beautiful / She scared me."

9. Marker here puns on the French word *tabou*, which was also the name of the Left Bank postwar cellar club, Le Tabou.

Marker undoubtedly refers here to Dermit's (whose surname appears with variations such as Dhermitte or Dhermite) recent appearance in the film adaptation of Cocteau's *Les Enfants terribles*, which was released on March 29, 1950, six months prior to the release of *Orpheus*. *Les Enfants terribles* was directed by Jean-Pierre Melville, who makes an uncredited appearance as the hotel director in *Orpheus*. In the late 1940s Dermit replaced Jean Marais in Cocteau's affections.

Siegfried and the Gaolers, or German Cinema Enchained

1. *Scipio Africanus: The Defeat of Hannibal* (1937): a historical film by Carmine Gallone that recounts the life of Scipio Africanus from the time of his election as proconsul until his defeat of Hannibal in 202 BCE. The Mussolini-funded film was propaganda for Italy's ambitions in North Africa.

2. *Film without a Title* (1948) is a comedy and also a *Trümmerfilm*, starring Hildegard Knef and Willy Fritsch.

3. Directed by H. C. Potter, *Hellzapoppin'* (1941) is the film version of the enormously popular Broadway musical revue that ran on Broadway from 1938 until 1941. Marker here alludes to the fact that the American film breaks the fourth wall.

4. Wolfgang Liebeneiner's *Love '47* was based on Wolfgang Borchert's play *Draußen von der Tür (The Man Outside)*.

The Aesthetics of Animated Film

1. Gilbert Cohen-Séat created the Filmology Institute in September 1948 to promote the scientific analysis of film.

2. Marie-Thérèse Poncet's groundbreaking dissertation was published the following year in two volumes: *Étude comparative des illustrations du Moyen Âge et des dessins animés* and *L'Esthétique du dessin animé*.

3. *The Three Little Pigs* (1933) is a Disney short that won an Oscar for Best Animated Short the following year.

4. The caricaturist and cartoonist Émile Courtet, better known by his pseudonym Émile Cohl (1857–1938), first became interested in cinema in 1907. A year later he created *Fantasmagorie*, the first animated film. During his lifetime, Cohl's most famous animated film was *The Neo-Impressionist Painter* (1910).

5. The Screen Cartoonists Guild was established in 1938. Marker here

refers to the five-week Disney animators' strike that began on May 29, 1941, prompted largely because of wage inequities. Marker here employs a French idiom popularized by Jean de la Fontaine's poem after the Aesop fable, *The Mountain in Labor.*

Gerald McBoing-Boing

1. *Van Gogh* (1948) is Resnais's twenty-minute documentary that won an Oscar in 1950 for Best Short Subject. *Malfray* is another Resnais short, also from 1948, whose subject is the French sculptor–painter Charles Malfray (1887–1940).

2. Marker's word choice here *talapouin* (sic for *talapoin*) is archaic and refers to either a Buddhist monk or a small monkey in Africa.

3. Marker here names two real towns: Châteauroux, the capital of the Indre department, and Ribérac, a small town in the Dordogne, as well as one imaginary one, Merlin-sur-Cloche.

4. Reference to the group of five prominent nineteenth-century Russian composers who sought to create a national style of music.

5. Beautiful maidens who await the faithful Muslim in Paradise.

6. Reference to René Clair's film *La Beauté du diable* (*Beauty and the Devil*, 1950), a loose adaptation of Goethe's *Faust* starring Michel Simon and Gérard Philipe.

7. This is a reference to Disney's animated musical film *Pinocchio* (1940).

8. Andrei Jhdanov (1896–1948) was the Soviet Union's propagandist-in-chief from 1945 to 1948.

An Ornamental Form

1. Marker refers here to the series of films on painters that Alain Resnais made in the immediate postwar period. In 1947 Resnais directed a series of silent shorts titled *Visit to...* that include Oscar Dominguez, Lucien Coutaud, Hans Hartung, Félix Labisse, César Doméla, Henri Goetz, and Max Ernst. A year later, he did a film on Van Gogh that he subsequently transferred to 35mm and that in 1950 won the Oscar for Best Short Subject. Two more films on art followed in 1949: *Gauguin* and *Guernica.* In this series we can also include Resnais and Marker's documentary short *Statues Also Die,* which sought to place African art, usually housed in anthropological museums, on equal footing with Western art, housed in fine art museums. Commissioned in 1950 and completed in 1953, *Statues Also Die* was immediately censured and was not released until 1964.

The Passion of Joan of Arc

1. Joseph-Marie Lo Doca (1905 or 1910–2004): Italian-born journalist, critic, and cofounder of the *Cahiers du cinéma* with André Bazin, Jacques Doniol-Valcroze, and Léonide Keigel in 1951.

2. Jules Lagneau (1851–1894) was a French professor of philosophy.

3. *Bajazet* (1672) is Racine's tragedy.

4. *Vampyr* (1932) is Dreyer's horror film.

5. Racine's final tragedy, *Athalie* (1691), is often described as a masterpiece.

Letter from Mexico City

1. Adolfo Ruiz Cortines assumed the presidency in December 1952 and remained in office until November 1958. He succeeded Miguel Alemán Valdés, who was the first civilian president of Mexico after a series of revolutionary generals.

2. The last French president of the Third Republic (1932 until July 11, 1940), Albert Lebrun was succeeded by Philippe Pétain.

3. Directed by Emilio Fernández and shot by Gabriel Figueroa, *María Candelaria* (1943) stars Dolores del Río and Pedro Armendáriz. It was the first Mexican film to be screened at the Cannes Film Festival, where, in 1946, it became the first Latin American film to win the Grand Prix. *Río Escondido* (1948) is Fernández's film starring María Félix.

4. *Soledad's Shawl* (1952) is a Mexican western directed by Roberto Gavaldón. "Grenier and Hussenot" refers to the theatrical troupe La Compagnie Grenier-Hussenot, founded by Jean-Pierre Grenier and Olivier Hussenot in 1946.

5. It is possible that Marker here refers to the Austrian film *Sodom and Gomorrah* (1922). Directed by Mihály Kertész (later known in Hollywood as Michael Curtiz), the film is remembered as the largest and most expensive Austrian film in history.

6. Alexandr Hackenschmied, a.k.a. Alexander Hammid (1907–2004), was a Czech-American photographer, filmmaker, cinematographer, and editor. He codirected *Meshes of the Afternoon* with his then-wife Maya Deren. Marker mentions him here because he was codirector and cinematographer on Herbert Kline's documentary *The Forgotten Village* (1941) on Mexican peasants whose life was essentially unchanged since the early nineteenth century. John Steinbeck wrote the screenplay.

7. In 1951 Luis Buñuel won the Best Director award at Cannes for *Los Olvidados*, which marked his return to the international stage.

Jorge Negrete (1911–1953) was a Mexican singer and actor nicknamed the "singing cowboy." The 1941 film *¡Ay Jalisco, no te rajes! (Hey Jalisco, Don't Back*

Down!) made him an international Latin star and helped to codify the charro film genre. Negrete cofounded the Mexican National Actors Association (ANDA) and replaced Cantinflas as its chairman. In 1952 Leticia Palma contested Negrete's leadership, actively campaigning for Cantinflas. On January 2, 1953, Palma was "rescued" by Major Manuel González, who helped her to safety after she had been heckled by an angry mob spurred on by Negrete. A special assembly ultimately voted to expel Palma from the ANDA, which terminated her career. Negrete, recently married to his costar María Félix, won the battle but didn't live long to enjoy his revenge. He died on December 5, 1953, of hepatic cirrhosis.

Leticia Palma (1926–2009) is best remembered for her performance in Roberto Gavaldón's *En la palma de tu mano* (1951, *In the Palm of Your Hand*). She starred in a dozen films before her dispute with Negrete led to her being banned by the Mexican film industry.

9. Cantinflas was the stage name of Mario Fortino Alfonso Moreno Reyes (1911–1993), an immensely popular Mexican comedian, actor, and filmmaker who developed a humor filled with Mexican features of intonation, vocabulary, and syntax that gave birth to various neologisms: *cantinflear, cantinflada, cantinflesco, cantinflero.* Charlie Chaplin called him the best comedian alive. In 1957, Cantinflas won a Golden Globe for his performance in *Around the World in Eighty Days.*

10. This is a reference to Our Lady of Guadalupe, which appeared miraculously on the cloak of Juan Diego, an Indigenous peasant, on the Hill of Tepeyac near Mexico City on December 12, 1531. Today the cloak is displayed in the nearby Basilica of Guadalupe, which is the most-visited Catholic shrine in the world.

Letter from Hollywood

1. André DeToth's horror film *House of Wax* (1953), starring Vincent Price, was a remake of the Warner Bros. film *Mystery of the Wax Museum* (1933). *House of Wax* was the first color 3-D feature film from a major studio.

2. System whereby two images of the same object are presented on screen, one in red for the left eye and one in blue for the right eye. The human brain combines them into a 3-D view.

3. *Bwana Devil* was an adventure B-movie written, directed, and produced by Arch Oboler, starring Robert Stack and Barbara Britton. The film is an adaptation of the story of the Tsavo man-eaters.

4. Reference presumably to Federico Sinibaldi, who codirected the Italian film *The White Angel* in 1943. Just what Sinibaldi's new technique was is unclear.

5. Austrian-born Fred Zinnemann shot *From Here to Eternity* in Hawaii. Huston was filming *Beat the Devil* (1953) on the Amalfi Coast and in London.

6. In *Prince Valiant*, the story of a Viking prince in the service of King Arthur, Henry Hathaway brings to life Hal Foster's popular comic strip in Technicolor and CinemaScope.

7. Marker's comment here echoes the *Variety* review of April 15, 1953: "This picture *[House of Wax]* will knock 'em for a ghoul. Warners' *House of Wax* is the post–mid-century *Jazz Singer*. What [. . .] Al Jolson did to sound, the Warners have repeated in the third dimension."

8. *Waxworks* (1924) was a German silent anthology film directed by Paul Leni.

9. Marker alludes here to André Breton's closing line in his novel *Nadja* (1928): "Beauty will be convulsive or will not be at all."

10. *Man in the Dark* (1953) is a 3-D film noir directed by Lew Landers, starring Edmond O'Brien and Audrey Totter, whom Marker mentions in his review of Robert Montgomery's *Lady in the Lake*.

11. André Bazin made depth of field a rallying cry in his February 1948 article "William Wyler, or the Jansenist of Mise-en-Scène," published in the *Revue du Cinéma*.

12. The phrase *no-man's land* is in English in the original.

13. "Sartre's dead" is a reference to Sartre's play *No Exit* (1944), where three dead characters are punished in the afterlife by being locked together in Hell for eternity.

14. *The Quiet One* (1948), a documentary directed by Sidney Meyers with commentary by James Agee, chronicles the rehabilitation of a young African American boy.

15. *A Place to Live* (1941), a short film directed by Irving Lerner and produced by the Philadelphia Housing Authority, was a call to action revealing the squalid living conditions of a family in a rat-infested neighborhood. Lerner was the uncredited producer of the Office of War Information's documentary short *Toscanini: Hymn of the Nations* (1944), directed by Alexander Hammid (a.k.a. Alexandr Hackenschmied) and featuring the Italian conductor Arturo Toscanini. Lerner's short *Muscle Beach* shows athletes and bodybuilders at the original Muscle Beach in Santa Monica, California.

16. Floyd Crosby (1899–1985) won an Academy Award for his cinematography on F. W. Murnau's *Tabu: A Story of the South Seas* (1931). In 1952, Crosby's work on Fred Zinnemann's *High Noon* earned him a Golden Globe. He was the father of musician David Crosby.

17. Marker refers here to Dassin's *Night and the City* (1950), partially shot on location in London, a striking example of noir expressionism.

18. With *Picture,* Lillian Ross introduced a new literary genre, the nonfiction novel, more than a decade before Truman Capote's *In Cold Blood* (1966). Graham Greene described Ross's book as providing "a terrifying picture of how a great film, directed by one of the best living directors, based on an American classic, can be slashed into incoherence through the timidities and the illiteracy of studio heads."

19. *Justice Is Done* (1950) is André Cayatte's film on the subject of euthanasia. The film won the Golden Lion at Venice but seems not to have overly impressed Marker.

20. Irving Lerner's *Man Crazy* does not appear to have been released in France. According to Florence Tissot's Chronology in the Cinémathèque française catalog, Marker befriended Lerner and in 1954 assisted him in putting together a documentary series for television. *Man Crazy* appears to have never been released on home video or DVD. According to the website "prabook.com," it is lost, a sad reminder of the fragility of even fairly recent films.

21. Marker will return to *Salt of the Earth* in his article "Hollywood on Location" a year later.

22. The phrase *mass medium* is in English in the original.

Cinerama

1. Reference to T. E. Lawrence, a.k.a. Lawrence of Arabia.

2. Reference to the German mathematician Athanasius Kircher. The inventor of a usable magic lantern was the Dutch scientist Christiaan Huygens; he did so in the 1650s.

3. *Aida* (1953) is Clemente Fracassi's film adaptation of the Verdi opera.

4. There is a typographical error here in the French: *"deux filles de talapoins"* should be *"deux files de talapoins."*

5. The phenakistoscope was the first widespread animation device that created a fluent illusion of motion. It was simultaneously invented in 1832 by the Belgian physicist Joseph Plateau and the Austrian mathematician Simon Stampfer.

6. Duško Popov (1912–1981) was a Serbian double agent for the British MI6 and the German *Abwehr.* Popov convinced German military leaders that the Allies were planning to invade mainland Europe in Calais, not Normandy. He is thought to have inspired Ian Fleming's 007.

7. Published in 1929, Paul Claudel's *The Satin Slipper* had to wait until 1943 for its first (partial) staging for a Comédie-Française production with Jean-Louis Barrault. At the end of the performance, Sacha Guitry is reported to have said that it was fortunate there was only one shoe!

8. With his Theatre of Cruelty, Antonin Artaud sought to abolish aesthetic distance and bring the audience into direct contact with life's dangers. Artaud

strove to make the theatre into a place where the spectator is exposed rather than protected. Marker worked briefly as secretary to Artaud at the end of 1946.

9. In Spanish in the original.

10. A founder of the Mexican Muralist movement along with David Alfaro Siqueiros and José Clemente Orozco, Diego Rivera was an exemplary socially committed artist who depicted Mexican history from its Mayan origins to the Revolution and post-Revolution.

11. This is a reference to Gance's spectacular triple-screen final sequence in *Napoléon* (1927).

12. The Waller Gunnery Trainer was a simulator designed to train World War II aerial gunners. It consisted of multiple film projectors.

13. Henri Colpi (1921–2006) pioneered the groundbreaking use of "flash-ins" that broke with the Hollywood classical tradition of "invisible" editing. He edited two of Resnais's masterpieces: *Hiroshima mon amour* (1959) and *Last Year at Marienbad* (1961).

The French Avant-Garde

1. This paragraph, starting with "Behind . . . it seems" is one long Proustian sentence in the original composed of 186 words. Marker extends the sentence with punctuation: a colon, a semicolon, and two parenthetical asides.

2. Marker vaguely echoes here a line by the poet Pierre Reverdy: "An image is not strong because it is brutal or fantastic—but because the association of ideas is distant and fitting."

3. In these articles Marker consistently uses the word *auteur* to designate a film author, anticipating François Truffaut's article in *Cahiers du cinéma* in January 1954, "A Certain Tendency of French Cinema."

4. Pierre Batcheff (1901?–1932) was a popular French film actor of Russian origin who acted in about twenty-five films until his untimely death, possibly by suicide.

5. The date of 1951 intimates that Marker wrote this article two years before it was published.

6. The Painlevé film is from 1947, the Soviet film from 1940, and the Grémillon documentary on Operation Overlord in Normandy from 1945.

7. Cocteau was certainly at odds with André Breton. But Cocteau's most recent biographer, Claude Arnaud, dispels the myth that Cocteau saw *Un chien andalou* only after finishing *The Blood of a Poet*. Arnaud adds that it was at Cocteau's urging that the de Noailles financed L'âge d'or, which Buñuel shot in 1930, just before *The Blood of a Poet*.

8. In her chronology for the Cinémathèque française catalog (2018),

Florence Tissot notes that in 1950 Marker had an epistolary exchange with Cocteau before publishing his review of *Orpheus*.

9. Anger moved to France after receiving a complimentary letter from Jean Cocteau after the poet saw the young American's film *Fireworks* at the Festival du cinéma maudit in Biarritz in 1949.

10. Victor Fleming directed *Dr. Jekyll and Mr. Hyde* (1941), Edward Dmytryk directed *Murder, My Sweet* (1944), and Hitchcock directed *Spellbound* (1945). Salvador Dalí oversaw the dream sequence in *Spellbound*.

An *Auteur*'s Film

1. Joseph Delteil, *Jeanne d'Arc* (Paris: Trémois, 1927).

2. Here is Sartre's exact phrase: "A fictional technique always relates back to the novelist's metaphysics. The critic's task is to define the latter before evaluating the former." It comes from his essay *Situations 1* (1947): "On *The Sound and the Fury*: Time in the Work of Faulkner," in *Literary and Philosophical Essays*, trans. Annette Michelson (New York: Criterion Books, 1955).

3. Racine traditionally used the prefaces to his works to outline his source material. *Bajazet* (1672) is the French dramatist's only play that refers to a recent historical event and is not based on a prior text. The event in question occurred in the Ottoman Empire in 1635 and thus was at a far remove from Racine's French audience.

4. Reference to the titular character in Racine's last play, *Athalie* (1691), considered his finest work.

5. Reference to Sartre's play *No Exit* (1944). The original title, *Huis clos*, is the French equivalent of the legal term *in camera*, referring to a private discussion behind closed doors.

6. Reference to the 1948 American film directed by Victor Fleming with Ingrid Bergman. The film is based on Maxwell Anderson's successful Broadway play *Joan of Lorraine*, which also starred Bergman.

7. *Gilda* (1946) is a film noir directed by Charles Vidor and starring Rita Hayworth.

Cinema, Art of the Twenty-first Century?

1. The British film pioneer Raymond Spottiswoode (circa 1913–1970) is credited with coining the term *3-D film*.

2. Reference to the 1951 Festival of Britain, a national exhibition and fair that attracted millions of visitors from throughout the United Kingdom. No doubt Chris Marker attended it.

3. The French astronomer and inventor Henri Chrétien (1879–1956) invented the anamorphic wide-screen process using an anamorphic lens system

called Hypergonar, which resulted in the CinemaScope wide-screen technique.

Farewell to German Cinema?

1. *Beauty and the Devil* (1950) is René Clair's retelling of the Faust story, starring Michel Simon and Gérard Philipe. Based on the clandestine Vercors novel, *The Silence of the Sea* was Jean-Pierre Melville's groundbreaking first film, shot without authorization.

2. *Rotation* does not seem to have been released theatrically in France. *The Kaiser's Lackey* was released in France in 1956 under the title *Pour le roi de Prusse*. Simultaneously with this article, Marker published a separate one on Wolfgang Staudte in *Cinéma 55* (November 1955): 33–36.

3. Reference to Banquo, a general in Shakespeare's *Macbeth*.

4. An American, a French, and a Russian film, respectively.

5. "The Sorcerer's Apprentice" is a segment in Disney's anthology film *Fantasia* (1940), based on a Goethe poem.

6. Chris Marker misattributes the authorship of *08/15* (1954) to Heinz Paul. Its director was Paul May. The film's title refers to the German army's standard machine gun, the 08/15.

7. *Man on a Tightrope* (1953) is Elia Kazan's film noir, starring Fredric March and Gloria Grahame.

8. Marker refers here to Vicas's Franco-German production *A Double Life*, based on Giraudoux's play *Siegfried* (1928).

9. The most influential of Stalin's secret police, Lavrentiy Beria (1899–1953) was a ruthless administrator and mass murderer.

10. The French title of the book and film was *Tant qu'il y aura des hommes (As Long as There Are Men)*.

11. The "Revenge" generation refers specifically to French men born between 1855 and 1895, who would have grown up hearing about the Franco-Prussian war of 1870 in which France lost two of its Eastern regions, Alsace and Lorraine. Georges Courteline (1858–1929) was a French satirist known for his sharp wit and cynical humor.

12. The Nuremberg trials, held between 1945 and 1949, were widely covered in the press. One wonders if Marker, who was frequently in Germany at the time, might have attended one of these trials.

13. See also Marker's repetition of the adjective *vrai* (real) in his review of Cocteau's *Orpheus*.

14. *In Those Days* is example of a *Trümmer* or rubble film. Marker misspells the name of the town Ilhlienworth, located in lower Saxony.

15. The Oder–Neisse Line constitutes the majority of the international border between Germany and Poland along the Oder and Neisse Rivers.

Hollywood on Location

1. The Silent Movie repertory cinema, which opened in 1942, was located at 611 North Fairfax Avenue in Los Angeles. Founded by Dorothy and John Edward Hampton, it was originally called The Movie Theatre.

2. M. G. Galkovitch was the Soviet Consul-General at the time. The aforementioned Michel (Mikhail) Eisenstein is presumably not a reference to Sergei Mikhailovich Eisenstein. In 1934, the latter was teaching at the State Institute of Cinematography in Moscow, after a visit to Hollywood followed by his Mexican odyssey when he shot footage for the film that would ultimately become ¡Qué viva México! (1979).

3. Martin Dies and Samuel Dickstein created the House Committee Investigating Un-American Activities, initially called the Dies Committee, which later became HUAC in 1946. The committee targeted communist infiltrators and sympathizers.

4. Edward Dmytryk (1908–1999) was named one of the Hollywood Ten, a group of blacklisted film industry professionals who refused to comply with HUAC and were cited for contempt of Congress and sentenced to prison. In 1951 Dmytryk changed course and testified before the HUAC, salvaging his career if not his reputation.

5. In 1952, Elia Kazan named Bromberg and seven other Group Theatre members as Communist Party members in testimony before HUAC.

6. At producer Darryl Zanuck's insistence, Kazan's Pinky (1949) cast a white actress, Jeanne Crain, as a light-skinned Black woman returning to the South, overlooking rising stars such as Dorothy Dandridge and Lena Horne.

7. Stevens's A Place in the Sun won six Oscars.

8. The Technicolor film What Price Glory (1952), starring James Cagney, Dan Dailey, and Corinne Calvet, is based on Maxwell Anderson and Laurence Stallings's enormously popular antiwar play from 1924. Raoul Walsh directed a silent version in 1926 on which Ford worked as an uncredited second-unit director. Marker was right in his conjecture that the film would never be theatrically released in France, but in 2007 Gaumont Columbia Tristar brought it out on DVD.

9. In 1952 Huston moved to Ireland as a result of his "disgust" at the "witch hunt" and the "moral rot" he felt was created by the HUAC investigation and hearings that were having a profoundly deleterious effect on the movie industry. In response to HUAC and before moving to Ireland, Huston cofounded, with director William Wyler and screenwriter Philip Dunne, the "Committee for the First Amendment" as a response to the ongoing government investigations into communists within the film industry.

10. See Marker's review of Olivier's Henry V earlier in this book.

11. Marker's "misspelling" is an intertextual citation to Alfred Jarry's satirical play *King Ubu* (1896).

12. *Little Fugitive* (1953) tells the story of a child alone on Coney Island. Hailed by critics, the film inspired the future young filmmakers of the French New Wave.

13. *Salt of the Earth* (1954) focuses on a protracted strike. In true neorealist style, the director Herbert J. Biberman employed real miners and their families in the film.

14. The Mexican star whom Marker references here is Rosaura Revueltas (1910–1996), a well-known Mexican stage and screen actor. Biberman's *Salt of the Earth* (1954) is her best-known film. She plays Esperanza Quintero, the wife of a mine worker. During the shoot, Revueltas was detained by immigration authorities for an alleged passport violation and deported to Mexico. She was subsequently labeled a communist and her career in American film abruptly ended. Biberman then had to hire a double to replace her. Revueltas is reputed to have later said: since [the INS] "had no evidence to present of my 'subversive' character, I can only conclude that I was 'dangerous' because I had been playing a role that gave status and dignity to the character of a Mexican-American woman." *Salt of the Earth* was the only film outright blacklisted during the McCarthy period. In 1956 at the Académie du cinéma de Paris, Revueltas was awarded the Best Actress award for her performance.

Marker cites, in passing, Georges Rouquier, who directed his own *Le Sel de la terre* in 1950, a documentary on salt mining in the Camargue.

Animation Film

1. By the mid-1930s, the animation work of German-born Oskar Fischinger (1900–1967) was labeled as degenerate by the Nazis. After moving to Los Angeles in 1936, he joined the Disney studio to animate the "Toccata and Fugue in D Minor" of *Fantasia* (1940). He resigned without credit when Disney altered his drawings, making them more realistic.

2. The French animator Paul Grimault (1905–1994) is sometimes called the French Walt Disney. In 1936, Grimault cofounded his own production company, Les Gémeaux, which went bankrupt in 1952 after producing *La Bergère et le ramoneur (The Shepherdess and the Chimney Sweep)* based on Jacques Prévert's adaptation of the Hans Christian Andersen story.

3. The Canadian-born film producer Stephen Bosustow (1911–1981) quit Disney during the 1941 animators' strike. In 1943 he cofounded the Industrial Film and Poster Service that evolved into the UPA. At UPA in the 1950s he produced a series of *Mr. Magoo* and *Gerald McBoing-Boing* cartoons, three of which won Oscars.

4. In 1932, German publisher Kurt Wolff commissioned the Czechoslova-

kian animator Berthold Bartosch to create an animated adaptation of Frans
Masereel's novel *The Idea*. Bartosch had earlier collaborated with Lotte Reiniger on *The Adventures of Prince Achmed* (1926), the world's oldest surviving
animated feature.

5. For more on *Gerald McBoing-Boing*, see Marker's essay in this book.

6. Stanley Kramer produced *The Four Poster* (1952), which Irving Reis directed.

7. For more on Cocteau's *The Blood of a Poet* (1930), see Marker's essay "The
French Avant-Garde" in this book.

8. The film's full title is *The Romance of Transportation in Canada* (1952).
Its French release was titled *Sports et transports*.

On the Waterfront

1. The New York School focused on street photography in gritty, candid
shots. Among its main proponents were Diane Arbus, Robert Frank, William
Klein, Weegee, and Lisette Model.

2. "Attorney" is Marker's usage.

3. "Investigators" is Marker's usage. Schulberg was not the only one to have
testified in the HUAC hearings. Kazan and actor Lee J. Cobb did as well.

4. Marker's quotation here ("Nous vivons sous un Prince ennemi de l'in-
trigue. . . .") slightly modifies a line from Molière's *Tartuffe* (act 5, scene 7) when
the police officer says to Tartuffe: "Nous vivons sous un prince ennemi de la
fraude." Molière, *Tartuffe*, trans. H. Baker and J. Miller (Mineola, New York:
Dover, 2000).

5. Schulberg based his screenplay on Malcolm Johnson's twenty-four articles that earned him a Pulitzer Prize in 1949.

6. "This hidden gem": Marker here employs a rare substantive in French,
sapate, which is misgendered as feminine.

7. Marker's observation here is borne out even in what seems a throw-
away line that undoubtedly was intended to circumvent censorship. Early in
the film, Charlie tells Johnny Friendly that Terry (Marlon Brando) has become
soft because of "too much Marquis of Queensbury." The phrase operates as a
double entendre for boxing and more obliquely for Brando's bisexuality. The
Marquis of Queensbury, who endorsed a code of conduct in boxing, helped
bring about the downfall of Oscar Wilde for his relationship with his son.

8. In a rare interview, Marker recalls first encountering Resnais when he
played a priest in a Luigi Pirandello play. See Jean-Louis Pays, "Des humanistes
agissants [Entretien avec Chris Marker et Armand Gatti]," *Miroir du Cinéma*,
no. 2 (May 1962): 5; quoted in Darke, *La Jetée*, 30. Preliminary research has not
uncovered the Pirandello play in question. Little is known about Resnais's concrete work in the theatre in the immediate postwar period. Special thanks to

Laurence Moreau of the Bibliothèque nationale de la France for her help on this question.

9. *Pieds-Nickelés*, literally "nickel-plated feet," is one of the earliest and longest-running French comics. It is about a group of French youthful anarchists resistant to work—"slackers," in modern parlance. It was created in 1908 by Louis Forton.

SELECTED SOURCES AND FILMOGRAPHY

Films by Chris Marker (with English subtitles)

Chris Marker Collection. London: SODA Film + Art, 2014. (*Sunday in Peking, Letter from Siberia,* and *A Grin without a Cat*).

Immemory: a cd-rom. Cambridge, Mass.: Exact Change, 2008. Also available at http://gorgomancy.net.

La Jetée / Sans Soleil. Irvington, N.Y.: Criterion Collection, 2007.

Le Joli Mai. Brooklyn, N.Y.: Icarus Films, 2013.

Books on Chris Marker

Alter, Nora M. *Chris Marker.* Urbana: University of Illinois Press, 2006.

Bartos, Adam, and Colin MacCabe. *Studio: Remembering Chris Marker.* New York: OR Books, 2017.

Cooper, Sarah. *Chris Marker.* Manchester: Manchester University Press/ Palgrave, 2008.

Darke, Chris. *La Jetée.* London: Palgrave/BFI, 2016.

Darke, Chris, and Habda Rashid, eds. *Chris Marker: A Grin without a Cat.* London: Whitechapel Gallery, 2014.

Lupton, Catherine. *Chris Marker: Memories of the Future.* London: Reaktion, 2005.

Website

Chazalon, Christophe. *Chris Marker.ch: Plongée en immémoire.* http:// chrismarker.ch/

Filmography

A chronological list of films cited by Chris Marker in the essays in this book. In most instances, the years listed are for the original release.

The Great Train Robbery. Edwin S. Porter, director. USA, 1903.

L'Assassinat du duc de Guise (The Assassination of the Duke of Guise). Charles le Bargy and André Calmettes, directors. France, 1908.

Cabiria. Giovanni Pastrone, director. Italy, 1914.

Intolerance. D. W. Griffith, director. USA, 1916.

Das Cabinet des Dr. Caligari (The Cabinet of Dr. Caligari). Robert Wiene, director. Germany, 1920.

When the Clouds Roll By. Victor Fleming, director. USA, 1920.

Blade af Satans Bog (Leaves from Satan's Book). Carl Theodor Dreyer, director. Denmark, 1921.

Der müde Tod (Destiny). Fritz Lang, director. Germany, 1921.

Dr. Mabuse, der Spieler (Dr. Mabuse). Fritz Lang, director. Germany, 1922.

Sodom und Gomorrha: Die Legende von Sünde und Strafe (Sodom and Go-morrah). Mihály Kertész, director (later Michael Curtiz in USA). Austria, 1922.

Nosferatu—Eine Symphonie des Grauens (Nosferatu). F. W. Murnau, director. Germany, 1922.

Entr'acte. René Clair, director. France, 1924.

Die Nibelungen. Fritz Lang, director. Germany, 1924.

Das Wachsfigurenkabinett (Waxworks). Paul Leni, director. Germany, 1924.

Kniaz Potyomkin Tavricheskiy (Battleship Potemkin). Sergei Eisenstein, director. Soviet Union, 1925.

Ben-Hur. Fred Niblo, director. USA, 1925.

The Freshman. Fred Newmeyer and Sam Taylor, directors. USA, 1925.

Grass: A Nation's Battle for Life. Merian C. Cooper and Ernest Schoedsack, directors. USA, 1925.

Du skal ære din hustru (Master of the House). Carl Theodor Dreyer, director. Denmark, 1925.

Die Abenteuer des Prinzen Achmed (The Adventures of Prince Achmed). Lotte Reiniger, director. Germany, 1926.

Chang: A Drama of the Wilderness. Merian C. Cooper and Ernest Schoed-sack, directors. USA, 1927.

The Jazz Singer. Alan Crosland, director. USA, 1927.

Metropolis. Fritz Lang, director. Germany, 1927.

Napoléon. Abel Gance, director. France, 1927.

La Passion de Jeanne d'Arc (The Passion of Joan of Arc). Carl Theodor Dreyer, director. France, 1928.

Un chien andalou. Luis Buñuel and Salvador Dalí, directors. France, 1929.

L'age d'or. Luis Buñuel, director. France, 1930.

Le Sang d'un poète (The Blood of a Poet). Jean Cocteau, director. France, 1930.

L'Idée (The Idea). Berthold Bartosch, director. France, 1932.

The Most Dangerous Game. Ernest B. Schoedsack and Irving Pichel, directors. USA, 1932.

Vampyr—Der Traum des Allan Gray (Vampyr). Carl Theodor Dreyer, director. Germany, 1932.

King Kong. Merian C. Cooper and Ernest Schoedsack, directors. USA, 1932.

Las Hurdes (Land without Bread). Luis Buñuel, director. Spain, 1933.

The Three Little Pigs. Walt Disney, director. USA, 1933.

La Joie de vivre (Joy of Life). Anthony Gross and Hector Hoppin, directors. USA, 1934.

Scipione l'Africano (Scipio Africanus: The Defeat of Hannibal). Carmine Gallone, director. Italy, 1937.

Alexander Nevsky. Sergei Eisenstein, director. Soviet Union, 1938.

Confessions of a Nazi Spy. Anatole Litvak, director. USA, 1939.

Experiments in the Revival of Organisms. David Yashin, director. Soviet Union, 1940.

Fantasia. Walt Disney, director. USA, 1940.

The Grapes of Wrath. John Ford, director. USA, 1940.

Pinocchio. Walt Disney, director. USA, 1940.

The Sorcerer's Apprentice. Walt Disney, director. USA, 1940.

Die drei Codonas (The Three Codonas). Arthur Maria Rabenalt, director. Germany, 1940.

Valley Town. Willard Van Dyke, director. USA, 1940.

Vénus aveugle (Blind Venus). Abel Gance, director. France, 1941.

Citizen Kane. Orson Welles, director. USA, 1941.

Dr. Jekyll and Mr. Hyde. Victor Fleming, director. USA, 1941.

The Forgotten Village. Herbert Kline and Alexander Hammid, directors. USA, 1941.

Hellzapoppin'. H. C. Potter, director. USA, 1941.

A Place to Live. Irving Lerner, director. USA, 1941.

The Land. Robert Flaherty, director. USA, 1942.

The Magnificent Ambersons. Orson Welles, director. USA, 1942.

Vredens dag (Day of Wrath). Carl Theodor Dreyer, director. Denmark, 1943.

L'Éternel retour (The Eternal Return). Jean Delannoy, director. France, 1943.

María Candelaria. Emilio Fernández, director. Mexico, 1943.

Meshes of the Afternoon. Maya Deren and Alexandr Hackenschmied (a.k.a. Alexander Hammid), directors. USA, 1943.

Mission to Moscow. Michael Curtiz, director. USA, 1943.

The North Star. Lewis Milestone, director. USA, 1943.

Henry V. Laurence Olivier, director. United Kingdom, 1944.

Ivan Grozny (Ivan the Terrible). Sergei Eisenstein, director. Soviet Union, 1944.

Murder, My Sweet. Edward Dmytryk, director. USA, 1944.

To Have and Have Not. Howard Hawks, director. USA, 1944.

Toscanini, Hymn of the Nations. Alexander Hammid, director. USA, 1944.

Brief Encounter. David Lean, director. United Kingdom, 1945.

Les Enfants du paradis (Children of Paradise). Marcel Carné, director. France, 1945.

Pride of the Marines. Delmer Daves, director. USA, 1945.

Spellbound. Alfred Hitchcock, director. USA, 1945.

Två människor (Two People). Carl Theodor Dreyer, director. Denmark, 1945.

Le 6 juin à l'aube (The Sixth of June at Dawn). Jean Grémillon, director. France, 1946.

The Best Years of Our Lives. William Wyler, director. USA, 1946.

The Big Sleep. Howard Hawks, director. USA, 1946.

The Brotherhood of Man. Robert Cannon, director. USA, 1946.

Gilda. Charles Vidor, director. USA, 1946.

Die Mörder sind unter uns (The Murderers Are among Us). Wolfgang Staudte, director. Germany, 1946.

Paisà. Roberto Rossellini, director. Italy, 1946.

Sciuscià (Shoeshine). Vittorio De Sica, director. Italy, 1946.

The Stranger. Orson Welles, director. USA, 1946.

Brute Force. Jules Dassin, director. USA, 1947.

Assassins d'eau douce (Freshwater Assassins). Jean Painlevé, director. France, 1947.

Gran Casino. Luis Buñuel, director. Mexico, 1947.

In jenen Tagen (In Those Days). Helmut Käutner, director. West Germany, 1947.

Kiss of Death. Henry Hathaway, director. USA, 1947.

The Lady from Shanghai. Orson Welles, director. USA, 1947.

Lady in the Lake. Robert Montgomery, director. USA, 1947.

Ehe im Schatten (Marriage in the Shadows). Kurt Maetzig, director. East Germany, 1947.

Caccia tragica (Tragic Hunt). Giuseppe De Santis, director. Italy, 1947.

Wozzeck. Georg C. Klaren, director. East Germany, 1947.

Berliner Ballade (The Berliner). Robert Stemmle, director. West Germany, 1948.

Affaire Blum (The Blum Affair). Erich Engel, director. East Germany, 1948.

Anni difficili (Difficult Years). Luigi Zampa, director. Italy, 1948.

Film ohne Titel (Film without a Title). Rudolf Jugert, director. West Germany, 1948.

Hamlet. Laurence Olivier, director. United Kingdom, 1948.

Macbeth. Orson Welles, director. USA, 1948.

Malfray. Alain Resnais, director. France, 1948.

Muscle Beach. Irving Lerner and Joseph Strick, directors. USA, 1948.

The Quiet One. Sidney Meyers, director. USA, 1948.

Río Escondido (Hidden River). Emilio Fernández, director. Mexico, 1948.

Robin Hoodlum. John Hubley, director. USA, 1948.

Ruy Blas. Pierre Billon, director. France, 1948.

Van Gogh. Alain Resnais, director. France, 1948.

Nachtwache (Keepers of the Night). Harald Braun, director. West Germany, 1949.

King of the Rocket Men. Fred C. Brannon, director. USA, 1949.

Liebe 47 (Love '47). Wolfgang Liebeneiner, director. West Germany, 1949.

The Magic Fluke. John Hubley, director. USA, 1949.

On the Town. Gene Kelly and Stanley Donen, directors. USA, 1949.

Pinky. Elia Kazan, director. USA, 1949.

Rotation. Wolfgang Staudte, director. East Germany, 1949.

Le Silence de la mer (The Silence of the Sea). Jean-Pierre Melville, director. France, 1949.

Es kommt ein Tag (A Day Will Come). Rudolf Jugert, director. West Germany, 1950.

La Beauté du diable (Beauty and the Devil). René Clair, director. France, 1950.

Das kalte Herz (Heart of Stone). Paul Verhoeven, director. East Germany, 1950.

Der Rat der Götter (The Council of the Gods). Kurt Maetzig, director. East Germany, 1950.

Padeniye Berlina (The Fall of Berlin). Mikheil Chiaureli, director. Soviet Union, 1950.

Der fallende Stern (The Falling Star). Harald Braun, director. West Germany, 1950.

Gerald McBoing-Boing. Robert Cannon, director. USA, 1950.

Justice est faite (Justice Is Done). André Cayatte, director. France, 1950.

The Next Voice You Hear. William A. Wellman, director. USA, 1950.

Night and the City. Jules Dassin, director. United Kingdom, 1950.

Orphée (Orpheus). Jean Cocteau, director. France, 1950.

Bayaya (Prince Bayaya). Jiří Trnka, director. Czechoslovakia, 1950.

Le Sel de la terre (Salt of the Earth). Georges Rouquier, director. France, 1950.

Sunset Boulevard. Billy Wilder, director. USA, 1950.

Herrliche Zeiten (Wonderful Times). Günter Neumann, director. West Germany, 1950.

Los Olvidados (The Young and the Damned). Luis Buñuel, director. Mexico, 1950.

The African Queen. John Huston, director. USA, 1951.

An American in Paris. Vincente Minnelli, director. USA, 1951.

Journal d'un curé de campagne (Diary of a Country Priest). Robert Bresson, director. France, 1951.

Fourteen Hours. Henry Hathaway, director. USA, 1951.

En la palma de tu mano (In the Palm of Your Hand). Roberto Gavaldón, director. Mexico, 1951.

Der Untertan (The Kaiser's Lackey). Wolfgang Staudte, director. East Germany, 1951.

Die letzte Heuer (The Last Year). E. W. Fiedler and Hans Heinrich, directors. East Germany, 1951.

Miracolo a Milano (Miracle in Milan). Vittorio De Sica, director. Italy, 1951.

Now Is the Time. Norman McLaren, director. United Kingdom, 1951.

A Place in the Sun. George Stevens, director. USA, 1951.

Quo Vadis. Mervyn LeRoy, director. USA, 1951.

The Red Badge of Courage. John Huston, director. USA, 1951.

Die Sünderin (The Sinner). Willi Forst, director. West Germany, 1951.

Susana. Luis Buñuel, director. Mexico, 1951.

Around Is Around. Norman McLaren, director. United Kingdom, 1952.

The Bad and the Beautiful. Vincente Minnelli, director. USA, 1952.

Bwana Devil. Arch Oboler, director. USA, 1952.

Casque d'or. Jacques Becker, director. France, 1952.

Dreamboat. Claude Binyon, director. USA, 1952.

The Four Poster. Irving Reis, director. USA, 1952.

High Noon. Fred Zinnemann, director. USA, 1952.

Ivanhoe. Richard Thorpe, director. USA, 1952.

Kangaroo (a.k.a. The Australian Story). Lewis Milestone, director. USA, 1952.

Vadvízország (Kingdom on the Waters). István Homoki Nagy, director. Hungary, 1952.

Limelight. Charlie Chaplin, director. USA, 1952.

Madeline. Robert Cannon and John Hubley, directors. USA, 1952.

The Member of the Wedding. Fred Zinnemann, director. USA, 1952.

Moulin Rouge. John Huston, director. USA, 1952.

Plymouth Adventure. Clarence Brown, director. USA, 1952.

The Quiet Man. John Ford, director. USA, 1952.

Red Skies of Montana. Joseph M. Newman, director. USA, 1952.

The Romance of Transportation in Canada. Colin Low, director. Canada, 1952.

Singin' in the Rain. Stanley Donen and Gene Kelly, directors. USA, 1952.

El Rebozo de Soledad (Soledad's Shawl). Roberto Gavaldón, director. Mexico, 1952.

Something to Live For. George Stevens, director. USA, 1952.

This Is Cinerama. Mike Todd Jr., Walter A. Thompson, and Fred Rickey, directors. USA, 1952.

What Price Glory. John Ford, director. USA, 1952.

Beat the Devil. John Huston, director. USA, 1953.

Le Rideau cramoisi (The Crimson Curtain). Alexandre Astruc, director. France, 1953.

From Here to Eternity. Fred Zinnemann, director. USA, 1953.

Gerald McBoing-Boing's Symphony. Robert Cannon, director. USA, 1953.

The Girl Next Door. Richard Sale, director. USA, 1953.

House of Wax. André DeToth, director. USA, 1953.

Johann Mouse. Joseph Barbera and William Hanna, directors. USA, 1953.

Julius Caesar. Joseph L. Mankiewicz, director. USA, 1953.

Lili. Charles Walters, director. USA, 1953.

Little Fugitive. Raymond Abrashkin, Morris Engel, and Ruth Orkin, directors. USA, 1953.

Man Crazy. Irving Lerner, director. USA, 1953.

Man in the Dark. Lew Landers, director. USA, 1953.

Man on a Tightrope. Elia Kazan, director. USA, 1953.

Niagara. Henry Hathaway, director. USA, 1953.

Peter Pan. Hamilton Luske, director. USA, 1953.

Weg ohne Umkehr (No Way Back). Victor Vicas, director. West Germany, 1953.

Shane. George Stevens, director. USA, 1953.

Sombrero. Norman Foster, director. USA, 1953.

The Story of Three Loves. Vincente Minnelli and Gottfried Reinhardt, directors. USA, 1953.

The Sun Shines Bright. John Ford, director. USA, 1953.

08/15. Paul May, director. West Germany, 1954.

Touchez pas au grisbi (Don't Touch the Loot). Jacques Becker, director. France, 1954.

Double Destin (A Double Life). Victor Vicas, director. France–West Germany, 1954.

On the Waterfront. Elia Kazan, director. USA, 1954.

Prince Valiant. Henry Hathaway, director. USA, 1954.

Robinson Crusoe. Luis Buñuel, director. Mexico, 1954.

Salt of the Earth. Herbert Biberman, director. USA, 1954.

Abismos de pasión (Wuthering Heights). Luis Buñuel, director. Mexico, 1954.

Hoheit lassen bitten (Your Highness, Please Leave). Paul Verhoeven, director. West Germany, 1954.

Tom and Jerry. Fred Quimby, producer. USA, 1946–54.

Invitation to the Dance. Gene Kelly, director. USA, 1956.

Moby Dick. John Huston, director. USA, 1956.

INDEX

Apollinaire, Guillaume, xlii, 15,
  157n8
Aragon, Louis, xxxviii–xxxix, 89
Arbus, Diane, 168n1
Armendáriz, Pedro, 159n3
Arnaud, Claude, 163n7
Around Is Around (McLaren), 146
Around the World in Eighty Days,
  160n9
Artaud, Antonin, 84, 97, 162–63n8
Asherson, Renée, 5
*Assassination of the Duke of Guise
  (L'assassinat du Duc de Guise)* (le
  Bargy and Calmettes), 22–23
Astruc, Alexandre, xxxii, xliv
Athalie (Ataliah) (Racine), 61–62,
  101, 159n5, 164n4
Audioscope, 70
Auric, Georges, 94
Avery, Tex, xlv, 51
*¡Ay Jalisco, no te rajes! (Hey Jalisco,
  Don't Back Down!)* (Negrete),
  159–60n7

Baceque, Antoine de, xiv
Bajazet (Racine), 59, 99, 159n3, 164n3
Ball, Lucille, 127
Bandar-Logs, 154n12
Banks, Leslie, 9
Banquo, 110, 165n3
Barrault, Jean-Louis, 9, 162n7
Barthes, Roland, xiv, xl, xxvii
Bartosch, Berthold, 142, 168n4
Batcheff, Pierre, 93, 94, 163n4
Battle of Agincourt, 3–4, 5, 6, 7, 8, 9
*Battleship Potemkin (Kniaz Potyom-
  kin Tavrichevsky)* (Eisenstein), 17,
  39, 101
Baudelaire, Charles, lv
Bayeux Tapestry, xlii, xlv, 1, 48, 49
Bayreuth Festival, 24

Bazin, André, xi, xv, xxviii, xxxii, 117,
  140, 153n1, 159n1, 161n11; death of,
  xxvi; *DOC* and, xxiv; on Marker,
  xvii, xviii; PEC and, xxvii
Beat the Devil (Huston), 161n5
Beauty and the Devil (Clair), 108,
  165n1
Becker, Jacques, 108, 135, 148
Beethoven, Ludwig van, 56–57
Bemelman, Ludwig, 144
Ben-Hur (Niblo), xxii, xlii, 9, 18,
  154n15
Benga, Féral, 94
Berenizi, Jacopo, lviin2
Berg, Alban, xxxix
Berger, Christian, lviin2
Bergman, Ingrid, 164n6
Beria, Lavrentiy, 112, 165n9
Berliet, Jimmy, 93
*Berlin: Die Sinfonie der Großstadt
  (Berlin: Symphony of a Metropolis)*
  (Ruttmann), xxx
Berliner, The (Stemmle), 39
Berritz, Sabine, xxxv
Berton, Yvonne-Yacinthe ("Yéva"),
  xxiv
Best Years of Our Lives, The (Wyler),
  128
Betty Boop, xlv, 50
Beuve-Méry, Hubert, xxxvii
Bevan, Richard, lxiin46
Biberman, Herbert J., 139, 167n13,
  167n14
Big Sleep, The (Hawks), 15
Billon, Pierre, 155n5
Biquefarre (Rouquier), lviiin10
blacklists, 124, 127, 128, 139, 166n4,
  167n14
Blanchar, Dominique, 19
Blanchar, Pierre, xliv, 19
Blanchot, Maurice, xxxviii

CHRIS MARKER (born Christian Hippolyte François Georges Bouche-Villeneuve, 1921–2012) was a French writer, artist, and director. At the lycée Pasteur, he cofounded the literary magazine *Le Trait d'union* (The Hyphen) and signed contributions as Marc Dornier. After serving in World War II (including for the American army), he began writing under pseudonyms, the most popular and long-lasting being the Americanized Chris Marker. Associated with the so-called Left Bank directors, he experimented with film from 1947, making nontraditional documentaries that were later associated with the essay film. His time-travel film *La Jétee* (1962), one of the most celebrated shorts ever made, marked his breakthrough among film societies and international art house audiences. A true polymath, his later creations ranged from videos and the interactive CD-ROM *Immemory* to the multimedia digital platform Second Life.

STEVEN UNGAR is professor emeritus of cinematic arts and French at the University of Iowa. His previous books published by the University of Minnesota Press are *Scandal and Aftereffect: Blanchot and France since 1930* (1995), *Identity Papers: Contested Nationhood in Twentieth-Century France* (1996), and *Critical Mass: Social Documentary in France from the Silent Era to the New Wave* (2018). He has also written *Roland Barthes: The Professor of Desire* and *Cléo de 5 à 7*.

SALLY SHAFTO is an interdisciplinary film scholar and specialist of the French New Wave, Maghrebi cinema, and international art cinema. She is the author of *The Zanzibar Films and the Dandies of May 1968*. Her many translations include Jean-Marie Straub and Danièle Huillet's *Writings*; Jean-Michel Frodon's *The World of Jia Zhangke*. She teaches at Framingham State University.